LAZEROWITZ, Morris. Philosophical theories, by Morris Lazerowitz and Alice Ambrose. Mouton (dist. by Humanities), 1976. 304p bibl index 76-379136. 15.00 ISBN 90-279-7501-9

A penetrating study of philosophical theories that is a superb demonstration of teaching experience on all levels of inquiry. Two features dominate throughout, linguistic discrimination and concept refinement. Continuous clarification and analytical criticism of theories serve as the foci of traditional and contemporary philosophy. Widely recognized as logicians and philosophical analysts, the authors offer an extensive treatment of the wider ranges of historic philosophical thought. The searching "Doubts and queries" at the end of each chapter provide an invaluable asset. Espousal of any particular school of philosophy is graciously avoided. The empirical and the a priori, the contingent and the necessary are skillfully interwoven. While fully aware of the claims of empirical knowledge today, the authors state that, in philosophy at any rate, "it is by no means certain whether *anything* which could be correctly described as an empirical investigation occurs" (p.37). In an otherwise discerning treatment of speculative idealism one wonders why Bradley rather than Hegel is cited as the representative of absolute idealism — especi̶ ̶ince, according to the

Continued

LAZEROWITZ

authors, self-consistency would seem to take precedence over the more adequate coherence. Excellent general bibliography. Index of names only. Despite minor strictures, including a few unfortunate typographical errors, the book is without doubt one of the best critiques of philosophical theories this reviewer has seen. Highly recommended, especially for the more mature student and one's philosophical colleagues.

Philosophical Theories

MORRIS LAZEROWITZ
AND ALICE AMBROSE

Professors of Philosophy
Smith College

Philosophical Theories

MOUTON · THE HAGUE · PARIS

ISBN: 90-279-7501-9
© 1976, Mouton & Co, The Hague, Netherlands
Printed in Hungary

Preface

This book on philosophical theories is the outgrowth of introductory and advanced courses in philosophy we have given at Smith College and at various universities. John Burnet asserted that 'no one will ever succeed in writing a history of philosophy; for philosophies, like works of art, are intensely personal things'. It would seem that in philosophy, more so than in mathematics or physics, subjective factors are involved, which perhaps is part of the explanation of the widespread and stubborn disagreements found in philosophy. The thinking of no two philosophers is ever quite the same, and instead of having to compromise over differences of opinion we decided at the outset to write different parts of the book independently of each other. Alice Ambrose is responsible for chapters I, II, VII, and VIII; Morris Lazerowitz is responsible for chapters III, IV, V, and VI .All the chapters, however, were thoroughly discussed and criticized by both.

Our approach in this book is that philosophy in all its branches, despite its subjective determinants, is capable of being a reasoned discipline, in which clarity in the expression of the theories and articulation of the arguments not only are desirable but are essential. Accordingly we have throughout presented chains of reasoning in support of views and in criticism of views. We have tried to make perspicuous the complexities of philosophical reasoning in order to help show why it is so difficult to arrive at firmly established propositions. For many, of course, the charm of philosophy is that it always leaves open the possibility of a personal choice of position. In a number of places we have come out in favor of certain positions, but this was done primarily to make the book more challenging to the reader. Ludwig Wittgenstein has become an important influence in philosophical thought, and we have woven ideas of his into the text wherever we thought it useful to do so.

Conway, Massachusetts

Morris Lazerowitz

September 1975

Alice Ambrose

Contents

1. The Subject Matter and Methods of Philosophy

When Western philosophy came into existence in Ionia it had three intellectual predecessors, mathematics, natural science, and religion, with which it has continued up to the present day to overlap both in subject matter and method of investigation. In respect of method, pursuit of knowledge in philosophy and in mathematics have a feature in common: both are concerned to follow out the implications of concepts. In respect of subject matter, philosophy, at least in certain of its branches, seems to overlap with the natural sciences. Like science, philosophy professes to investigate the world of natural phenomena, although its investigations are not confined to things in space and time. One difference, however, between philosophy and natural science is evident. Science from the beginning had a special purpose, to make the world conform to our needs by discovering laws which could be applied to things. And in this respect it differs markedly from philosophy. Kant said that philosophy bakes no bread, and Aristotle before him remarked that 'all men by nature desire to know' but that in philosophy men do not seek knowledge for any advantage. Thus, while astronomy has had its uses, e.g., in constructing a calendar and in seafaring, the concerns of philosophy were only with the ultimate stuff of the heavenly bodies in space and with the nature of space itself, without a utilitarian end in view. Theoretical science also pursues knowledge for its own sake, but its findings are of a different order from those of philosophy. Science conducts its investigations and makes its speculations on a foundation of presuppositions which philosophy undertakes to examine. Thus, science assumes the validity of inductive procedures, which presuppose the uniformity of nature and the existence of a world independent of our perception, whereas philosophy looks into the foundations of induction and the warrants for belief in an external world. The scientist accepts the commonsense belief that the future will be like the past, whereas philosophers like Hume are concerned with its

9

justification. And the scientist accepts the everyday belief that there is a common objective world, while philosophers, for example, Descartes, investigate its rational justification.

Many of the ideas in terms of which it was most natural in the beginnings of philosophy for reflective people to interpret their world came from religion. Death is one of the phenomena around which religions revolve, and it is bound up with the great questions for which both religion and philosophy have sought answers. Schopenhauer said that 'if it were not for death, people would hardly philosophize'. Not only death but other universally experienced phenomena present men's minds with equally persistent questions: the reign of law throughout nature, which raises a doubt about one's own freedom from bondage to natural forces; the existence of moral evil, for which the doer's responsibility and the reasonableness of retributive justice both come in question; the difference between ourselves and other animate beings, which may be one of degree only. Regarding those phenomena which present an enigma to our understanding, religion has provided explanations framed in terms of things lying beyond what we meet with in sense experience; the supersensible is brought in to help explain the sensible. Because 'ultimate questions' have been the concern of both religion and philosophy, ideas such as God, freedom of the will, the immortality of the soul made their way into the content of philosophy. In the case of religion, faith and the authority of others were the determinants of beliefs rather than evidence and reasoned argument, while in philosophy, ideally at least, faith and authority play no role. Roughly speaking, philosophy has its subject matter in common with religion and natural science, but it shares its procedures for discovering and establishing truth with the underlying method of mathematics, namely, reasoning on concepts, and also, it would seem, with at least some of the rules of evidence used by the natural sciences.

A preliminary glance, however, at the methods which philosophers have in fact or in appearance used in their investigations raises the question whether results such as natural scientists obtain about phenomena are obtainable by any of the methods used in philosophy. On the surface there appear to be two general methods employed in philosophy, one empirical, to which experience is relevant, and the other *a priori*, which employs only reasoning. When G. E. Moore in his *Some main problems of philosophy* said that the philosopher must consider, among other things, 'how far it is likely that there are in the world important kinds of things which we do not absolutely *know* to be in it' (p. 1), his words suggest a procedure resorted to in the natural sciences, careful and controlled observation so conducted as to make conclusions probable if not certain. David Hume, for example, in his *A treatise of human nature*, gives the impression of observing introspectively the contents of his own experience in a search for a continuously existing self, a 'simple and continu'd' thing which is the subject of various mental activities. According to his claim, his self-examination discovers for him no such entity, and he proceeds from this to a generalization concerning others: '...setting aside some metaphysicians... I may venture to affirm of the rest of mankind, that they are nothing but a bundle or collection of different perceptions.' (Bk. I, Pt. IV, Sec. VI). Though Hume does not go so far here as to conclude that no substantival self exists, he seems to think himself entitled to infer that *probably* none exists.

Some inferences made from empirical data are deductive rather than problematic, that is, the inferential step is *a priori*, such that if the premises are true, then it is logically certain that the conclusion is. But of course the conclusion, like the premises, is an empirical truth or falsity: Both the antecedent and consequent are empirical, but the connection between them is not. For example, an argument from Moore proceeds deductively from the empirical premise 'Here is a hand' to the empirical conclusion 'There exists at least one material object'. His 'proof of an external world' consists of uniting observation with logical deduction.

Much of what philosophers do by way of describing the nature and relations of existent things looks like a simple observational report. John Locke, for example, describes what he calls 'sensitive knowledge' (knowledge of the physical objects whose existence is taken for granted by common sense) as resting on an inference from sense presentations. From how things appear, that is, from observational data, we proceed, according to him, to an inference beyond the data to how things *are*, what is inferred being held to have only practical certainty and often a degree of probability falling short of this. Hume's account of causation is another instance of a conclusion apparently founded on experience, in this case on careful observation of an assumed causal object, for the purpose of discovering the force which produces the effect. The result of his observation, that no causal 'tie' was to be found, leaves no doubt tha the considered his investigation to be comparable to investigations in genetics and mechanics.

There are great differences between the empirical-seeming observations of the philosopher concerning the existence and nature of phenomena and evidential data in the sciences which raise the question whether his procedure is ever in fact the same as that of the natural scientist. But that he constantly and predominantly employs a method which in essential respects is that used in mathematics and formal logic is not to be questioned. This is the method of reasoning on concepts. Analytic penetration into concepts, which explicates what the concepts entail, may be called the *a priori* method in philosophy, and it is the central method to which the others are secondary. Independently of observation, by mere contemplation of concepts, it can be known that anyone who is a father of twins is a parent of siblings. Similarly, by contemplating the concept *justice* we can hope to know, by following out its logical implications, what features any actual just act must have. A secure knowledge of the nature of things falling under the concept will be arrived at by delineating their necessary features. Anyone acquainted with procedures in geometry will recognize their counterpart in philosophical reasoning. An important difference between mathematics and philosophy is of course apparent: In mathematics we proceed from explicitly formulated postulates and precise definitions to conclusions rigorously circumscribed by the rules of deduction. In philosophy only Spinoza, whom we might call the Euclid of metaphysics, attempted to construct a body of theorems and postulates modelled after geometry. His *Ethics*, which professes to give a comprehensive and detailed picture of reality, supersensible as well as natural, uses analysis as its central technique.

Some illustration of the various things philosophers have tried to do will help make more concrete the subject matter of philosophy and also its methodology. Plato gives us a picture of the philosopher as 'spectator of all time and all existence', which is in agreement with Moore's idea that the task of philosophy is to 'give a general description of the *whole* of the universe' (p. 1). In their attempt to delineate the cosmos, philosophers seek to discover new existents, to lay bare new facts about the nature of familiar things, and to determine what must be and what cannot be. To illustrate the latter, consider Aristotle's attempt to demonstrate that time necessarily exists. A variant of his argument is the following: It is self-evident that time *could* exist. Suppose now that it does not exist. This implies that it could not exist. For whatever does not exist must, in order to exist, come into being at a particular time. But if time did not exist, there could be no time at which it would begin to be. Hence if time did not exist it could not come into existence, and therefore could never exist, which goes against the fact that it could exist. The proposition that time does not exist is thus shown to be self-contradictory, and the proposition that time does exist is necessarily true.

Philosophers have asserted the existence of various noncontingent necessary realities, and a general argument for their existence can be given, as follows. We have the idea of realities that are contingent, realities which could conceivably exist whether they in fact exist or not. Paradise, for example, might be held by sceptics not to exist, but no one would deny that it is theoretically possible. From this it can be shown that a noncontingent reality must exist. The concept of a contingent reality entails the concept of one that is not contingent, since otherwise the concept of a contingent reality would not be different from the mere concept of a reality. But a noncontingent reality is one whose nonexistence is inconceivable. It is, in other words, one which necessarily exists.

It will be clear that whatever exists necessarily will exist in all possible universes and that a proposition stating its existence will be true of all possible universes. In addition to such truths philosophers have also attempted to set out general truths holding for this universe but not necessarily for others. Thus, some philosophers have tried to show the existence of teleology in the actual world, that is, to show that nature is purposive. To establish this something more than the analysis of concepts is required. Appeal is made to observable facts, such as symbiosis in nature and the adaptation of species.

The methods philosophers use find application not only in attempts to establish what exists or what exists necessarily, but also in attempts to establish that a certain kind of thing – usually something taken for granted by common sense – does not or cannot exist. The nonexistence of a causal tie between events or things was argued by Hume on the basis, apparently, of observation. His conclusion was that there is no such thing as causal necessitation, in his words, that the idea of causation is a 'fiction of the imagination'. Usually, however, the unreality of a phenomenon is established by reasoning on concepts, in particular, by showing that they imply a contradiction. This was F. H. Bradley's method of establishing the unreality of change. His argument was that in order for a thing to change two conditions must be fulfilled: one, that it retain its identity, i.e., that the subject of change remain the same subject throughout the change, and the other that the thing itself alter. But these two conditions are incompatible. A, the subject of change, becomes different in undergoing change, and is replaced by A_1, which is not the original subject, but a new one, and A has disappeared. Even to say the subject 'becomes different' is illegitimate, as that implies that there is an invariant subject which undergoes change. Hence the concept of change taking place in a thing implies that the thing both changes and does not change, or to put it differently, that the subject continues to exist throughout the change and also does not. To turn to another field of philosophy, philosophical psychology, Thomas Hobbes reasoned against the possibility of unselfish desires somewhat as follows: The satisfaction of an agent's desire is always *his* satisfaction, no matter what the desire is. Hence in acting to satisfy a desire he acts in a purely selfish way, that is, to obtain satisfaction for himself. An act of charity, and even one of self-sacrifice, if done from a desire is selfish.

Discovery of new existents is another achievement philosophy has claimed for itself. Bertrand Russell wrote concerning abstract entities such as justice, as distinct from particular just acts, or football as against particular football games, that 'it is strange that hardly anybody except students of philosophy ever realizes that there are such entities' (1943, p. 146); and the same thing has been said about sense data. Thus C. D. Broad writes: 'The plain man does not clearly distinguish between physical objects and sensa... We first come to recognise them as distinct from physical objects by reflecting on the fact of sensible appearance, and the supposed contrast between it and the supposed properties of physical reality' (1927, p. 266). One argument for sense data is the following: When a white thing looks blue there must be *something* which *is* blue and is not identical with any part of the surface of the white thing. This something which the senses disclose in perception has the color the physical thing only looks to have and is an object in its own right. Everyone who perceives any of the things around him is directly aware of sense data, without their coming to his special attention. Singling them out with a name, like 'sense datum' or 'sensum', brings them to our conscious notice and leads to the examination of their properties and their relation to things.

In addition to the discovery of new objects philosophers have often claimed to have discovered new connections between important concepts, connections which have their counterpart in the world. By following out the implications of concepts they hoped to reveal the relations of things falling under them. For example, the relation between present truths and future occurrences. If present propositions about the future are either true or false, then what the future will be is already determined, that is, it is true now that the world will be so-and-so. Furthermore, from this relationship between present truths and the future some philosophers have gone on to the proposition that freely willed action is impossible, on the ground that the exercise of free will requires a world with a future not already fixed. In particular, if there is a set of true propositions about an agent's future behavior, then how the agent will act is already predetermined, and alternative courses of action are mere illusion. Another example is Moore's analysis of the concepts *sense datum* and *physical object*, one conclusion being that a sense datum cannot be related to a physical object as part of its surface.

About the nature of familiar things there occur in every branch of philosophy claimed (though often disputed) discoveries of new facts. Consider the familiar idea of a class. It used to be held that all classes must have members. Against this notion it may be argued that if it is correct, as it seems to be, to interpret the statement that there are lions as 'The class of lions has at least one member', then the statement that there are no lions is to be interpreted as 'It is not the case that the class of lions has members', which is to say that the class of lions has no members, or is empty. Another example of the familiar being thrown into a new and unusual light is provided by the various philosophical theories about material objects such as trees, books, and sheets of writing paper. Some of these go beyond anything ever dreamed of by common sense and some positively contradict it. To mention only two theories: Locke held that a physical object is an unknowable substratum in which experienceable attributes inhere. The attributes are knowable, but *that which has them* lies byond the range of possible experience. On the other hand, some philosophers, for example, George Berkeley, have denied the existence of an inexperienceable subject underlying attributes and have gone on to an account of the nature of physical objects which is even more surprising to common sense: Things are really systems of ideas.

The purpose of analyzing a concept is frequently to explicate general features of the things falling under the concept; but apart from special objectives, the aim every case of analysis has in common with every other is clarification. Broad writes about the importance of analyzing concepts in everyday use and ordinary beliefs, and it is worthwhile quoting him at some length.

'Common-sense constantly makes use of a number of concepts, in terms of which it interprets its experience. It talks of *things* of various kinds; it says that they have *places* and *dates*, that they *change*, and that changes in one *cause* changes in others, and so on. Thus it makes constant

they have not had before?); (b) Is the surveyor's conclusion from his data (e.g., that the side is a particular length x) comparable to Moore's conclusion? If his conclusion is correctly calculated but is false, consider the difference between establishing its falsity with establishing the falsity of the general proposition 'There are material objects'. Suppose the surveyor had deduced from his particular data that *there is a length*. Would establishing the falsity of this conclusion present the same peculiar difficulty as establishing the falsity of Moore's conclusion?; and (c) Does Moore's showing his two hands presuppose that others are aware of his body, and does this assume that the bodies of those in his audience exist? Must he go through the same procedure of calling attention ot his body to prove its existence, and then go on to prove in the same way the existence of others' bodies? I.e., does his kind of evidence *necessarily* assume what he set out to prove? (It has been charged that his proof begs the question.)

2. A number of philosophers, among them Plato and Descartes, have produced arguments which throw doubt on our claimed knowledge of the existence of an external world. These are arguments in which no agreed on mistake has yet been discovered. If correct, they show that Moore's demonstration is circular in a somewhat different way: in taking for granted that the existence of material objects can be known by placing ourseves in the proper position to obtain such knowledge. Do these arguments place the surveyor also in the position of taking for granted what needs to be proved?

3. Hume's invitation to 'cast our eyes on any two objects, which we call cause and effect, and turn them on all sides' in order to discover the alleged necessary connection between them, looks to challenge us to an empirical procedure. It was so taken by Russell, who said: 'The controversy is thus reduced to one of empirical fact, Do we, or do we not, sometimes perceive a relation which can be called causal? Hume says no, and his adversaries say yes, and it is not easy to see how evidence could be produced by either side.' (*A history of Western philosophy*, p. 669) If Hume's careful observation was an empirical procedure, (a) why was his report on what he found not accepted by others who were in a position to make equally accurate observations? (b) Supposing that observation of occurrences can decide whether *in fact* a force operates between them, why are the impressive regularities in nature not taken to render the existence of a necessitating force at least probable? What evidence would make it likely that causation exists? Can one describe the evidence which,

although not obtainable, would make this certain? In general, do philosophers support a theory by collecting new evidence which makes it increasingly likely? Broad's remark that philosophy, unlike any of the natural sciences, has no use for experiment, is borne out by the fact that philosophers have no laboratories nor do they gather statistics.

4. Hume's language in describing the search for a causal tie is the language appropriate to an empirical generalization based on observed instances: 'Upon the whole, there appears not, throughout all nature, any one instance of connexion which is conceivable by us.' (*An enquiry concerning human understanding*, Sec. VII, Pt. II) Can there be a search for what cannot be conceived? Is looking for what cannot be conceived like looking for a four-sided triangle or is it like a blind person's looking for a blue hat?

5. The above questions throw some doubt on whether Hume's investigation is empirical. Can it be reconstrued as an attempt to analyze the concept of causation? Would this analysis show anything about the *existence* of causation, or only something about its nature? Hume arrives at the view that causation is nothing more than constant conjunction. Is this conclusion one about what causation is, or does it deny the existence of causation?

REFERENCES

Recommended reading:
   G. E. Moore (1953), *Some main problems of philosophy*, Ch. 1.
Further readings:
   C. D. Broad (1927), *Scientific thought*, Introduction.
   C. I. Lewis (1926), *Mind and the world-order*, Ch. 1.
   Bertrand Russell (1943), *The problems of philosophy*, Chs. 14, 15.

2. The Logic of Propositions and Kinds of Knowledge

A number of thinkers from Aristotle to the present day have called attention to the importance for philosophy of assessing the character of propositions in relation to the means by which they are established. Aristotle viewed logic as a discipline the study of which would 'enable one to know for what sorts of proposition he should demand proof and what sorts of proof he should demand for them' (Ross, 1930, p. 20). Different classes of propositions are connected with different modes of investigation. As Wittgenstein put it, the answer to the question concerning whether and how a proposition can be verified 'is a contribution to the grammar of the proposition' (1953, p. 112), which is to say that it is a contribution to our understanding of its logical character, i.e., of the type of proposition it is. The classification of a proposition is bound up with the kind of procedure relevant to its confirmation or rejection; and if its classification is in doubt, examining the way one would go about verification or refutation can be helpful both as to what its character is and the kind of knowledge it yields. To different kinds of propositions quite different kinds of verification procedures are relevant.

Some philosopheres have held that certain categories of propositions are open to belief only, that knowledge of their truth or falsity is not possible. Thus, A. J. Ayer holds that 'empirical propositions are one and all hypotheses', that 'it is only tautologies that are certain' (1951, pp. 93–94). Other philosophers, like John Locke, claim for propositions referring to things attested to by the senses 'an assurance that deserves the name of knowledge' (1928, Bk. IV, Ch. 11). Locke distinguishes three degress of knowledge, his examples indicating the kinds of proposition with which each sort of knowledge is associated. The mind's perception of the agreement or disagreement of two ideas – that they are the same or diverse – is 'the most certain that human frailty is capable of'. 'Thus the mind perceives, that white is not black, that a circle is not a triangle, that three are more than two, and equal to one and two. Such kinds of truths the mind perceives at the first sight of the ideas together, by bare intuition, without the intervention of any other idea.' (1928, Bk. IV, Ch. 2). But we can be equally certain 'that the idea we receive from an external object is in our minds', and thus what Locke called 'intuitive' knowledge can be had of such a fact as well. 'Demonstrative' knowledge, which is also certain, can be had by proving the agreement or disagreement of ideas, say, between the three angles of a triangle and two right angles, by means of intermediate ideas of which we have either intuitive knowledge or prior demonstrative knowledge. Here it is clear from the example that the connection between the ideas is necessary, and that it is established *a priori*. To these two kinds of knowledge, intuitive and demonstrative, Locke includes yet another 'which going beyond bare probability, and yet not reaching perfectly to either of the foregoing degrees of certainty, passes under the name of knowledge' (*Ibid*). This is 'sensitive' knowledge of the existence of particular external objects corresponding to our ideas, for which he considers our senses provide us 'an evidence that puts us past doubting' (*Ibid.*).

The importance of making clear what John Wisdom calls "the modes of verification" proper to different kinds of statements becomes evident when the character of a statement and the relevant means of establishing the statement are in question. Determining the mode of verification in some ways resembles what are called decision procedures in systems of logic. It is sometimes possible to formulate a general procedure for deciding whether a certain proposition is provable from the postulates of a system in advance of carrying out the proof. The decision procedure shows whether or not the proposition is capable of demonstration by the rules of the system. The character of the proposition is internally bound up with its deducibility or nondeducibility, so that certain types of proposition are excluded from the possibility of proof whereas other types can be known, in advance of proof, to be capable of being deduced. How to decide, for formulas of greater and greater complexity, whether they *can* be proved has been a central problem of formal logic.

There is a parallel problem in philosophy of deciding for different classes of propositions what kinds of evidence are relevant to establishing them. It frequently happens that evidence produced for or against a position carries weight with one philosopher and not with another. Moore complained that disagreements in philosophy occur because philosophers 'attempt to answer questions, without first discovering precisely what question they desire to answer' (1922, p. VI), and this can occur because it is unclear what *kind* of considerations bear on a question. However difficult it may be to devise the specific means for determining the truth-value of a philosophical position (its truth or falsity), there is a prior difficulty which it is of first importance to solve, namely, that of deciding the *nature* of the evidence required and the character of the proposition for which evidence is sought. It is clear, for example, that Galileo's scientific experiment of dropping objects from the tower of Pisa was pertinent to determining the velocity of their fall, and also that his specific means was sufficient. But the matter is not so clearcut in the case of the controversial proposition that there are sense-data. What sort of evidence is relevant to deciding its truth-value? Examination of the sensible appearances of things and of things? or analysis of the concepts *sensible appearance* and *thing*? If the first, the proposition would appear to be empirical; if the second, then the opposite would seem to be the case. Both the nature of the proposition and the nature of the evidence presented for it come into question. The fact is that ascertaining the kind of evidence required for a proposition is internally bound up with deciding the character of the proposition, but the problem presents itself now in one aspect, now in the other. We may say that deciding the mode of verifying a proposition and deciding the logical character of a proposition, that is, its category, are two sides of the same coin.

Philosophical theology provides many instances which show the need of bringing the character of a proposition into explicit connection with its mode or modes of verification. Consider two of the classical arguments for the existence of God. One of these is the so-called ontological argument, which, without going into it here, professes to deduce God's existence from the conception of perfection. The other, the so-called teleological proof, infers His existence from what is taken to be evidence of design in the universe. The first argument has been described as being wholly *a priori*, obtaining its conclusion from concepts alone without drawing on empirical evidence. The teleological argument is at best a probable inference from observed matter of fact. One proceeds from concepts alone, the other uses observation, which is to say that two different modes of verification are employed. This raises the question whether the same proposition can have different modes of verification or whether different modes of verification imply a difference in the propositions they are related to. The specific question raised in this context is whether the words 'God exists' express only one proposition for which two different kinds of evidence are presented or two logically different propositions each with its own type of evidence. Deciding whether two logically different modes of procedure can be different modes of verifying the same proposition will enable us to see in this case whether two propositions are involved or only one, and if two, what they are.

It is to be noted that in nonphilosophical contexts the result of an empirical procedure is a proposition which conveys factual information. It would seem that for the most part, if not altogether, philosophical investigations have proceeded *a priori*. This raises the question whether the necessary propositions arrived at by reasoning on concepts alone can also give information about the world. If they can, then they would have to correspond to matter of fact if true, and matters of fact would bear on their truth or falsity. In the *Notebooks, 1914–16* Wittgenstein wrote: 'The *great* problem about which everything I write turns is: Is there an order in the world *a priori* ...?' (1961, p. 53e), that is, a structure to which all things must conform. Leibniz answered this question affirmatively. In his *Monadology* he clearly implied that any proposition which results from a correct analysis of concepts, being true of all possible worlds is also true of ours. For example, 'All squares are four-sided', which is analytic, according to him asserts features common to all possible squares and hence to all actual squares. To be a square is of necessity to be a four-sided figure, and this necessity determines our thought rather than is determined by our thought. As Descartes put it, thought cannot 'impose any necessity on things, but ... the necessity which lies in the thing itself ... determines me to think in this way'. (Immanuel Kant maintained that some propositions are synthetic *a priori*, which according to him implies that some necessary connections are not analytic and are mind determined. This will be discussed later.) The three necessary propositions which were singled out by Aristotle as 'the fundamental laws of thought' are on this way of looking at necessary propositions primarily laws of things. The law of identity, that everything is identical with itself, the law of contradiction, that nothing can be both φ and not φ, and the law of excluded middle, that everything must be either φ or not φ, are such that even God's thinking must conform to them, inasmuch as they are *necessary* laws of things. '...Though these are called laws of thought, and in fact we cannot think except in accordance with them yet they are really statements which we cannot but hold true of things ... the so-called necessity of thought is really the apprehension of a necessity in the being of things' (Joseph, 1934, p. 13).

Against this position stands the denial that these propositions say anything whatever about things. One ground for denying it is the difference between such statements as the following: (a) Either there are oak trees or there are no oak trees; (b) Either there are oak trees or there are maples. In respect of the information these provide about what there is, these two are radically different. (a) does not imply that a tree exists, whereas (b) does imply this. In fact (a) does not tell us that anything exists, nor does it tell us that anything does not. Consider now the denials of (a) and (b): It is false that oak trees either do or do not exist, or equivalently, oak trees both do and do not exist; it is false that there are either oaks or maples, that is, neither oaks nor maples exist. The second tells us what does not exist, whereas the first is an inconceivability. To see that it is false that oak trees both do and do not exist an inventory of things need not be taken, nor would such an inventory be relevant, whereas the falsity of 'neither oaks nor maples exist' can be known only by observing what there is, i.e., by finding an oak or a maple. The method of confirming (b), and of disconfirming it as well, is entirely different from calculating the truth, or falsity, of (a) With this difference goes a difference in the logical character of the statements. The truth-value of (b) is contingent upon what in fact is the case, and a different state of affairs would impose on it a different truth-value. (b) conveys one piece of information, its denial the opposite. The truth-value of (a) is by contrast invariant under all possible conditions; it is true *no matter what* is the case. This raises the important question whether, in general, propositions whose truth remains invariant under all conditions can be informative about the world. Kant thought some propositions belonging to this class, namely those he called synthetic *a priori*, were about the world, but he maintained that analytic propositions did not function to convey information about things. Wittgenstein in the *Tractatus Logico-Philosophicus* came to the view that analytic propositions, specifically, tautologies, say nothing at all about the world. It must be admitted that there are no ordinary circumstances in which anyone would feel informed on being presented with the tautology that something either is or is not the case.

Ayer, in common with a number of philosophers, does claim for them an informative function, but the information they yield is according to him verbal only; they record linguistic conventions. Something like this 'conventionalist' position is expressed by Wittgenstein in works later than the *Tractatus* when he characterizes them as 'rules of grammar'.

That there is any ground for characterizing them in this way, when the sentences expressing them appear to *use* words rather than mention them, may come as a surprise. But if one observes the radical difference in the modes of verifying the contingent proposition 'Donkeys are stubborn beasts' and the *a priori* proposition 'Donkeys are animals', the relevance of verbal considerations emerges plainly. The first proposition rests on observation of the behavior of donkeys, whereas there is no resorting to sense testimony in the case of the second. Anyone who knows the meaning of the words 'donkey' and 'animal' would know that a donkey is an animal. If anyone challenged this assertion one would not ask him to examine donkeys; one would ask him to consider the use of words. It is for this reason that such propositions as 'Donkeys are animals' are sometimes described as being true in virtue of the definition of the words occurring in their expression. Why Ayer should have said that in uttering a sentence for an *a priori* proposition he is 'simply calling attention to the implications of a certain linguistic usage' (1951, p. 79) thus becomes clear. And it is also clear why Wittgenstein characterized an *a priori* proposition as a rule of grammar: he was calling attention to the different functions *a priori* and empirical propositions have. The former function as does a rule of language, namely, to preclude the use of certain expressions to describe anything. The fact, for example, that 'A donkey is an animal' expresses an *a priori* proposition has as a consequence that the phrase 'donkey but not an animal' has no use in our language. It might be the case that the phrase 'donkey but not a stubborn beast' in fact applies to nothing, but it nevertheless is descriptive. 'Donkey but not an animal' is ruled out from descriptive use by the fact that 'A donkey is an animal' expresses in English a necessary proposition.

There are objections to these claims which cannot be gone into here, but which will be touched on later. For the present we return to the question whether sentences expressing analytic propositions assert any nonlinguistic fact. On this question Kant, Wittgenstein, and Ayer are in agreement that they are noninformative, that knowing them to be true adds nothing to our knowledge of things. On their view, if the *a priori* procedures of philosophers lead to analytic propositions, and to these only, then philosophy in Moore's sense, as a quest for knowledge about the whole of the universe, vanishes.

A great part of philosophy, if not all, can be saved from the charge that its propositions make no addition to knowledge if they can be shown to fall into a class of propositions which are informative even though they are *a priori*. In opposition to Kant there is the claim that no such propositions exist. Kant held that there are propositions which are both synthetic and *a priori*, that is, propositions which have in common with empirical propositions the important feature of giving information about their subjects while differing from these in being in principle irrefutable. Their truth is as certain as that of analytic propositions and their content as factual as that of empirical propositions. That a cube has twelve edges has been cited as an example of a proposition falling in this category (See Langford, 1942, p. 335). Experience, it has been urged, is required to make the connection between subject and predicate, between being a cube and having twelve edges, just as it is in the case of any empirical proposition, e.g., 'Elephants are herbivorous'. It is the experience of counting the edges of an actual cube or turning one over in the imagination which first informs us of the connection. An analysis – what Kant called 'dissection of concepts' – will not show the predicate to be merely a component of the subject. The predicate is 'ampliative', so that its ascription to the subject conveys additional information about what the subject term refers to. Some philosophers deny this by maintaining that all *a priori* propositions are analytic. Certainly Leibniz would have maintained that a sufficiently enlightened mind would see that it had the form *ab is a*. But if Kant's account is correct, then the generalization about cubes will be importantly different from such a proposition as 'A rectangle has right angles', which does have this form. Clearly it is similar in having 'strict necessity'; it is not open to theoretical falsification by any possible cube.

It is customary to classify propositions as either empirical (contingent) or *a priori*, a classification with which Kant's third category of propositions having the features of both, is consistent. In recent years the dichotomy empirical-*a priori* has been challenged, but this need not concern us for the present. It is nevertheless necessary to be clear on the dichotomy that is being challenged. In general, an empirical proposition is one whose actual truth-value is not its only possible truth-value. That is, two possibilities are open to it, truth and falsity. Thus, an empirical proposition, though in fact true, could conceivably be false, and though in fact false, could conceivably be true. For example, 'Elephants are herbivorous' is true but can be conceived to be false. Despite important differences among empirical propositions, this is the feature which characterizes them all. Their truth-value is contingent upon some circumstance which might be otherwise. What is the case determines the truth-value they have, and a different state of affairs would impose on them a different truth-value. In contrast to this category of propositions, *a priori* propositions are all such that their actual truth-value is their only possible one. Possessing one truth-value precludes the possibility of their possessing the other. The truth of 'All squares are rectangles' is necessary, and the falsity of 'Some squares are not rectangles' is likewise necessary. It is inconceivable that the first be false or that the second be true.

Descriptions of necessary propositions which go beyond this basic characterization fall within disputed territory. For example, there is some consensus that experience will not establish that all cubes have twelve edges and that in this respect this proposition differs from 'All elephants are herbivorous', which requires the observation of more than one elephant and is arrived at inductively. But the consensus is not complete. J. S. Mill held that necessary propositions are nothing more than empirical generalizations to which experience shows no exception and, on the contrary, constantly confirms. So-called necessary propositions, like laws of nature, are according to him inductions from observation. C. I. Lewis, without agreeing with Mill that *a priori* truths are at the same time empirical truths, has within recent years subscribed to the view that they are open to confirmation by inductive procedures. Of the analytic proposition 'Cats are animals' he allows it may be established without recourse to empirical evidence, but that 'also it might be established – as well established as most laws of science, for example, by generalization from observed instances of cats' (1946, p. 91). Another and quite different controversial account is Leibniz's characterization of true *a priori* propositions – what he called 'truths of reason' or 'identical propositions' – as being such that their negations are, or imply, a self-contradiction. But this characterization would rule out synthetic *a priori* propositions. According to Kant, true synthetic *a priori* propositions, like analytic propositions, are such that no other truth-value is possible for them, but unlike analytic propositions, their negations are not self-contradictory. They have, in Kant's words, the 'inner necessity' of an analytic proposition of the form *ab is a*, but since the predicate is not a conjunctive component of the subject (e.g., 'All cubes have twelve edges'), negation creates no contradiction between subject and denied predicate. Among *a priori* propositions there are yet other differences: some have no demonstration; the necessary connection between their constituent concepts is evident upon inspection – as Locke said, 'at the first sight of the ideas together'. Examples are 'All squares are plane

figures', 'Every statement is either true or false'. Other *a priori* propositions are such that the connection of their concepts is not discoverable
by an immediate view, but by finding mediating ideas that effect the connection by proof. A sufficently extended piece of analysis constitutes a
deduction. The line between a stepwise deduction and an immediate
apprehension is not always definite. The statement '31 is a prime number'
is a case in point.

There are differences between empirical propositions, as well as between
a priori propositions. These become perspicuous when one considers the
means of establishing them. In the case of empirical propositions, whose
negations are not inconceivable, it is correct for the most part to describe
their mode of verification as observation and experiment. But among
empirical propositions there is a special class, sometimes called 'basic'
propositions, which has been subject to extended debate in philosophy.
Some philosophers have even refused to them the title 'empirical',
because they are not linked with any mode of verification. These are
propositions about one's own immediate experience, what might be
called subjective reports. Examples are 'I have a pain', 'There looks to me
to be a lake in the distance'. It is evident that they do meet the condition
for being empirical, viz., that their negations are neither self-contradictory
nor in principle inconceivable. Anyone who says 'I am in pain' could be
saying something false; but if he is, he knows that he is. The reason why
some philosophers have refused to call these statements empirical is that
unlike statements that require sense testing or experimentation, these are
subject to no sort of testing by those who utter them. What has happened,
perhaps unwittingly, is that the term 'empirical' has been identified with
'verifiable in possible experience'. It is tempting to think of this identification as a mistake, but it may be that philosophers introduce it in order to
mark an important point of difference between basic propositions and
propositions subject to verification techniques by everyone. Basic propositions are such that the person who utters them does not *learn*, or get to
know, what their truth-values are. Their truth-values are not arrived at by
a verification procedure. In Locke's words, they are 'past doubting'; for
they are not correctible by any future experience. When Ayer, in answer
to the question, 'How do I know I really am in pain?', says 'I know it by
feeling it' (1937, p. 154), his language suggests that we discover we have
pains by doing something – by going through a kind of verification
process. The implication is that we might have pains without knowing
that we have them and that we *learn* that we have them by feeling them.

But there is no *coming to know* such a fact, as there is in the case of the experiences of someone other than oneself. First-person and third-person statements of this kind, although alike empirical, are manifestly different in respect of verification.

A cluster of problems surrounds descriptions of the character of *a priori* and empirical propositions, and of various classes of propositions within the two categories. For example, the proposition 'I shall live forever' is *in principle* unfalsifiable by me, i.e., I could not conceivably establish its falsity. And it would seem that unless I could know what it would be like to establish that it is false I could not know what it would be like for it to be false. It has been claimed that from this it follows that it does not make sense to say it *is* false. Universal propositions of the form 'All *a* is *b*' whose range of possible confirming instances extends through the infinity of time and space raise an analagous question: whether one can know what it is like for them to be true if it cannot be known what it is like to run through the totality of cases which would establish that they are true. We know what it would be to falsify the proposition that friction between two bodies produces heat; a single counter-case would do. But to run through the infinity of verifying instances is logically impossible. The question is then whether we know what it is like for it to be true. The same question can be raised about an 'unbounded' negative existential statement such as 'There are no griffins'. The characterizing feature of an empirical proposition is that both it and its denial are theoretically possible, which implies that both its truth and its falsity are conceivable. The two propositions, 'Friction between bodies produces heat' and 'There are griffins' appear to answer to the characterizing condition for being empirical and yet not to possess the feature implied by it: Like an *a priori* false proposition, the first is such that we do not know what it is like for it to be true since we have no idea what it would be for it to be verified. It is logically impossible to examine all possible confirming cases covered by it, past, present, and future. And like an *a priori* true proposition, the second is such that we do not know what it would be for it to be falsified. For it is logically impossible to establish its falsity by looking at each of an infinity of places where there might be a griffin. It seems proper to say of these two propositions, and of many propositions like them, that they and their denials are both theoretically possible; yet it is doubtful whether it is proper to say that both their truth and their falsity are conceivable.

In philosophy we constantly find that there is uncertainty regarding the logical character of its propositions, uncertainty which often spans centuries and reflects itself in confusion over the appropriate ways of establishing them. Thus, sentences expressing philosophical theories have in the history of philosophy had a variety of interpretations placed on them. Some philosophers take them to express a proposition about things, others a proposition about relations between concepts, and still others a proposition about words. We have seen that the teleological argument for the existence of God and the Anselmic proof raise a question about what the words 'God exists' express. Confusion about the character of a proposition is often due, as Wittgenstein pointed out, to the fact that the words of a metaphysician can be used to state a fact of experience (1958, pp. 56–57), and that we reject them as expressing something false when in fact we are rejecting a form of symbolism. (From notes taken by M. Masterman and Alice Ambrose in the intervals between dictation of *The blue book*. To be referred to as *The yellow book*.) Thus, a form of language which Rudolf Carnap has called the material mode of speech permits the expression of verbal propositions whose character is concealed by its representing them as referring to things. To cite his example: 'A rose is a thing'. Some years ago a book appeared under the title *Words and things* by Ernest Gellner (1959), a title which points up the need in many instances of deciding whether what is under philosophical discussion is the nature and existence of an object or the use of a term. The question, 'What sort of things are meanings?', is a case in point. This question has been given different answers by different schools of philosophy. Plato and Russell answer the question in one way, namely, that meanings are abstract objects, or 'universals', and Wittgenstein answers it in another: the meaning of a word is not an object; it is the use the word has in the language. One answer to the question suggests that it is about things, the other suggests that it is about words. That is to say, the question, 'What sort of things are meanings?', itself raises the question whether it is, or is not, a request for information about things.

Asking this latter question is the same as trying to determine whether 'The meaning of a word is a kind of thing' is a 'pseudo-object sentence' (Carnap, 1960, p. 60) and has a translation comparable to Carnap's translation of 'A rose is a thing'. From this sentence, he says, '...we cannot learn any quality of the rose, neither as to its colour, nor size, nor form, nor anything else .... We can ascertain its truth without observing any rose, by only considering to what syntactical kind the word "rose" belongs, namely that it is a thing-word' (*Ibid.*, p. 62). That is, the word 'rose' belongs to the category of nouns which are names of things. Is the question, 'Is a meaning a kind of thing?', also a request for verbal information, formulated in the material mode of speech? It might be and apparently sometimes has been construed verbally, as the question whether the word 'meaning' is a thing-denoting name, i.e., belongs to the category of names of objects – objects given by the senses or in some other way. If 'The meaning of a word is a kind of thing' does in an indirect way give verbal information, then the type of investigation appropriate to ascertaining the truth of what it asserts would be a linguistic one. Classical nominalist positions, or for that matter, Wittgenstein's position, imply that the sentence is a pseudo-object sentence. The Russell-Platonic position implies that the question about the nature of meanings is not a concealed verbal question, but is instead a request for ontological information. A similar question about the nature of numbers comes up in the philosophy of mathematics (See Hardy, 1940, pp. 63–64). The Platonic view is that numbers are abstract objects. Determining the character of the statements, 'Meanings are a kind of thing', 'Numbers are abstract objects', comes to deciding whether the appropriate procedure for ascertaining their truth is a kind of interior looking – an inspection of what is before one's mind when one understands a general word or a number word. Is a meaning something that lies beneath the verbal surface, 'something that lies within, which we see when we look into the thing, and which an analysis digs out'? (Wittgenstein, 1953, p. 43) Which procedure for determining the nature of meanings is relevant, turning the outward eye upon language or the inward eye upon the mind's contents? It is easy to see that laying bare the character of the question and the character of the two answers given to it is a prerequisite for solving 'the problem of universals'. This is but one example of philosophical positions whose character and mode of establishment have persistently remained unclear.

There are a number of propositions which in nonphilosophical contexts would be taken to be empirical, but whose character remains still to be uncovered if one is to take seriously the long standing disputes over it. Two such propositions are 'Other people than myself exist' and 'There are in the world a number of physical objects'. Moore lists these among the propositions of Common Sense which each of us knows to be true. Philosophers have raised questions about the status both of the pair mentioned and of the correlated claims, 'I know other people exist', 'I know there are physical objects'. F. H. Bradley argued that the concept *person* and the concept *physical object* are both self-contradictory, from which it follows that the assertion that there are people, or trees and houses, is on a par with assertions that there are roud squares. It likewise follows that to know that there are people and physical objects is also logically impossible. Far from being true empirical propositions, as Moore holds, they are on Bradley's view *a priori* false.

Sceptical philosophers who have not gone so far as to deny the reality of things and people have denied the possibility of knowing them to be real. One reason given is that to know that things external to us exist would require knowing, for one thing, that we are not dreaming. And they have denied that this is possible. As Descartes pointed out, every waking-life experience could conceivably be reproduced in dream-experience, with no internal feature possessed by the one which is lacking to the other. Sceptics conclude that sense experience can neither establish nor even make probable that a real world of persons and things exists. Moore insists that he does know it to be in fact true that trees, houses, and other people exist, though he allows that he does not know how he knows this nor how he could prove that he is not in a dream. Ayer makes the stronger claim that it is not false but nonsensical to assert that the world of sense experience is unreal (1951, p. 39). These claims and counterclaims throw into doubt the status of the proposition concerned. If experience will neither establish nor render it probable that there are things and other people, can the proposition be the proposition it seems to be? Could an analysis show it to be *a priori*? And does any empirical consideration support the claim that it is never conceivably true that we have knowledge of the existence of things and other minds? If what is requisite for knowing this is knowing that we are not dreaming, then an examination of the possibility of knowing the difference between dream and waking life is in order. How would one go about deciding that he is not dreaming? By tests and careful observation? The sceptic would deny that these, and apparentily any other means, will serve the purpose. Then is the statement 'I am not dreaming' empirical?

Hume's view that the idea of an underlying substance in which sense qualities inhere is a fiction of the imagination raises a similar question about the character of the proposition 'Substance is a fiction'. To arrive at this conclusion Hume appeared to make use of observation – the kind of procedure relevant to an empirical proposition. Sight, he said, acquainted him with color and shape, touch with smoothness, etc., but no impression was to be had of substance. Locke would have replied that this is not surprising inasmuch as substance is unknowable. But he asserted that it exists nonetheless, inasmuch as we cannot imagine how these qualities 'can subsist by themselves' without something to support them 'and from which they do result' (1928, Bk. II, Ch. 23). Locke seems to be saying that qualities which constantly go together cannot be conceived to exist without belonging to something, and Hume that this something is a fiction. But what sort of fiction? Griffins are fictions, but a griffin is a conceivable existent and we have an idea of what it would be like to encounter one. But despite leaving the impression that he has failed in an empirical search to find a subject of attributes, Hume asserts that he has no idea of substance, and if there is no such idea, then substance and griffins are fictions of a logically different kind. The mode of verification relevant to one is different in kind from the mode of verification relevant to the other.

Many philosophical positions, like Hume's on substance and the sceptic's on our knowledge, have an empirical air about them. But philosophical controversy makes it suspect whether they are empirical even where the temptation is greatest to suppose them to be such, namely, where the matter appears to be capable of settlement by introspecion. The question whether one can feel pleasure without being aware of it, and the question whether a mental image can appear to have a color it in fact lacks, would both seem to have, on introspection, a ready answer. But they do not; controversy continues. Does this imply that experience is not relevant, that an analysis of the notions of 'felt pleasure' and of 'mental image' is the proper means of deciding on their truth? And will an analysis also leave their truth-value in dispute?

DOUBTS AND QUERIES

1. We have seen that *a priori* propositions which are either intuitively or demonstratively certain can be determined to be such by inspection of or reasoning upon their constituent concepts. For example, 'A man who has a widow is dead', 'A cube has twelve edges'. C. I. Lewis has raised the question whether they might not also be established – 'as well established as most laws of science' – inductively. Since observation first suggests that a cube has twelve edges, is it not plausible to suppose that inductive evidence is relevant to showing it to be true? But is the inductive procedure appropriate to general empirical propositions also appropriate to general mathematical propositions? Is it correct to say, as Mill does, that necessary propositions such as 'Two straight lines cannot enclose a

plane' 'receive confirmation in almost every instant of our lives' and that 'experimental proof crowds in upon us in ... endless profusion' (1956, Bk. II, Ch. 5, Sec. 4)? If it is, then it is correct to say at a certain point in confirming a necessary proposition p that p is probable. And if p is probable, then not-p is improbable. But what is improbable *could* be true. Yet if p is necessary, could not-p be possibly true?

2. In the history of mathematics attempts at demonstration of a theorem have sometimes been preceded by the kind of examination of cases involved in inductive procedures. Thus, Fermat examined the first five numbers of the form $2^{2^n}+1$ and proceeded to the general proposition that all numbers of this form are prime. Euler had recourse to the same procedure and discovered that the sixth number of this form was not prime. Could Fermat have been conceiving to be true what is logically impossible? And is it proper to characterize as inductive the procedure of confirming by calculation even such a limited theorem as 'For $n = 0, 1, 2, 3, 4, 2^{2^n}+1$ is prime'? Is this like confirming that the first five cows in Brown's barn are black? An important point of difference which deserves thinking about is that each cow which observation shows to be black *could* be shown by observation to be some other color. (We can imagine a black cow changing its color.) But a number which inspection shows to have a certain property inspection could not possibly show to lack it. (It is inconceivable for $2^{2^3}+1$ to lose its property of being prime and become divisible without remainder by a number other than itself and 1.)

3. To suppose that instances of a generalization have a bearing on its truth even when it is *a priori* presupposes that the generalization gives information about those instances. We have seen that according to the conventionalist view of *a priori* propositions they have no factual content and serve to report usage; they are about words rather than about what the words denote. How then explain the relevance of testing a number theory generalization by examining its instances?

4. On the face of it, there would seem to be no bridge from a statement about terminology to a statement about things, from verbal usage to ontology. For the two statements move in different planes. Consider Ayer's claim that 'the fact that you *can* restate propositions [about physical objects] in terms of sense data, *if* you can, tells you something important about them' (1954, p. 141). What sort of 'can' is this? If it is the logical 'can' which occurs in 'Griffins can exist but round squares cannot', then to assert that the nature of physical objects can be described in terms of sense data is to assert an *a priori* proposition. On the conventionalist

view will this be a statement about physical objects? Is there a valid way of inferring a fact about things from a fact of usage?

5. The conventionalist view itself, as an account of *a priori* propositions, raises a number of unanswered questions. For one thing, it raises the question whether the view that necessary propositions are verbal implies that there are no necessary propositions. The question is startling, and some philosophers have answered it in the affirmative. Consider equating 'All squares are rectangles' with the verbal proposition 'The word "rectangle" applies to every figure the word "square" applies to'. The latter is a mere matter of fact about English usage, which is to say that it might be otherwise. What conclusion must be drawn from holding that the two can be identified?

6. Suppose now that it is incorrect to hold that propositions we all take to be necessary report usage. Then why is it often sufficient to appeal to usage to determine whether they assert a truth? That it is relevant to do this cannot be denied. There is something to be said for the claim that necessary propositions are true in virtue of the definitions of terms used to express them. In some way the truth of 'All squares are rectangles' would seem to be bound up with the verbal statement ' "Rectangle" applies to whatever "square" applies to'. But are they bound by identity? If a necessary proposition is verbal, that is, a report of usage, can you argue that a person who grasps the necessary *proposition, All squares are rectangles*, whether expressed in English, French, Chinese, ... etc., will know English if this proposition is equated with '*Rectangle*' *applies to whatever* '*square*' *applies to*?

7. Could there be a true proposition even though no language existed? If there could not be, that is, if the proposition *A rose is a thing* is identical with '*Rose*' *is a thing-word*, could the proposition be a necessary truth, one holding *at all times*, even before language existed?

8. Opposed to the conventionalist position is the general view that necessary truths convey information, not about words, but about things. It will be recalled that one of the chief exponents of this counterview was Leibniz, and that his claim was challenged by Wittgenstein. According to Leibniz a necessary truth is an identical proposition whose negation implies a self-contradiction. It therefore falls into the general category of analytical or tautologous propositions. Wittgenstein held that such propositions say nothing, the underlying reason being that a proposition that is compatible with all the possibilities is empty of information about any of them. The implication is that identical truths say nothing about the

3*

totality of possible worlds. It is useful to consider this conclusion in relation to W. H. B. Joseph's claim that an identical truth is both a law of thought and a law of things. What sort of procedure is relevant to deciding between claim and counter-claim? In general, what is the mode of verification for determining the truth of rival claims about the nature of *a priori* necessity? What means are relevant to deciding whether or not necessary propositions convey only verbal information, whether or not they give us facts common to all possible worlds, whether some of them, those Kant called synthetic *a priori*, give us new information about things, or whether all *a priori* propositions are empty of factual content?

REFERENCES

Recommended reading:
  A. J. Ayer (1951), *Language, truth and logic*, Chs. 2, 3.
Further readings:
  John Locke (1928), *An essay concerning human understanding*, Book IV, Chs. 1, 2, 3, 9, 10, 11.
  John Wisdom, *Philosophy and psychoanalysis*, 'Metaphysics and verification'.
  Ludwig Wittgenstein, *Tractatus logico-philosophicus*, Propositions 3.34–4.5.

3. The External World

The attempt to arrive at a philosophical understanding of the nature of objects constituting the external world – of such objects as chairs, houses, trees, and stars – i.e., the attempt to reach an understanding of the ultimate structure of things, has brought to light a host of problems to which new problems are constantly being added. All of these problems connect up with the question whether, and how far, our senses are capable of revealing to us what things are in their inner nature, and even whether they exist. If the instruments which we must use to obtain knowledge of things are our senses, then their adequacy requires careful investigation.

It will be clear from the various proposed answers to the question about the constitution of physical objects that it is not to be identified with the similar-sounding question asked by scientists. Laboratory procedures do not figure in the work of the philosopher: Philosophy has no laboratories. And it is by no means certain whether *anything* which could be correctly described as an empirical investigation occurs. Philosophers sometimes give the impression of resorting to observation, as Hume seemed to do in his investigation of causation, but there is no doubt that none of their results is obtained with the help of scientific instruments. In coming to the conclusion that what we take to be productive causes are nothing more than constant joint occurrences, Hume did not inspect instances of causation through a magnifying glass. His instrument was *analysis*, and the object of his analytical scrutiny was the concept of causation. At times the philosopher represents his investigation as being a kind of experiment conducted in the imagination, and it will be of particular importance to get clear what the nature of such an experiment is, or whether, indeed, it is an experiment. It will be useful to keep in mind throughout the ensuing discussion of theories about the nature of things the question regarding the modes of verification relevant to the theories.

We begin with what we may suppose to be the metaphysics of the man in the street, that is, with the idea which he has, in an inarticulate form, of what the constitution of things is. Some philosophical theories make explicit the features of things implicit in this idea, some go on to subject it to criticism, deriving consequences that the ordinary man is not aware of. What this idea is can be gathered from everyday talk about things: The ordinary language descriptive of things has their features embedded in it. And ordinary language is, of course, the language of Everyman, including philosophers of all persuasions, who in the conduct of their daily life are not different from Everyman. The generic traits things are taken for granted to have may according to some philosophers be sifted out from common speech because common speech has grown up on the basis of an antecedent metaphysical theory.

As the subject-predicate structure of our language indicates, we distinguish between things and their properties. Things present themselves to our senses by means of organized clusters of attributes, as Locke put it, attributes 'united in a common subject'. Smells, colors, tastes, etc. are given to the senses as in some way belonging together; their organization does not seem to be accidental. And a given thing, such as a chair, gets its character from the attributes which inhere in it and which it as a substance holds together. The most general notion of things, which is reflected in our everyday talk about them, is that they are characterized by properties but are something in addition to the properties characterizing them. Things are the subjects of multi-attribution, and are sometimes described as being the 'support' of a variety of qualities. Many philosophers reject the substance-attribute theory of things as mistaken, and some of them explain the mistake as being due to superimposing the noun-adjective structure of our language upon things, in Russell's words, as being due to 'transference to the world-structure of the structure of sentences composed of a subject and a predicate' (1945, p. 202). Other philosophers, who can be understood to be making the theory of the ordinary man explicit, would maintain that facts about things dictate the structure of language – such facts as that a thing is something which has properties but is not itself just the collection of properties.

Within this very general conception of a thing one can by being attentive to everyday talk about things make further specifications. It is proper to say of a chair or a table, whether truly or not, that we see the same one twice and that other people see the same one we see. That is, it is intelligible English to speak of the same physical object being perceived at different times by the same person and of its being perceived by different people at the same time. Of a mental image this can perhaps be said intelligibly, but is in fact not true. (This will be discussed later.) It is an important point of contrast between physical objects and mental images that the existence of a physical object is not confined to a single perception nor to a single perceiver, whereas the existence of a mental image is. A mental image is such that just *that* image does not reappear, nor exist between perceptions, nor is it accessible to other people. It is said to be subjective, that is, to depend for its existence on being perceived. As Tweedledum said of the Red King, were he to awake the things in his dream would 'go out – bang!' The span of their existence is completely subject to the person who apprehends them. They do not, to use Hume's expression, have 'continu'd and independent existence'. Nor are they open to observation by more than one perceiver; they are private to the perceiver as well as dependent for their existence on him.

The way in which we talk of mental images and of physical objects reflects their contrasting features. Our language indicates that physical objects are conceived of as existing while unperceived, consequently between perceptions, and as being publicly accessible. That is, embedded in common speech we find along with the general conception of a physical object as a substance which supports qualities the more specific notions that it is independent of perception, temporally continuous, and public. These features do not exhaust what is comprehended in the ordinary conception of a physical object. One further feature is its preservation of identity throughout a series of changes. It can change, and remain the same thing. Another is its spatial unity. The properties a thing has have a common spatial location, for example, the smell of a lemon is localized where the color and shape are. Still another is its accessibility not only to different people but to our different senses. Certain attributes are accessible to one sense only, as color, taste, and smell, but the physical thing is accessible to more than one sense. A final and very important characteristic is causal efficacy, the power a physical object has to cause change in something else. By virtue of this power it produces physical change by acting on other physical things, and sensory occurrences by acting on a mind. A billiard ball, for example, causes motion in the ball it strikes and auditory and visual sensations in the person who observes it.

Philosophical reflection on these commonplace characteristics of physical objects has given rise to views which it is not natural for the uncritical man to hold. One natural idea about things is that they have properties of every kind they appear to have. We all recognize the fact that things can appear to have properties they do not have, e.g., that the apparent color of a thing, the apparent size, the apparent shape, may not be the real color, size, or shape. But though a particular apparent property may be different from the real property, it is taken for granted that a thing has properties of every *kind* it appears to have: It may not have the color it appears to have, but it has some color oɪ other; and similarily for the roster of other sense properties. Some philosophers have challenged this assumption, notably Locke and Descartes, and long before them, Democritus. Locke put forward a view to the effect that properties of some kinds which a physical object appears to have it could not by its very nature have. Such a view will strike the ordinary man as untrue since it goes so strongly against what his senses attest to.

Another view about the nature of physical objects which will be foreign to the thinking of the ordinary man is, however, consistent with his unreflective assumptions. This is the view that a thing, as opposed to its experienceable attributes, is unknowable: The subject of attribution – that in which properties inhere – is beyond the reach of the senses. Locke held that 'those qualities we find existing... we imagine cannot subsist ... without something to support them' (1928, Bk. II, Ch. 23), but that this support is an 'I know not what'. And Aristotle likewise held that the bearer of attributes, what he called matter, was 'unknowable in itself'. The unfamiliar idea that a thing has as a component an inexperienceable substance underlying its qualities has its backing in a number of considerations stemming from familiar facts, especially the facts that a thing is accessible to the different senses and that it is temporally continuous throughout changes. A thing is given equally to all the senses, but it is given to none of them in the way in which a particular sense-property is given, for it is not itself a sense-property. Color and taste, for example, have nothing in common, so that *what* we see and taste, because it is neither a color nor a taste, is neutral between them. It is itself not perceived in the way in which its sense-properties are perceived. This neutrality between the senses implied by its accessibility to more than one sense is one of the reasons behind the distinction between direct and indirect perception. It is natural to distinguish between perceiving a thing and perceiving its color or shape, inasmuch as the thing is not *given* to the senses as are its properties. Perception is not of a shape and *also* of the thing which has the shape, and in consequence some philosophers hold that we apprehend the *thing* only indirectly.

The fact that a physical object is capable of enduring continuously while changing, that is, of remaining the same thing throughout a series of alterations in size, shape, etc., also bolsters this distinction, and provides an additional reason for the view that an unknowable substratum underlies sense-given properties. A thing could conceivably change in such a way that *all* of its sense-properties are replaced by others. But though in this hypothetical case it is altogether different at the end of the process of change than it was at the beginning, we still say it is the same thing. Consider now what the senses disclose: the series of changes. By hypothesis there is nothing in the perception of the thing that has endured throughout. Consequently we must say that what has remained the same is hidden from our perception. The invariant subject of changes, because *it* is never given to the senses, is unknowable. This point was put graphically by Descartes as follows.

'Let us take for example, this piece of wax: it has been taken quite freshly from the hive and it has not yet lost the sweetness of the honey which it contains; it still retains somewhat of the odour of the flowers from which it has been culled; its colour, figure, its size are apparent; it is hard, cold, easily handled, and if you strike it with the finger, it will emit a sound. Finally all the things which are requisite to cause us distinctly to recognise a body, are met with in it. But notice that while I speak and approach the fire what remained of it becomes liquid, it heats, scarcely can one handle it, and when one strikes it no sound is emitted. Does the same wax remain after this change? We must confess that it remains; none would judge otherwise. What then did I know so distinctly in this piece of wax? It could certainly be nothing of all that the senses brought to my notice, since all these things which fall under taste, smell, sight, touch and hearing are found to be changed, and yet the same wax remains. . . . But what must particularly be observed is that its perception er is neither an act of vision, nor of touch. . .' (*Meditation* II).

The body whose changing forms are perceptible is not itself capable of being perceived.

There is a further and perhaps more fundamental consideration which supports the view that the bearer of attributes is unknowable. Suppose we conduct an experiment in the imagination of stripping away all the properties of the wax, in an attempt to comprehend the thing which is distinct from and in addition to its properties. Let us one by one imagine its color, shape, solidity, smell abstracted from it. What remains is something of which we can form no conception other than that it supports attributes. Yet something must remain. A thing is something more than its attributes; being a thing entails being something in addition to them. But a careful examination of our sense contents never reveals this additional something. Thinking away a thing's properties is a way of trying to reveal substratum, which as the experiment shows, eludes our conception. The result of the experiment is that what is left after stripping, as an examination of the content of perception reveals, is a mere x, beyond describing and beyond knowing. As Kant said, '. . . in all substance the proper subject, that which remains after all accidents (as predicates) are abstracted, consequently that which forms the substance of things, remains unknown...substance itself can never be thought by our understanding, however deep we may penetrate, even if all of nature were unveiled to us.' (1929b, sec. 46). The difference between physical geology and what we might call metaphysical geology should not go unnoticed here. For the field geologist, substrata are discoverable by excavation or other physical tests, if not practically, then in principle. But there is no metaphysical excavation which will lay bare for us the subject of attributes. That lowest layer is not in principle discoverable, nor do we know what it is that a search would disclose.

Among the attributes substance has, some philosophers, for example Locke, have distinguished two kinds, those which a thing must have in virtue of being a physical thing, and those which it merely appears to have but which it is impossible that it should have. (This characterization is ambiguous in Locke, but is implied by his argument.) Both types of property present themselves to our senses, but of the properties a thing appears to have, some it could have and some it cannot. The first are its spatially or temporally *quantitative* properties such as size, shape, solidity, motion or rest, duration. These are not only possible properties, but essential – as Locke said, 'utterly inseparable from the body'. Without them a physical thing cannot be, that is, being a physical thing *entails* having size, shape, etc. These qualities Locke denominated 'primary and real'. By contrast such sense qualities as color, taste, odor, temperature, sound are not real qualities of a body: '. . .yellowness is not actually in gold, but is a power in gold to produce that idea in us by our eyes, when placed in due light' (Locke, 1928, Bk. II, Ch. 23).' Let not the eyes see light, or colours, nor the ears hear sounds; let the palate not taste, nor the nose smell; and all colours, tastes, odours, and sounds . . . vanish and cease, and are reduced to their causes, i.e. bulk, figure, and motion of parts' (*Ibid*, Bk. II, Ch. 8). Unlike the first kind of properties, which 'are in the things themselves, whether they are perceived or no', the 'secondary' qualities are 'but the powers of several combinations of those primary ones...' and would not exist were there no perceptions. Locke's view was anticipated many centuries earlier by Democritus, who said: 'By convention, there is sweet; by convention, bitter; by convention, hot; by convention, cold; by convention, colour; but in truth there exist atoms and the void' (Sextus Empiricus, in: Nahm, p. 269).

The view that certain kinds of qualities which appear to characterize physical objects 'do not really exist in the bodies themselves' has its support in an argument from the divisibility of matter. Anaxagoras maintained that there is no least of that which is small; there is always a smaller: However minute the divisions in matter are, further division is still conceivable. In opposition to this view, those like Democritus 'who believe in atoms said that division stops at the indivisible substances and does not continue to infinity' (Aetius, in: Nahm, p. 173). There comes a point, they said, at which the parts of matter can be no further divided. These parts, to use Russell's distinction, though geometrically divisible are physically indivisible. They are the ultimate constituents composing that which occupies space. The composite, or what is divisible, consists of the parts into which it can be divided. Now the parts finally reached in a process of division are *too small* to have color, sound, odor, taste. But every part, *however small*, must have size and shape. 'Take a grain of wheat', said Locke, 'divide it into two parts, each part has still solidity, extension, figure, mobility; divide it again, and it retains still the same qualities. For division (which is all that a mill, or pestle ... does upon another, in reducing it to insensible parts) can never take away either solidity, extension, figure, or mobility from any body' (Locke, 1928, Bk. II, Ch. 8). 'Had we senses acute enough to discern the minute particles of bodies, and the real constitution on which their sensible qualities depend ... that which is now the yellow colour of gold, would then disappear, and instead of it we should see an admirable texture of parts of a certain size and figure' (*Ibid.*, Bk. II, Ch. 23).

As a corollary of this account of the attributes the ordinary man ascribes to things we have an account of perception as effecting a partial correspondence between the data of sense and their outer causes. The qualities of our data, if primary, duplicate the qualities of the perceived physical object; if secondary, they belong to the data only, and it would be an error to suppose them to belong to the object. We *say* the grass is green, but taken literally, this is false. Descartes asserted that 'the principal error and the commonest which we may meet with ... consists in judging that the ideas which are in [us] are similar or conformable to the things which are outside [us]' (*Meditation* III). And as we have already seen, the ultimate cause of our sensations, namely, the bearer of the perceived qualities, has no correlate whatever among our sense contents.

The thesis that an unknowable substratum is a component of physical things came under attack by Locke's successor, Bishop Berkeley. From him the view commonly known as phenomenalism received its important formulation, although it had its roots in the ancient theory of Protagoras, to the effect, roughly speaking, that a thing is a sum of seemings, or appearances, to perceivers. The substratum view of physical objects, being bound up with our subject-predicate talk about things, would seem to be an outcome of views very natural to the ordinary man, even though it itself is alien. Some philosophers have claimed that ordinary language has misled people into holding the substratum view about things and have put forward a rival metaphysical view which would seem to be associated with a remodelling of the structure of language used to refer to things. To put the matter briefly, their view is bound up with a replacement of ordinary subject-predicate thing-language by a form of speech which uses a different grammar. The subject-predicate language remains, of course, and the philosopher's using it is a concession to the demands of everyday life. The phenomenalist philosopher follows Berkeley's advice to 'think with the learned and speak with the vulgar.'

The source of this reconstruction of language is the critique of the notion of substratum. It can readily be seen that substratum is not only unknowable to us but also resists God's comprehension. The arguments showing it to be unknowable show that it is *intrinsically* unknowable: It is logically impossible for substratum to be known by a mind regardless of how great its power. Not even God's omniscience could penetrate substratum, any more than it could enable him to think a four-sided triangle. The existence of substratum would have had for Berkeley disconcerting implications: Not only that it was beyond the ken of even an Infinite Mind but also that it is something God could not have created. For He could not have thought into being what He cannot think. Genesis tells us that God said, 'Let there be', and there was. But God could not have said, 'Let substratum be', for He, no more than anyone else, could think substratum. Paradoxes might be multiplied: To suppose that He created substance would imply that He could never know what He had created.

Berkeley's view about the nature of what exists can be stated in various ways. His famous dictum, 'Esse est percipi', 'to be is to be perceived', does not, without qualification, state his position. For inasmuch as minds, as against their contents, are not perceived, the dictum would imply that nothing whatever exists. Minds, not being possible objects of perception, would not exist, and things would not exist because there would be no perceivers. The accurate statement of Berkeley's position is: To be is to be perceived or to be a perceiver. Alternatively, to be other than a perceiver is to be perceived. The implication is that what the ordinary man classifies as physical objects – such things as chairs, human bodies, the planets – are mind-dependent. As it turns out, on Berkeley's view their dependency is ultimately on God: To be a physical thing is to be perceived by an Infinite Perceiver. G. E. Moore's way of putting it (in a discussion) is that a physical object is an idea in the mind of God.

The critique of the notion of substratum is central to the doctrine of phenomenalism. Locke admits that 'if anyone will examine himself concerning his notion of pure substance in general, he will find he has no other idea of it at all, but only as a supposition of he knows not what support of such qualities, which are capable of producing simple ideas in us' (1928, Bk. II, Ch. 23). The Bishop of Worcester, in his criticism of this assertion, summed up Locke's position on substance as follows: '...without knowing what it is, it is that which supports accidents; so that of substance we have no idea of what it is, but only a confused and obscure idea of what it does' (See, Locke 1812, Vol. IV, p. 448). The question is whether we have even an obscure idea of what it does if we have no idea of what it is, and conversely, whether describing it in terms of its function of supporting attributes provides any idea of what it is. To say substratum is unknowable is to imply that we have no idea whatever of what it is. Berkeley called substratum an 'abstract idea', that is, an idea that could not be framed. And if it is in principle impossible to say what it is, it is in principle impossible to say what it does. We can no more conceive what it would be for substratum to support attributes than to conceive of substratum itself. We cannot intelligibly speak of attributes being supported if in principle the support cannot be specified. And this is to say that the term 'substratum' is completely contentless, that no conception is attached to it. It is literally meaningless, a pseudo-term. The same holds for the phrase 'support of attributes', which conveys no idea of what it denotes nor of the function of what it denotes. Ayer makes ordinary language responsible for anyone's supposing 'substance' stands for something.

'It happens to be the case, that we cannot, in our language, refer to the sensible properties of a thing without introducing a word or phrase which appears to stand for the thing itself as opposed to anything which may be said about it .... But from the fact that we happen to employ a single word "substance" to refer to a thing, and make that word the grammatical subject of the sentences 'n which we refer to the sensible appearances of the thing, it does not by any means follow that the thing itself is a "simple entity"... It is true that in talking of "its" appearances we appear to distinguish the thing from its appearances, but that is simply an accident of linguistic usage' (1951, p. 42).

A further critique of substratum theory is connected with the distinction between primary and secondary qualities. This critique has two sides, one directed against substratum, the other oriented towards a new account of the nature of physical objects, the phenomenalistic theory that they are sets of ideas. This theory is arrived at via a consideration concerning secondary qualities which can be extended to primary qualities, namely, that there is no way of distinguishing, amongst the qualities a physical thing presents under various conditions, between its real qualities and those which are only apparent. Consider the secondary quality, color. The ordinary man assumes that though the color a table appears to have may not be its real color, some color which on other occasions the table appears to have or which it could appear to have really belongs to it. Locke's argument from the divisibility of matter was directed to showing that no color belongs to the minute particles constituting matter, and the color a material thing appears to have is only the effect produced by those particles in virtue of their primary qualities. The present consideration, however, that there is no way, in principle, of picking out the real qualities of a thing from the totality of qualities it presents under different conditions, is quite independent of Locke's consideration. It could be used to argue that regardless of size, whether large or small, a body could not have color. Russell sets out the argument for this position as follows.

'There is no colour which preeminently appears to be *the* colour of the table, or even of any one particular part of the table – it appears to be of different colours from different points of view, and there is no reason for regarding some of them as more really its colour than others. And we know that even from a given point of view the colour will seem different by artificial light, or to a colour-blind man, or to a man wearing blue spectacles, while in the dark there will be no colour at all ... Thus colour is not something which is inherent in the table, but something depending upon the table and the spectator and the way the light falls on the table. When, in ordinary life, we speak of the colour of the table, we only mean the sort of colour which it will seem to have to a normal spectator from an ordinary point of view under usual conditions of light. But the other colours which appear under other conditions have just as good a right to be considered real; and therefore, to avoid favoritism, we are compelled to deny that, in itself, the table has any one particular colour' (1943, pp. 13–14).

Only perceptual favoritism makes us call the color seen by the normal perceiver under standard conditions the *real* color of a thing. A little reflection shows that the standard condition is only one of a great number of possible conditions, all of which have the same theoretical status. And what is taken to be the standard or average perception is arrived at by counting heads, and the count could, in principle, be different from the present count. That is to say, what is normal now could come to count as abnormal and what is abnormal could come to count as normal. Thus, with respect to color there is no non-arbitrary way of deciding, among the different colors a thing is seen as having, which is real and which merely apparent. All colors a thing looks to have are on the same footing, which is to say that all are equally apparent and hence not actual, or real, properties of the thing. They are properties of the perceptual appearances and not of the things themselves. It is obvious that the same consideration applies to the other so-called secondary qualities – temperature, odor, sound, taste. They are one and all merely apparent, and since these apparent qualities are perceiver-dependent, so are those among them the ordinary man calls real.

As we have seen, Locke admitted the subjectivity of the secondary qualities. It remained for Berkeley to direct against that 'deservedly esteemed philosopher' (1871, Pt. I, Intr., Sec. 11), a criticism undermining his claim that the primary qualities 'are in the things themselves, whether they are perceived or no'. In the *Dialogues between Hylas and Philonous*, and in his *Principles*, Berkeley notes the variability, one by one, of the primary qualities. Here again, only perceptual favoritism would make us single out any one of the qualities presented to perception as being a real character of the thing. They are generically the same. What is taken to be the actual size, for example, is but one among an indefinite number of sizes a thing does or could present. Motion and rest, duration, solidity, shape are in the same case. There is no ontological principle for placing any apparent quality on a different footing from any other. All are equally perceiver-dependent. In fact even the sense contents we call delusive differ in no qualitative way from those we call veridical. The conclusion to be drawn from these considerations is that a physical substance can in principle no more have primary qualities than it can have secondary qualitites. What then is our idea of a substance? It is the idea of a completely qualityless object, not conceivable in terms of any properties we encounter in experience. But this is no idea at all. The supposed idea of something uncharacterized by properties is not the idea of anything. We cannot envisage anything theoretical to which we should apply the term 'propertyless thing'. And this means that the term has been given no application and has no intelligible meaning.

If it turns out that instead of the idea of something mysterious that eludes both perception and conception there is no idea, and that the subject of attributes, or alternatively, the thing which presents appearances, vanishes, then we are left with a quite different conception of a physical object. Unable to distinguish that which presents appearances from the appearances themselves, because 'that which presents appearances' denotes nothing, we are left merely with the appearances. The phrase 'thing plus its appearances', which looks as though it stands for a sum of components, reduces to 'appearances'. Once the conception of a thing is freed from the spurious notion of a subject of appearances, what remains is the conception of a thing as an organization of the appearances. As Ayer said, when we refer to the sensible appearances of a thing 'it does not by any means follow that the thing itself . . . cannot be defined in terms of the totality of appearances. . . Logical analysis shows that what makes these "appearances" the "appearances" of the same thing is not their relationship to an entity other than themselves, but their relationship to one another (1951, p. 50). Thus our talk of the properties a thing has or the appearances 'it' presents is a misleading though natural manner of speaking; 'it' is just the organized totality of shapes, colors, smells, tastes – or to use a term in present day currency, the organized collection of sense data. This is the phenomenalist position on the nature of physical objects. '. . . a "thing" will be defined as a certain series of aspects, namely those which would commonly be said to be *of* the thing. To say that a certain aspect is an aspect *of* a certain thing will merely mean that it is one of those which, taken serially, *are* the thing' (Russell, 1929, p. 113). A thing turns out to be a construct of experienceable components, instead of a whole constituted of these components plus their inferred unknowable possessor. It is interesting to note a similarity between the phenomenalist account of a physical object and the modern explanation of irrational numbers. It is natural to look upon $\sqrt{2}$ as the limit of the sequence of rational numbers 1, 1.1, 1.14, 1.141, etc. Mathematicians, however, define $\sqrt{2}$ as just the sequence itself.

Inasmuch as 'unknowable substance' has no meaning attached to it, nothing is lost by the phenomenalistic description of a physical object as a system of appearances. Nevertheless, the picture of the external world seems somehow changed. Appearances, being dependent on perceivers for their existence, constitute a world from which all that was stable and substantial seems to have vanished. In fact, Berkeley's form of phenomenalism was attacked for denying the existence of physical objects. Dr. Johnson, in response to Boswell's claim that though Berkeley's doctrine was untrue it could not be refuted, 'struck his foot with mighty force against a large stone, till he rebounded from it' (Boswell 1893, Vol. I, p. 271), with the defiant words 'I refute it *thus*'. The existence of physical objects, which Dr. Johnson supposed Berkeley to have denied, was thus thought to have been established. But the refutation was not to the point and the doctrine he tried to refute was not Berkeley's. Berkeley's argument against the existence of matter was not an argument against the existence of chairs, tables, etc., and those who took it to be such misinterpreted Berkeley's immaterialism. The view that matter does not exist implies only that chairs and tables are not composed of matter in which attributes inhere; its force is not to deny that there are such things. Rather, its force is to deny the existence of a claimed component of things. However paradoxical it may seem, the view that matter does not exist does not imply that chairs, mountains, the moon, in short, 'all the choir of heaven and furniture of the earth', are unreal. Berkeley's theory, and in general, phenomenalism, is a theory about the nature of things, that is, their constitution, and is not a theory about what exists.

When Berkeley undermined the distinction between primary and secondary qualities the negative consequence was that the x which was thought to manifest itself through its appearances vanished into the appearances. The corollary positive consequence was the theory that physical objects are just the systems of appearances. This theory is supported by a further consideration, a *Gedankenexperiment* to ascertain what it is we think when we conceive of a physical thing. Berkeley asks us to 'attend to what is meant by the term *exist* when applied to sensible things'. He goes on to assert: 'The table I write on I say exists; that is, I see and feel it; and if I

4

were out of my study some other spirit actually does perceive it' (1871, Pt. I, Sec. 3). And what is it that he perceives, or would perceive? 'Lights and colours, heat and cold, extension and figures' (*Ibid*, Sec. 5). That is, what exists and is perceivable can only be thought of in terms of the appearances it presents to perception. To think of one's writing table is to think of how it would look or feel. As Bradley put it, 'Try to discover any sense in which you can still continue to speak of it, when all perception and feeling have been removed; or point out ... any aspect of its being, which ... is not still relative to this source. When the experiment is made strictly, I can myself conceive of nothing else than the experienced (1925, p. 145).

The conception of a physical object as a set of appearances of course does not imply that the appearances must be present to oneself alone, that is, that the object must be perceived by oneself alone. It does not even imply that the object is being perceived by oneself. Berkeley's dictum is that to be is to be perceived, not 'to be is to be perceived by me'. The latter is the dictum of one form of solipsism. In this respect the phenomenalist position is consonant with the commonsense assumption that a number of people see the same thing and that there are things not perceived by oneself. The view that a thing is conceivable only as a set of appearances, together with the dependency of appearances for their existence on being perceived, merely implies that when one thinks of a thing not perceived by oneself one is thinking of an appearance apprehended by some other mind. Thus, that I conceive of an apple as something that looks red, feels hard, tastes sweet implies that I conceive of it as looking, feeling, and tasting thus to some perceiver not necessarily myself, or to a number of perceivers, all of whom can sensibly be said to be perceiving the same apple. The phenomenalist conception of a thing in terms of how it appears or would appear, that is, as a set of actual and possible appearances, in no way upsets the use of such a sentence as 'Twenty tourists are seeing the Statue of Liberty, but I have never seen it'. In effect phenomenalists assign to the term 'physical object' the meaning 'system of actual and possible sensible appearances', and as Berkeley maintains, 'the common use of language will receive no manner of alteration ... from the admission of our tenets' (Berkeley, 1871, Pt. I, Sec. 51).

Something further should be said in explanation of the phrase '*possible* sensible appearances'. Again we turn to the conception we have of a physical thing. A thing is always thought of as being something more than the particular appearances present to any one sense or even to all the senses of any one perceiver. For example, when one sees an apple one expects to experience an odor and taste as well. No one of the senses discloses all the appearances which make up our idea of an apple. And even with respect to a single sense, say the sense of sight, the actual appearance seen is taken to be but one of those which would be seen from other perspectives. Were a thing constituted of the appearances present at one time to a single perceiver, the thing would shrink into a fragment of what we conceive it to be, and we could not sensibly ask about the shape or color of parts hidden from view. When we see a thing we never see its entire surface. Moore, for example, maintained that the two expressions 'sees a thing' and 'sees a good part of the surface of a thing' were synonymous, and he went on to maintain further that when one sees part of the surface of a thing one is seeing one of its possible appearances.

Many contemporary philosophers have adopted the language of sense data as an alternative to the more usual appearance-terminology. The following consideration serves to introduce the term 'sense datum'. When we see a white page that looks yellow or a stick half immersed in water that looks bent we do see *something* that *is* yellow, or *is* bent, though of course that something is not identical with the sheet of paper (which is not yellow) or the stick (which is not bent). The term 'sense datum' is used to refer to the entity which actually has the properties the physical object appears to have. The sense datum of the sheet of paper is the thing that *is* yellow, the sense datum of the stick, the thing that *is* bent, and neither datum is identical with the thing, or the surface of the thing, of which it is an appearance. The phenomenalist position on the nature of physical things can now be expressed in sense datum terminology: A thing is a unified class of sense data. We turn now to the arguments, which are not all of equal value, by which the position has been supported. The first is the so-called argument from illusion.

Consider again the white sheet of paper, now seen as white. We are in this case inclined to think that we are seeing the sheet itself as against one of its appearances, and that the difference between seeing the paper when it looks yellow and seeing it when it looks white is the difference between seeing a sense datum of the paper and seeing the paper. But phenomenalists have argued that what is present to our senses when we see a white sheet of paper which does not look yellow is not less a sense datum than what is present to us when it does look yellow. In the one case we see a white sense datum, in the other a yellow one. The experience of looking at a sheet of paper that looks to be yellow is qualitatively the same as the

4*

experience of looking at a sheet of paper which really is yellow. Ayer argues that 'if, when our perceptions were delusive, we were always perceiving something of a different kind from what we perceived when they were veridical, we should expect our experience to be qualitatively different in the two cases. We should expect to be able to tell from the intrinsic character of a perception whether it was a perception of a sense-datum or of a material thing. But this is not possible...' (1947, p. 7). What is more, the content of a perception of what we take to be the surface of a physical object could in principle be duplicated exactly by the content of a dream experience or of an hallucination, i.e., when no physical object is being perceived. As Berkeley said, '...what happens in dreams, frensies, and the like, puts it beyond dispute that it is possible we might be affected with all the ideas we have now, even though no bodies existed without...' (1871, Pt. I, Sec. 18).

Another consideration indicating that the contents of delusive and veridical perceptions are intrinsically indistinguishable is the fact that these contents form a continuous series.

Ayer argues as follows:

'If I gradually approach an object from a distance I may begin by having a series of perceptions which are delusive in the sense that the object appears to be smaller than it really is. Let us assume that the series terminates in a veridical perception. Then the difference in quality between this perception and its immediate predecessor will be of the same order as the difference between any two delusive perceptions that are next to one another in the series ... these are differences of degree and not of kind ... [which] is not what we should expect if the veridical perception were a perception of an object of a different sort, a material thing as opposed to a sense-datum' (1947, pp. 8–9). The conclusion is that what is commonly taken to be the thing as against its appearances belongs to a continuum of appearances and hence is itself merely one among the appearances. The objects of awareness in veridical and delusive perceptions are generically the same, and all equally sense data.

Moore uses the phenomenon of double images to argue for the same point, viz., that there is no way in principle of distinguishing what is taken to be the surface of a thing from a sense datum which is not the surface. 'Double images have convinced me', he wrote, 'that the sense-datum of which I am speaking when I say "That's a sofa" is *not* identical with any part of the surface of the sofa' (1962, p. 78). '...When we see a thing double, we certainly have *two* sense data each of which is *of* the

surface seen, and which cannot therefore both be identical with it . . .'
'Nor can it be that one of the two is the surface, and the other something
else, not identical with any physical object' (1959, p. 56). The two kinds of
sense contents are qualitatively indistinguishable, i.e., not different in
kind. Ayer proceeded to the conclusion that all that one's senses reveal
to him is the presence of sense data (1954, p. 141). Physical objects will be
sets of data conjoined in a unity. Anything other than sense data will
elude perception. Gorgias made a comparable claim two thousand years
earlier. We can imagine him arguing, were he to express himself in a more
modern idiom, as follows: 'Whenever I try to compare my perception of
a thing with the thing itself I find myself in the egocentric predicament of
comparing one perception with another. I never am able to compare my
perception of a thing with the thing. I only find myself comparing one
sense datum of it with another sense datum of it.' This we might think
leaves us with two alternatives, one that a thing as something in addition
to a system of sense data is a metaphysical entity which, by Occam's
razor, may be dispensed with, the other that the thing *is* just the system of
sense data. (This is a principle of scientific parsimony, one version of
which is that entities should not be multiplied unnecessarily.) The
phenomenalist implies that the second alternative is the only possible one,
because his argument shows, if it shows anything, that the conception of a
thing is identical with the conception, without remainder, of an organization of appearances.

It will be recalled that a thing was defined as an organization of actual
and possible sense data, and this raises a question concerning the ontological status of possible sense data. Is a possible sense datum to be identified
with the possibility of *there being* a sense datum, comparable to the
possibility of there being a centaur, i.e., something which could exist but
does not? Or is a possible datum an existent entity which could be
someone's sense content even though it happens not to be? Which of
these two senses enters into the phenomenalist definition of a thing? It is
important to note the difference between the two senses, either of which
would distinguish possible from actual data. An actual datum is a sense
presentation. Is the difference between an actual and a possible sense
datum like the difference between a dollar with which a purchase is being
made and a dollar in one's wallet with which the purchase could be made?
Or is it like the difference between an actual and an imaginary dollar? The
possibility of there being a sense datum, like the possibility of there being
a dollar, does not imply the existence of a sense datum, or a dollar. If all

one's dollars were mere possibilities, then one would have no dollars. Were the conception of a thing the conception of a set of actual data plus the mere possibility of there being further data, then a thing would reduce to the data actually present to some perceiver. The sheet of paper which I take myself to be perceiving would be no more than the white oblong patch given to my visual perception, no part of which would be unperceived. But in this case the object of my perception could not be a physical thing: It could not be a sheet of paper. For the conception of a physical thing is the conception of something more than what is perceived of it at any one time. In this respect a physical object differs from one of the data it presents. Although a datum present to someone's awareness may be linked with other data not yet present, it is not true to say of that datum that there are unperceived parts. The whole of a datum is given in awareness, but not the whole of a physical object. And the parts which exist unperceived by a particular perceiver are possible data for him. A possible datum is an existent which could be presented to his awareness. It differs from an actual datum of his, not because it might but does not exist, but because it might be, but is not, perceived. The term 'possible data' in the phrase 'actual and possible data' must be interpreted to denote existent entities if the conception of a thing is to be the conception of something more than what is presented of it to limited perceivers, that is, to perceivers like ourselves from whom some parts or qualities of physical things are always hidden.

Mill's characterization of a thing as a *permanent* possibility of sensation, and the distinction between an actual datum, presented to awareness, and a possible datum which exists though unperceived by a particular perceiver, suggest the idea that a thing *could* exist unperceived by anyone. In fact Russell made a distinction between a sense datum and a sensibile which was intended to avoid the subjectivity of the Berkeleian form of phenomenalism which makes the existence of a thing contingent on its being perceived. A thing was defined by Russell as a class of sensibilia, where these were 'objects which have the same ... status as sense data, without necessarily being data to any mind ... the relation of a *sensibile* to a sense-datum is like that of a man to a husband; a man becomes a husband by entering into the relation of marriage, and similarly a *sensibile* becomes a sense-datum by entering into the relation of acquaintance' (1917, pp. 148–149). Russell granted that 'it may be thought monstrous to maintain that a thing can present any appearances at all in a place where no sense organs and nervous structure exist through which it could appear', but says, 'I do not myself feel the monstrosity' (*Ibid*, p. 150). His reason was that as soon as the necessary distinction is made, within a perceptual experience, between the object of awareness and the awareness of it – this distinction was also made by Moore in his 'Refutation of idealism' – there remains no ground for supposing the object of awareness, alike with the act of awareness directed upon it, must be mental, i.e., perceiver-dependent. Therefore on his theory that a thing is a construct of sensibilia, a thing could exist without presenting an appearance to any mind.

The objection to the view that sensibilia could exist apart from being sensed is that any sensibile could be duplicated by a precisely similar mental image, which implies that sensibilia and mental images are qualitatively indistinguishable. They are no more distinguishable than is one mental image from another: Generically they belong together. Hence if a mental image could not exist apart from an awareness of it, that is to say, could not exist and not be someone's mental image, then sensibilia cannot both exist and not be the content of a perception. A sensibile, like a mental image which is not my sense content, must then be an actual datum to some mind or other. Consequently a physical thing, which with respect to any ordinary perceiver consists of a small number of actual data and an indefinite number of possible data, will exist only if, nevertheless, the possible data are actually perceived. The unperceived parts of a thing which I am perceiving will have to be perceived if the object of my perception is a thing and not just the contents of my present perception.

Phenomenalism, it can be seen, implies two things. It implies that a physical thing reduces to a system of *actual* data, and it also implies that the existence of a thing entails the existence of a Superperceiver to whose perceptions *all* data are given. A thing, being more than the sense content of any limited perceiver, must be wholly the sense content of a Superperceiver. Berkeley's view is usually called subjective idealism, but perhaps a more appropriate name for it would be theological phenomenalism. The existence of a grain of sand, alike with the existence of a planet or a cluster of stars, entails the existence of a cosmic Mind. With respect to *us*, a physical thing is *objective*, that is, it can exist unperceived by us. But with respect to God it is subjective; its existence is dependent on His perception, and the world of things may be described as his cosmic dream, parts of which we are privileged to perceive. His perception holds it continuously in existence, and has done so throughout the history of the cosmos. Ronald Knox's limerick summarizes the view:

> There once was a man who said, 'God
> Must think it exceedingly odd
> To find that this tree
> Continues to be
> With no one about on the Quad.'
>   *Reply:*
> 'Dear Sir: Your astonishment's odd;
> *I* am always about on the Quad.
> And that's why the tree
> Continues to be
> Since observed by
>   Yours faithfully', God.

That the world of things, which we perceive intermittently, does not depend for its existence on *our* perception is supported by a fact which Berkeley notes, namely, that many of our sense impressions are not subject to the control of our will. Berkeley used this fact as an argument for the existence of God; but it can be used to give some credence to there being external objects at least partly constituted of sense data which exist independently of our perception of them. (It is curious that Locke did not use his claim with regard to what he called simple ideas to argue to the existence of external objects. According to him such ideas – e.g., redness, loudness, sweetness – in contrast to complex ideas compounded from them, the mind is incapable of framing by itself. They obviously could not depend on a mind which is incapable of framing them and which therefore must be a passive recipient. The consequence is that simple ideas have an *external* source.) We might call Berkeley's argument the argument from 'the ineluctable modality of the visible' (from James Joyce, *Ulysses*). In his words: 'I find I can excite ideas in my mind at pleasure, and vary and shift the scene as oft as I think fit... But, whatever power I may have over my own thoughts, I find the ideas actually perceiv-ed by Sense have not a like dependence on *my* will. When in broad daylight I open my eyes, it is not in my power to choose whether I shall see or not, or to determine what particular objects shall present themselves to my view: and so likewise as to hearing and other senses; the ideas imprinted on them are not creatures of *my* will. There is therefore some other Will or Spirit that produces them' (1871, Pt. I, Secs. 28–29). Thus the necessity of accounting for the occurrence of one's involuntary data leads to a causal proof of the existence of God. It must be admitted, however, that this argument no more proves the existence of God than it proves the existence of a Cartesian demon. (An 'evil genius, not less powerful than deceitful, who has employed his whole energies in deceiving me', *Meditation* I.)

It has to be pointed out that the existence of a thing, and of a world of things, has not been proved. Consequently, given that a thing is a system of data too wide for the capacities of a limited perceiver, in default of a proof of the existence of at least one such thing, the existence of God likewise has not been proved. And proof of the existence of such a thing will prove what is entailed by it, the existence of God. It is a point of logic that what proves or renders probable the antecedent of an 'if..., then –' statement also proves or renders probable its consequent. Thus, God's existence can be proved or rendered probable by a demonstrative or probabilistic proof that there is at least one thing.

Now there are a number of considerations which make it at least highly probable that things exist. We need only invoke common sense, as did Moore when he held up his two hands, saying, as he made 'a certain gesture with the right hand, "Here is one hand", and adding, as [he made] a certain gesture with the left, "and here is another" (1959, p. 146). In this 'proof' he appeals to the testimony of the senses. And in an abundance of instances sense evidence is accepted as attesting to the existence of physical objects. Locke also invoked common sense when he said, 'I think nobody can in earnest be so sceptical as to be uncertain of the existence of those things which he sees and feels' (1912, Bk. IV, Ch. 11), his implication being that it would be irrational to doubt the existence of chairs, coats, and the like. Such experiences as repeated similar perceptions, reflections of things seen in a mirror, and data which are not 'creatures of our own will' fortify this belief. And not only is it undoubted that present sense evidence attests to the existence of perceived physical objects but also that it makes probable the existence of objects which lie wholly beyond our present perceptions. Consider Moore's example of a train whose wheels are not being perceived while it is in motion (1953, pp. 132–133). To passengers in the train various appearances present themselves – sights, sounds, pressures, motion, but not the appearances of wheels. Can anyone doubt that these appearances make it extremely probable that the carriage is running on and supported by wheels, i.e., that things exist which are unperceived by the passengers?

In general, if what the senses disclose cannot count as evidence for the existence of physical things, then there is no conceivable evidence for this. We might argue in the following way. Physical things could, conceivably, exist. And if it is conceivable that there are things, then it is conceivable that there is evidence which would establish or make probable their existence. Now the only evidence, in principle, for the existence of physical things is sense evidence. Our senses are the only possible avenues of information concerning the existence of things. And this information, it must in all sobriety be allowed, the senses abundantly provide. Either of two related conclusions may be drawn here, and it is unnecessary for the purposes of this chapter to adjudicate between them. Some philosophers have drawn the conclusion that the available sense evidence makes the existence of things more or less probable, but only probable (e.g., Hans Reichenbach). Other philosophers have drawn the conclusion that our senses make this certain. Thus Moore wrote: 'Suppose that now, instead of saying... "I have got some clothes on", I were to say "I think I've got some clothes on, but it's just possible that I haven't." Would it not sound rather ridiculous for me now, under these circumstances, to say, "I *think* I've got some clothes on" or even to say "I not only think I have, I know that it is very likely indeed that I have, but I can't be quite sure?".... But for me, now, in full possession of my senses, it would be quite ridiculous to express myself in this way, because the circumstances are such as to make it quite obvious that I don't merely think that I have, but know that I have' (1959, pp. 227–228).

Some philosophers, including those who belonged to the ancient Greek school of scepticism, have argued, in effect, that although sense evidence is the only possible evidence for the existence of a physical world, nevertheless our senses are not trustworthy witnesses and that therefore no inference from sense evidence to things can be justified. Now it must be granted that the senses sometimes deceive us, and many philosophers have used this fact as an argument for scepticism with respect to the senses. The objection to this conclusion is that we would have no idea what it would be like to be deceived by our senses unless we had an idea of what it would be like not to be deceived by them. As J. L. Austin put it, '...talk of deception only *makes sense* against a background of general non-deception' (1962, p. 11). Controlled observation, the conditions of which cannot be gone into here, alone will enable us to decide when our perceptions are veridical and when not. Wittgenstein has remarked that philosophers frequently use terms in dissociation from their antitheses in the language (1958, p. 46). And it will be clear that a philosopher who holds that since our senses sometimes deceive us we cannot be sure that they do not always do so, and hence that all of our perceptions may be delusive, is in a concealed way using the term 'delusive perception' in dissociation from its antithesis 'veridical perception'. Complete distrust of the senses, regardless of how watertight the argument in support of it may seem to be, is illegitimate. To use Moore's words, 'It would always be at least as easy to deny the argument as to deny that we do know external facts' (1922, p. 163).

Some philosophers, for example Bradley, have held a type of view according to which the available sense evidence, that is, the sensible appearances, is not evidence for the existence of physical objects, on the ground that the proposition that physical objects exist implies a contradiction. Their view, curiously enough, is that the only possible evidence for the existence of things is not possible evidence. But these philosophers held that the existence of things is inconceivable, which in itself is highly paradoxical. If we allow that the existence of physical objects *is* conceivable, then sense evidence, i.e., the appearances, is evidence for their existence.

The view arrived at about a physical object – about the nature of such things as chairs, tables, etc. – is not that it is constituted of a substance which presents appearances with none of which it can be identified, but that it is an organization of mind-dependent components which are nevertheless public. It will be helpful to remind ourselves of the general properties assigned by common sense to things: temporal continuity, spatial unity, multiple accessibility, neutrality as between the senses, causal efficacy. Theological phenomenalism can give an account of all of these attributes, but it gives a special non-commonsense account of the causal power attributed to things. Berkeley stated that ideas, i.e., sense data, are 'visibly inactive' (1871, Pt. I, Sec. 25), and since causal powers cannot be housed in a material substratum, he attributed causal efficacy only to a mind, 'an incorporeal active Substance' (*Ibid.*, Sec. 26). Putting aside questions about causation, an important question that comes up at this point is the relationship between mind dependence and multiple accessibility. Theological phenomenalism rests on the idea that privacy and mind dependence are distinct and that mind dependence does not imply privacy. We ordinarily distinguish between our pains, sensations, mental images, and the like, which are thought of as being 'private' to ourselves, and 'objective' things like chairs and shoes. The conception of a chair is, to use Hume's expression, that of something 'independent and continu'd', which is to say that the span of its existence does not necessarily coincide with the duration of anyone's perception of it and that it exists between perceptions. And of course we have the further idea that it is capable of being perceived by any number of perceivers. The view that things are organizations of sense data which are kept in continuous existence by a Superperceiver and some of the components of which we sometimes perceive implies that sense data can be shared perceptually and are not necessarily private to a single mind. By contrast a pain or a mental image is thought of as being private to its possessor, that is, as something to which he has privileged access, from which other minds are excluded. We normally think of a dream as being the dream of only one dreamer and the number of dreams as being no fewer than the number of dreamers, although of course there are fewer Statues of Liberty than there are sightseers. If two people had what we should call the same dream, because of the point for point similarity of their descriptions, we should say that nevertheless there were numerically two dreams. We should not be inclined to say that there was one dream which the two dreamers dreamt. And some philosophers have maintained that it is *logically* impossible for dream images to be the objects of more than one dreamer. Each dreamer has his own dream, which is private to himself. A dream does not enter into the sense-history of more than one mind. The same can be said of pains, sensations, afterimages, and the like. They do not exist between our awarenesses of them and therefore are not subject to repeated perceptions. The span of their existence is identical with the duration of the awareness of them, and what seem to be repeated awarenesses are awarenesses of numerically distinct objects.

It will be clear then that if being perceiver dependent entails being private to the perceiver, theological phenomenalism must be ruled out as a false doctrine. Hume appears to have held that mind dependence entails privacy: '...since nothing is ever really present to the mind, besides its own perceptions...' (1888, Bk. I, Pt. IV, Sec. II, p. 197), and this led him to the view that what we call a thing is nothing more than a series of perishing sense impressions. One of the important properties attributed to things, the property of multiple accessibility, vanishes, and we no more could perceive a sense datum in God's mind than we could an afterimage that another person has. The world of relatively stable, public objects disappears into the private contents of separate minds. The so-called common world breaks up into a number of private worlds: Each mind is a hermetically sealed entity, an island universe out of connection with any other universe. Since all the sense contents of a mind are dependent on and private to it, no inference to anything external to a mind can be made from the occurrence of any sense content. This implies that no one can know that any other mind exists. According to this line of reasoning it can be known that a common world, one which is perceived by more than one mind, does not exist. Hume's view that sense data are private to their perceivers implies that nothing exists which could be a common object of perception. It also implies that there is no sense evidence which would make probable anyone's belief that a mind other than his own exists. The view that no one can know that anyone else exists is one of the traditional forms of solipsism.

More important for the present purpose than the solipsistic outcome of Hume's position are the consequences of the position on the common notion of a thing. One consequence that becomes immediately evident is that a thing cannot be constituted of an indefinite number of sense data of which only some are actually perceived by one mind. On this view I could not with truth say that the coin before me has an underside which I am not perceiving. The whole of the coin contracts into my perceived sense datum, which is another way of saying that there is no coin. The identification of privacy with mind dependence not only causes the common world to vanish but also brings about (conceptually of course) the annihilation of physical things. Hume's line of reasoning implies that there are no things. There are merely successions of evanescent sense data, perceptual contents which make only single momentary appearances in the theatre of the mind. Not only is no sense datum capable of being perceived by two minds but no sense datum is capable of being perceived twice by the same mind.

It might be held that Hume's reasoning does not imply the nonexistence of things but rather that it implies something about what things are, their nature. Heraclitus held that nothing remains the same for any two moments of time, and philosophers have divided on the consequence of this claim, some holding that there are no things and others that things are processes. And a Humean Heraclitus would seem to be free to draw either the conclusion that there are no things, there is only a subjective parade of impressions, or the conclusion that a thing *is* a stream of impressions satisfying certain conditions of connectedness and orderliness. The objection against the second alternative is that it does not correspond to the usual conception of a thing, and in fact introduces a new idea. It introduces, in effect, a redefinition of the term 'physical object'. The implication of Hume's line of reasoning in conjunction with the ordinary conception of a thing is that there are no things. It has already been remarked that the identification of privacy and mind dependence implies that a thing contracts into a sense content no part of which is unperceived, whereas on the ordinary conception of a thing, a thing has unperceived parts and must be more than the sense content of a limited perceiver. Hume gives recognition to the existence of the usual conception of a thing by his attempt to explain how we come to form the idea of 'continu'd and independent' objects. His explanation, in his own words, is the following:

'tis evident, that whenever we infer the continu'd existence of the objects of sense from their coherence, and the frequency of their union, 'tis in order to bestow on the objects a greater regularity than what is observed in our mere perceptions (p. 197). ... Our perceptions are broken and interrupted, and however like, are still different from each other (p. 213). But as this interruption of their existence is contrary to their perfect identity ... we disguise, as much as possible, the interruption, or rather remove it entirely, by supposing that these interrupted perceptions are connected by a real existence of which we are insensible (p. 199). The imagination is seduc'd into such an opinion only by means of the resemblance of certain perceptions, ... which we have a propension to suppose the same (p. 209). The imagination tells us, that our resembling perceptions have a continu'd and uninterrupted existence, and are not annihilated by their absence. Reflection tells us, that even our resembling perceptions are interrupted in their existence, and different from each other (p. 215). 'Tis evident, that as the ideas of the several distinct *successive* qualities of objects are united together by a very close relation, the mind, in looking along the succession, must be carry'd from one part of it to another by an easy transition, and will no more perceive the change, than if it contemplated the same unchangeable object ... The smooth and uninterrupted progress of the thought ... readily deceives the mind, and makes us ascribe an identity to the changeable succession of connected qualitites (p. 220). 'Tis a gross illusion to suppose, that our resembling perceptions are numerically the same; and 'tis this illusion, which leads us into the opinion, that these perceptions are uninterrupted, and are still existent, even when they are not present to our senses (p. 217). (1888, Bk. I, Pt. IV, Sec. II and III.)

In brief, the source of our concept of things is according to Hume in the occurrence of successive resembling sense data which are mistaken for one and the same sense datum perceived at different times. The important point to notice about Hume's explanation is that it does not deny that we do have a concept of physical things having the usual generic properties attributed to them: non-intermittent, objective existence, and the like. The explanation only tells us that we wrongly, although naturally, apply the concept to what we encounter in perception. In other words, Hume's view does not deny that there is the everyday concept of a thing, which is embedded in ordinary language; rather, it denies that anything in the world corresponds to it. It will be remembered that two alternative conclusions were open to the Humean Heraclitus, one that there are no things, the other, that a thing is nothing more than a stream of connected, evanescent sense data. The second alternative is not open to anyone who grants the existence of the common conception of things, as Hume does. The common conception of a thing is of something that answers to the properties already cited, and any view which implies that nothing answering to these properties exists makes an existential claim, that there are no things, comparable to the claim that there are no leprechauns. Dr. Johnson's refutation of Berkeley's immaterialism would seem to apply more relevantly to Hume's doctrine.

It has already been urged that we have sense evidence for the existence of stable, objective things, and an acute philosopher like Hume who holds by implication that there are no things is no less in possession of such evidence than is the man in the street. It would seem that there is only one explanation as to how he could hold the view against the forceful evidence of his senses, and this is that he was guilty of a confusion, difficult to avoid in philosophy, between two kinds of impossibility. It will be remembered that Hume arrived at his view via the bridge of identifying mind dependence with privacy. And the point regarding the distinction between the two kinds of impossibility can in the present connection be made by distinguishing two possible views with regard to privacy, one which might be called factual privacy and the other logical privacy. Some philosophers hold that pains and mental images are logically private to the minds that have them, and that they are logically inaccessible to other minds. Ayer, for example, has said, 'It is logically impossible for a sense-experience to belong to the sense-history of more than a single self' (1951, p. 125). And W. T. Stace said: 'I cannot experience anything except my own experience. I can see my red, but I can never see yours... I can feel my emotion, but not yours. Even if your anger infects me, so that I feel it in sympathy with you, it is yet, in so far as I feel it, *my* anger, not yours' (1932, p. 67).

Factual privacy is the kind of privacy possessed by an object which could, in principle at least, be public. Pepys' *Diary* was once private in this sense. Pepys wrote it in a private code, so that it was his exclusive possession, he alone having access to it. But his *Diary* was capable of becoming common property, as indeed it did when it was decoded and expressed in a public language. It will be clear that what is factually private could become public and what is public could become factually private. Thus, the inscriptions on the Rosetta stone were public at one time, and centuries later became factually private to Champollion, their decoder, until he made their meaning public again.

By contrast, what is logically private, unlike anything which is factually private, could not become public. If *a* is logically private, which is to say, necessarily private, then it is logically impossible for *a* to become public, just as it is logically impossible for a whole number which is odd to become an even number. It will be argued shortly that if the objects of sense experience are necessarily private, then it would be logically impossible for there to be any public objects of sense experience; and if there cannot be public sense objects, then there cannot be private sense objects either. The conceptual exclusion of the one is inconsistent with the conceptual retention of the other.

Attention was called earlier to the point made by Wittgenstein that a term which is used in dissociation from its antithesis loses its application. Expressed in terms of concepts rather than of words, Wittgenstein's maxim in the present context comes to saying that the concept of a private sense object is internally linked to the concept of a public sense object, such that if one kind of object is logically impossible so is the other. To put the matter more simply, we would not have the idea of a private sense object unless we had the idea of a public sense object. To make the term 'private' do even part of its work requires preserving the distinction between private and public sense objects, and the preservation of this distinction implies the theoretical possibility of there being public sense objects. The claim that all sense objects are logically private is thus ruled out. It is ruled out that in perceptual awareness – awareness of color patches, afterimages, etc. – we are presented with data that are logically inaccessible to others.

Another way of putting the matter is the following: The proposition that all sense contents are necessarily private, that is, the proposition that being a sense content entails being private, implies that there is no conceivable sense content which is not private, and this in turn implies that 'private' is a term which does not serve to distinguish between sense contents. It implies thus that the concept of a private sense content is identical with the concept of a sense content, just as the concept of a male brother is identical with the concept of a brother. It follows that the proposition that all sense contents are private sense contents is nothing more than the empty proposition that all sense contents are sense contents. In order to be able to speak of private sense contents it must be possible to speak of public sense contents. The preservation of the distinction implies the possibility of there being both kinds of contents.

It is necessary now to supplement the claim that publicly accessible sense contents are possible with the futher claim that *public* and *private* are external, not internal, features of sense contents. The argument just given with regard to private and public sense contents does no more than preserve the distinction between the terms 'public' and 'private'. It does not show that what is private could be public. To show this it needs to be shown that the distinction between private and public sense contents is not like the distinction between even and odd numbers. The conception of an even number requires the conception of an odd number, and conversely; we do not have the conception of the one without having a conception of the other. But this does not imply the conceivability of an even number becoming odd or of an odd number becoming even. Even numbers are not even merely as a matter of fact; they are even by internal necessity.

That being public and being private are external features of sense contents, and that a private sense content could become public, appears from the following consideration. Compare a yellow memory-image of a sheet of paper, which is taken to be private to the person who has it, with a yellow sheet of paper, which is taken to be public and accessible to more than one person. It has already been pointed out that a mental image is qualitatively the same as a visual sense datum, and thus that a yellow image of a sheet of paper is intrinsically indistinguishable from the content of a perception of a yellow sheet of paper. And this implies, if the distinction between public and private sense objects is preserved, that being public and being private are external, accidental features of sense data. This comes to saying that if a sense datum is private it is factually private, where what is in fact private could, like Pepys' *Diary*, become public property. Thus, a pain that is private to me could in principle be felt by others and a mental image which is mine could in principle be perceived by others. It is in fact not the case that these are accessible to more than one perceiver; but it is not logically impossible that they should be. Their existence and duration are perceiver dependent. That is, they could not exist without being someone's sense content, nor have a duration beyond the span of someone's perception. But they *need* not be exclusively the sense content of one person. They are not logically private.

This means that it is possible for a sense datum to belong to the sense-history of more than one mind, and thus to belong to the sensehistory of a limited perceiver and also to the sense-history of a Super-perceiver. An important consequence of the present thesis is that being perceiver dependent does not, as Hume apparently thought, imply being private to the perceiver. We have come back to the view that a thing is a permanent possibility of sensation. And to be a permanent possibility of sensation is to be constituted by an indefinitely large organization of actual sense data, all of which must be perceived if the thing is to exist, and a small selection of which are perceived by a limited perceiver at any given time. A number of important phenomenalistic philosophers would reject the theological implications of the view developed here. But these philosophers have never given a clearcut explanation of what they mean by 'possible sense data' in their philosophical description of a thing as 'a set of actual and possible sense data'. They may discover to their surprise that all along their doctrine has carried with it a hidden theology.

The position of theological phenomenalism which is given special prominence here is open to a number of objections which cannot be gone into. It is not out of place to remark that, as the history of philosophy abundantly shows, no position is free from objections. Taking this into account, the authors of this book conceive their role to be that of expositors of positions rather than as advocates of particular views. It will be understandable that sometimes a view is best presented in an atmosphere of advocacy; but actual advocacy should be discounted as much as possible in philosophy, which as yet has produced no secure results.

DOUBTS AND QUERIES

1. The idea of substratum was arrived at by what was called the stripping experiment, an experiment conducted in the imagination. Does this answer to the usual idea of making an experiment? Consider Archimedes' experimentation with a lever, which resulted in a physical law about the

distances from the fulcrum at which different weights must be attached if they are to balance. In advance of making the experiment the expected outcome may have differed from the actual outcome, but whether it did or not, with regard to the actual outcome it is nevertheless possible to conceive of a contrary outcome. It is easy enough to conceive of weight w at distance d from the fulcrum balancing another weight W at distance D in accordance with a quite different law from $wd = WD$. And in general, experimentation leads to a result the contrary of which is conceivable. Now the experiment conducted in the imagination with regard to the substratum subject of attribution appears to eventuate in a result the contrary of which is ruled out as inconceivable. The result of abstracting from a thing its attributes was that the subject of attribution is inconceivable, i.e., that the contrary result, the conceivability of the subject is in principle impossible. What then is the nature of the *Gedankenexperiment* with regard to substratum? An ordinary experiment does not show a conceivable result to be inconceivable; e.g., Galileo's experiment did not show the inconceivability of a heavier object falling faster than a lighter one. It established a matter of fact without blotting out a conceivable alternative. If the stripping experiment conducted in the imagination is not an experiment, what is it?

Further, in conducting this experiment, do we imagine a process of actually stripping away a thing's attributes? Do we strip away its color leaving its shape and odor, then its shape, leaving its odor, etc.? Is stripping away properties in the expectation of coming to a remainder comparable to removing the hat and coat from the man Descartes reported passing in his street, in the expectation of arriving at whatever it is the clothes covered? Stripping away clothing will reveal a *something*. Is this comparable to stripping away properties to find a substance; or is the stripping talk a colorful way of describing another kind of procedure? If properties are not stripped away in a literal sense, in what sense are they stripped away?

2. It was suggested that Locke could have inferred from the existence of simple ideas which the mind is incapable of framing by itself the existence of an external source for them, analogous to Berkeley's arguing from the existence of involuntary ideas to the existence of an external causal agency. Compare these arguments with Descartes' claim that because the mind is incapable by itself of forming the idea of an Infinite Being the idea must have been implanted by God. Are any of these inferences warranted? Consider Descartes' own query whether he might not be

'so constituted by nature that he might be deceived even in matters which seemed to him most certain' (*Meditation* VI), so that he might have created, unbeknownst to himself, all the ideas he has without the concurrence of any outer causes. Does Berkeley's admission of this fact, when he said that 'what happens in dreams, frensies, and the like, puts it beyond dispute that it is possible we might be affected with all the ideas we have now, even though no bodies existed without' (1871, Pt. I, Sec. 18) apply also to his argument that his involuntary ideas require a cause other than himself? If Berkeley accounts for ideas of sense, which are not the creatures of his own will, as being caused by God, how must he account for dream images and hallucinatory data which also are not subject to our control?

3. Berkeley wrote that 'when in broad daylight I open my eyes, it is not in my power to choose whether I shall see or not, or to determine what particular objects shall present themselves to my view'. (1871, Pt. I, Sec. 29) Does this imply that his eyes are not themselves ideas of sense, or does it imply that certain ideas, which are 'of external things', are subject to the control of his will? Presumably Berkeley intended the latter alternative, since God (and some finite minds) perceives his eyes. Is he then committed to the consequence that by means of ideas subject to the control of his will he places himself in a position of being the receiver of ideas not under the control of his will?

4. Berkeley maintained that 'the common use of language will receive no manner of alteration ... from the admission of our tenets'. Consider his claim that ideas are 'visibly inactive', which is presented as a fact of introspection: 'to be satisfied of the truth of this, there is nothing else requisite but a bare observation of our ideas.' (1971, Pt. I, Sec. 25) Nevertheless, he gives a reason which is not a fact of introspection: 'For, since they and every part of them exist only in the mind, it follows that there is nothing in them but what is perceived' (*Ibid.*). What is the logical character of the proposition that ideas are inactive? If it is arrived at by reasoning on the concept of an idea, and is therefore *a priori*, then it would be inconceivable that one should be frightened by the data of delirium tremens, or that one idea should give rise to another. Also, if minds alone have causal efficacy, and necessarily so, then things (which are classes of data) could not conceivably produce changes in other things or receive alterations from them. Would such expressions as 'fire heats water' be rendered false by the view? Or would they be unintelligible? Are they compatible with the 'common use of language'?

5. It was argued that the term 'private' requires for its intelligible use possible application of the antithetical term 'public', so that 'all sense contents are private' would say nothing if the privacy referred to is logical, that is, if the concept *private* does not distinguish between two classes of possible sense contents, those which are private and those which are public. Does the term 'perceiver dependent' in the same way require the term 'perceiver independent'? Does the claimed inconceivability of sense contents that are not dependent on a perceiver reduce the statement that all sense contents are perceiver dependent to a more tautology? Theological phenomenalism, according to which things are not dependent on *our* perception, distinguishes between perceiver dependent and perceiver independent objects. Does it preserve the required distinction between perceiver dependence and perceiver independence? If it does not, are we led back to Russell's distinction between sense data and sensibilia? What is the logical character of the statement, 'The existence of an appearance is possible only if there is a perceiver to whom it is an appearance'?

6. Hume lays down the maxim that we have no ideas which are not copies of impressions. The idea of continued and independent things according to him has its source in a confusion between identity and similarity. Is this a possible explanation? On his own accounting we have no impression of an uninterrupted sense object, one which continues to exist between perceptions; and this implies that we have no idea of such an existent. Is Hume's explanation of how we come to have the usual conception of a physical object an explanation of an idea we do not have? Wittgenstein observed that we can look for a person who does not exist but not hang a person who does not exist. Could Hume have looked, i.e., could he have known what impression he sought to find? Does his explanation, together with his conclusion that the idea of a continued and independent object has no correspondent impression, imply that we have an idea which we cannot have?

7. Gorgias put forward the following theses: Knowledge is impossible, communication is impossible. The connection between the two would seem to be that sense experience is subjective and private and that language cannot be used to communicate what is private. His two theses might be summarized in the statement that the privacy of experience implies the impossibility of a public language. Does Hume's position imply that if there were two minds it would be impossible for them to communicate? That is to say, does Hume's view imply linguistic solipsism, the view that no one else can know what the meanings are which I attach to words?

One of Locke's views about our knowledge is that it is confined to our perception of agreement and disagreement among our own ideas. Does this imply the impossibility of our having knowledge of 'real existence'? About words, Locke held that 'no one hath the power to make others have the same ideas in their minds that he has, when they use the same words that he does ... Words stand for nothing but the ideas in the mind of him that uses them ... it is evident that each can apply them only to his own ideas' (1928, Bk. III, Ch. II). Does this too imply linguistic solipsism with regard both to things and other minds? Does it, in other words, imply that we can use words neither to describe outer things to ourselves nor our ideas to others?

8. Hume takes what imagination tells us about our sense objects and what reflection tells us to be inconsistent with each other. The imagination tells us that 'our resembling perceptions have a continu'd and uninterrupted existence, and are not annihilated by their absence. Reflection tells us, that even our resembling perceptions are interrupted in their existence, and different from each other'. (1888, Bk. I, Pt. IV, Sec. II) Consider now what imagination and reflection, resp., issue in. What can be imagined may or may not have a counterpart in reality. Hence if one is 'seduc'd by the imagination' into an opinion, that opinion will be an empirical one. Reflection, on the other hand, if it is reflection on concepts rather than reflection in the popular sense of canvassing the empirical data, will issue in an *a priori* proposition. Presumably it is the former type of reflection which discloses that perceptions are interrupted in their existence and numerically distinct. For it shows the idea of a perception to be inconsistent with uninterrupted existence, which is to say that reflection on the content of a perception brings to light an entailment between the concepts *being a perceptual content* and *having a duration coincident with the span of awareness*.

The question now arises whether it is possible for an *a priori* proposition to be inconsistent with an empirical one. Suppose that it is necessarily the case that perceptions are interrupted. Then if the imagination shows that it is possible for the objects of perception to have a continued existence between acts of sense awareness, it would be possible for an *a priori* true statement to be false. That is, an *a priori* true statement could have more than one truth-value. Or if an *a priori* true statement cannot be false, which in this context would imply that our perceptions cannot be continued and uninterrupted, then it would be impossible for the empirical proposition, which has its source in the imagination, to be true. In consequence, a proposition which has either of two truth-values can by logical necessity have only one truth-value; alternatively, one of its possible truth-values is impossible. Since either consequence, that an *a priori* proposition is capable of having more than one truth-value, or that an empirical proposition is incapable of having more than one truth-value, is a logical absurdity, the proposition that entails them, namely, that an inconsistency exists between an *a priori* and an empirical proposition, must be rejected. This is to say that an *a priori* statement and an empirical statement cannot be related to each other as claim and counterclaim.

REFERENCES

Recommended readings:
　Bertrand Russell (1929), *Our knowledge of the external world*, Chs. 3, 4.
　– (1917), *Mysticism and logic*, Ch. 8.
Further readings:
　A. J. Ayer (1954), *Philosophical essays*, Chs. 1, 6.
　George Berkeley, *Three dialogues between Hylas and Philonous*, The
　　first dialogue.
　G. E. Moore (1953), *Some main problems of philosophy*, Chs. 7, 8, 9.
　– (1959), *Philosophical papers*: 'A defense of common sense'.

4. Metaphysical Systems

Classical writings such as Books VI and VII of Plato's *Republic* and Leibniz' *Monadology* illustrate two of the directions metaphysics has taken, one given it by a philosopher who sets himself the task of describing what lies beyond the physical horizon, the other, given it centuries later by a philosopher who tries to provide a systematic and detailed account of all the parts of reality. In the preceding chapter we were concerned with theories about the nature of things in the physical world, what Aristotle would call one portion of Being. 'There is a science', he says, 'which studies Being *qua* Being, and the properties inherent in it in virtue of its own nature. This science is not the same as any of the so-called particular sciences, for none of the others contemplates Being generally *qua* Being; they divide off some portion of it and study the attribute of this portion...' (*Metaphysics*, Bk. IV). This science is Metaphysics, which according to Descartes is the root of the tree of knowledge. Physics, he said, is its trunk, and the special sciences its branches.

It has already been pointed out how different is the investigation of physical objects conducted by the philosopher and the investigation conducted by physicists. So although in the preceding chapter we considered theories about one portion of Being, these theories are not physical. They are in fact metaphysical, and like M. Jourdain in *Le Bourgeois Gentilhomme* who was surprised to learn he had been speaking prose, we have already been doing metaphysics. In the present chapter the questions we shall ask will be larger questions than those just dealt with. They will be the sort which arise in the effort to 'comprehend the universe, not simply piecemeal or by fragments, but somehow as a whole' (Bradley, 1925, p. 1). For example, does the universe operate exclusively by mechanical causation, does teleology enter into it, or is it under the sway of pure chance? What are the basic materials entering into the composition of all that exists? And perhaps most fundamental,

What is real, and what is mere appearance? If there are parts of reality which transcend the bounds of experience, then metaphysics must look into their relation to the world which is given to sense. And it must show that these transcendent realities do exist.

In general, and very roughly, there are two types of metaphysics, one the metaphysics of transcendence, which asserts the existence and delineates the attributes of realities which we cannot represent to ourselves since they lie beyond what can be given either to sense experience or introspection, and the other, the metaphysics which concerns itself with the experienced world, both sensible and psychical, and attempts to give an integrated account of it without invoking unknowables. The first type tends to denigrate the world of phenomena investigated by the special sciences. It makes out the world of common sense, by comparison with the higher reality, to be 'a beggarly show' (Bradley's description) and on Plato's view it is a cosmic cave in which the ordinary man passes his life in the darkness of ignorance. The man 'who returns from above out of the light into the den' is laughed at by cave dwellers who have never attained to 'the beatific vision' and whose experience is too limited to grasp the vision he tries to communicate. Objects not to be encountered in any sense experience, transcending space and time, are beyond the ken of those confined to the prison-house of sight; and these objects are the realities. The common world of everyday experience Plato dismissed as a shadow world, time itself being nothing more than a 'moving image of eternity'. This is one metaphysics of transcendence. There are other such metaphysics, some portraying a reality which transcends both time and space, and in consequence condemning both time and space as unreal, others condemning space but conceding reality to time. By contrast, other comprehensive and systematic theories, instead of dismissing the world of everyday experience, confine themselves to attempts to explain its nature. Phenomena investigated by the various sciences, rather than objects of mystical contemplation, are accorded exclusive possession of the honorific term 'real'.

This classification of metaphysical positions as transcendental or non-transcendental, is, however, a very rough one. Leibniz, for example, in developing a theory about non-transcendent objects, at the same time created what might be called a metaphysics of sense-transcendence. The (non-transcendent) objects of sense were described in terms of elements not accessible to sense. Their basic constituents were held to be of the nature of minds. Although minds are not beyond the reach of experience, in particular, of introspection, they are beyond the reach of the physical senses. The Leibnizian position thus has both a similarity and a dissimilarity to a metaphysics of complete transcendence such as Bradley's, which delineates a reality not identifiable in terms of any ordinary experience. His Absolute transcends what is disclosed by either perception or introspection. In a later chapter we shall examine a theory about *abstract* realities, i.e., realitites which are neither minds nor sense objects and hence not open to introspection or the senses. They are 'intelligible objects', that is, objects grasped by the intellect.

Metaphysical theories, whether transcendental or not, can be classified in a number of different ways, each type representing a different outlook on the world. Some are monistic, some dualistic, some pluralistic, each of these descriptive adjectives referring to the number of basic substances which constitute reality. According to such system builders as Spinoza and Bradley, there is but one substance, according to Descartes there are two, according to Leibniz and Hobbes, there is a plurality of substances, but all are of one kind, in the one case mental, in the other material. And this latter difference provides classifications not only of pluralistic metaphysics but also of monistic metaphysics, as idealistic or materialistic. Acquaintance with the various types of position has the virtue of widening our intellectual horizon. As Russell puts it, they 'enlarge our conception of what is possible, enrich our intellectual imagination and diminish the dogmatic assurance which closes the mind against speculation' (1943, pp. 249–250).

In this chapter we shall develop two metaphysical views about the nature of reality, one a monistic system modelled after that set out by one of the most influential British philosophers of this century, F. H. Bradley, the other a modification of the pluralistic metaphysics of Leibniz' *Monadology*. The first, called Absolute Idealism, represents the world as being what William James called the block universe, an unchanging world in which the one Real transcends both space and time. The other, Pluralistic Idealism, represents the world as a dynamic development from an infinity of centers of force. Both systems belong to the rationalistic tradition, the tradition which maintains that knowledge of reality is attainable by reasoning alone, either from what is given in experience or even quite independently of experiential data. In the history of philosophy there have been various formulations of the thesis that reality is to be comprehended only through thought, the earliest clear-cut formulation being given by Parmenides who said that what is thinkable and what is are one and the same: '. . . it is the same thing that can be thought and that can be' (in: Nahm, 1947, p. 115). Spinoza laid a similar groundwork for the possibility of knowledge through conception in his view that the order of nature is the order of thought. In our own century Bradley expressed the view in his consistency theory of truth: The self-consistent is the real. It is clear, of course, that what is self-contradictory cannot be real: A round square cannot be. But it is another thing to hold, as Bradley does, that 'a thing is real when, and in so far as, its opposite is impossible' (1925, p. 538), that is, when its opposite is logically inconceivable. This expresses his 'absolute criterion' (*Ibid.*, p. 136) of ultimate reality. Hegel expressed it in the form, 'the real is the rational'.

The Bradleian position has had a long history of development, and it will be instructive to relate it to its first beginnings in the position and reasoning of Parmenides and his disciple Zeno of Elea. The much more sophisticated immaterial monism of Bradley grew out of the materialistic monism of Parmenides, according to whom reality is a single cosmic atom. This latter view as well as the Bradleian view stemmed from the rationalistic tenet that what is and what can be thought are the same. Parmenides proceeded to argue for this as follows: It is postulated that what is is thinkable, or alternatively, what is unthinkable, or implies a contradiction, is not. If it can be proved that what is thinkable also is, the identity between the conceivable and the existent will be established. Parmenides argued that thought must have an object. One cannot think without thinking of *something*. Thinking of nothing implies the existence of a thought which has no object. It is not, as some modern existentialists seem to suggest, thinking of a queer attenuated object; it is just not thinking. It will be remembered that in the last chapter there was a reference to Bradley's *Gedankenexperiment*, in which he attempted to conceive of something other than experience. We can imagine Parmenides inviting us to make the same kind of intellectual experiment with regard to nothing, or 'not-being', with a negative outcome: 'Thou canst not know what is not – that is impossible – nor utter it' (in: Nahm, 1947, p. 116). Parmenidean rationalism equates the existent with the conceivable or thinkable, and the nonexistent with the contradictory or inconceivable. Bradley's modern version of it is that inconsistency logically determines falsity, and consistency truth: A proposition which implies a contradiction makes a false claim about reality, while one which does not, i.e., a consistent proposition, makes a true statement about reality, true at least to a degree.

In 'The conception of reality' Moore has given an interesting argument for the rationalistic premise that whatever is thought of must be: 'How ... can a thing ... be thought of unless it is there to ... be thought of? To say that it ... is thought of, and that yet there is no such thing, is plainly self-contradictory. A thing cannot have a property, unless it is there to have it, and, since unicorns and temporal facts *do* have the property of being thought of, there certainly must be such things. When I think of a unicorn, what I am thinking of is certainly not nothing; if it were nothing, then, when I think of a griffin, I should also be thinking of nothing, and there would be no difference between thinking of a griffiin and thinking of a unicorn. But there certainly is a difference; and what can the difference be except that in the one case what I am thinking of is a unicorn, and in the other a griffin? And if the unicorn is what I am thinking of, then there certainly must *be* a unicorn, in spite of the fact that unicorns are unreal.' (1922, p. 215 – In this essay Moore rejects the rationalistic position and subjects this argument to a critique.)

It is worth pointing out that Aristotle, who is far removed from Parmenidean thinking, implied in his famous theory of the concrete universal the Parmenidean proposition that what is conceivable must exist. A universal is an object given to conception; and on his view a universal exists only if it is instantiated, the implication plainly being that the conceivability of an object implies its existence. Aristotle's view, expressed in terms of Mill's distinction between the connotation of a word and its denotation, is to the effect that no general word has a connotation unless it has a denotation, or alternatively, that no general word, for example 'justice', has meaning unless it has an application to something.

This view, and the Parmenidean theory as well, clearly flouts common sense. It would seem that we can think of unicorns and griffins even though they *are not*, and the words 'unicorn' and 'griffin' have meaning even though they fail to apply to anything. And as a concession to common sense some philosophers have distinguished between two modes of being. In the words of Prof. J. Laird: 'The question may be raised whether "being" and "existence" are identical. An apparently clear distinction between the two was familiar in British philosophy some little time after the turn of the century. The idea was that "being" was a genus of which "existence" and "subsistence" were the distinct species. Anything a man could name or appear to think about was said to "have being", but of the entities which were said to "have being" only some existed.' (1942, pp.

248–249). With this interpretation of 'being' the rationalistic tenet that what can be thought of must be could more plausibly be maintained.

The distinction was not made merely *ad hoc* to square with the fact that we apparently can think of unicorns and griffins. Russell at one time supported it by an argument. He wrote: 'If A be any term that can be counted as one, it is plain that A is something and therefore that A is. "*A* is not" must always be either false or meaningless. For if *A* were nothing, it could not be said not to be; "*A* is not" implies that there is a term *A* whose being is denied, and hence that *A* is. Thus unless "*A* is not" be an empty sound, it must be false – whatever *A* may be, it certainly is. Numbers, the Homeric gods, relations, chimeras . . . all have being, for it they were not entities of a kind, we could make no propositions about them. Thus being is a general attribute of everything, and to mention anything is to show that it is . . . *Existence,* on the contrary, is the prerogative of some only amongst beings' (1938, p. 449).

Leaving aside the question whether this argument is correct, or whether the distinction may be maintained, we shall accept for the time being the rationalistic criterion of reality in order to develop the Bradleian monistic system which rests on it. We now return to the Parmenidean system from which Bradley's system evolved. Parmenides' position is simple, primitive, and to many people baffling. The ancient world is said to have been rocked with laughter by it. Nevertheless the world-picture it presents has appeal, especially in moments when the mundane world is too much with us. When it appears that 'the whole temple of man's achievement must inevitably be buried beneath the debris of a universe in ruins' (1917, p. 48), then a negative metaphysics which demonstrates that 'death and change, and the irrevocableness of the past' (*Ibid.,* p. 55), are unreal is accepted with ease.

By taking the intellectual *via negativa* Parmenides offered to philosophers the means of dismissing as not real all that is given either introspectively or perceptually. His system undertakes two things: (1) to establish the existence of something, and (2) to demonstrate its properties. The first, that something exists, was argued as follows: Either something exists or nothing exists. Being an instance of the law of excluded middle, *p* or not-*p*, this premise is unassailable. Now it has already been argued that nothing is inconceivable and therefore cannot be. It follows then that something exists. The same thing can be argued by using a combination of Cartesian and Parmenidean premises: Thought exists and must have an object. Therefore something, which is its object, exists. This something, with attributes as yet unspecified, is simply called Being. It can be shown that not more than one such exists. If there were two things then there would have to be an empty space between them. But empty space, space where there is nothing, is inconceivable. Prof. A. E. Taylor expresses this point as follows: 'Strictly speaking, the notion of an empty space or an empty time is unmeaning, as the simple experiment of thinking of their existence is sufficient to show. We cannot in thought successfully separate the spatial and temporal aspects of experience from the rest of the whole to which they belong and take them as subsisting by themselves, any more than we can take timbre subsisting apart from musical pitch or colour-tone apart from saturation' (1912, p. 249).

It remains now to demonstrate the properties Being has in addition to the property just demonstrated, namely, that it is *one*. A corollary of this property is that it is continuous. Being cannot consist of parts in separation from each other, for this would mean the existence of empty spaces, however small, between the parts. And empty space is impossible. Thus Being is a continuum of matter, a plenum, which unlike a sponge contains no empty spaces within itself. As Parmenides says, 'thou canst not separate being in one place from contact with being in another place; it is not scattered here and there through the universe, nor is it compounded of parts' (in: Nahm, 1947, p. 117). We get some idea of Parmenidean Being if we imagine a cosmic Titan pressing together all the matter of the universe until the limit of compressibility is reached. This will only be attained when all the empty spaces within the mass of matter, however minute, are filled and all discontinuities eliminated. It is of interest that in 1927 the astronomer George Lemaitre constructed a hypothesis about the primary state of matter of the physical universe which has Parmenidean overtones. It was called the 'big bang' hypothesis, and was to the effect that the differentiated universe, the beginning of multiplicity, was formed by the flying apart of the components following an inner upheaval.

A further important attribute of the completely continuous One is its eternality. That Being is eternal implies that it could not have a beginning or end in time, which in turn implies that it is uncreated and indestructible. We can argue against its having a beginning in time by pointing out what this would imply: a time before Being existed, when there was nothing. The hypothesis that Being had a beginning implies the existence of not-being. It follows that Being could not have been created. By a comparable *reductio ad absurdum* argument it can be shown that Being cannot come to an end in time, as this would imply a time after which there is nothing. Hence Being is indestructible.

Parmenides gives us a picture of a frozen universe in which nothing happens and nothing changes. Being is all that there is and fills all of space. It therefore is incapable of motion, since motion implies an unoccupied space for it to move into. It is also incapable of any qualitative change. That 'things arise and perish ... that they change their position and vary in colour' ... 'all these things will be but a name' (in: Nahm, 1947, p. 117), that is, so many empty words. What is real neither waxes nor wanes, nor undergoes any change. To complete the Parmenidean picture of the universe, Being is finite, and a sphere. This claim was in fact one point for attack by Melissos.

'The hypothesis of the being of the one', which was treated with so much respect by Plato, is supported by the astonishingly acute, and so far unrefuted, arguments of Parmenides' pupil Zeno. These arguments, according to the words Plato places in the mouth of Zeno in his dialogue *Parmenides* (Sec. 128), 'were meant to protect the arguments of Parmenides against those who make fun of him and seek to show the many ridiculous and contradictory results which they suppose to follow from the affirmation of the one'. Zeno's counteroffensive was that the 'hypothesis of the being of the many ... appears to be still more ridiculous than the hypothesis of the being of the one'. In this dialogue we find Socrates complaining to Parmenides that Zeno merely 'puts what you say in another way, and would fain make us believe that he is telling us something which is new. For you, in your poems, say The All is one, and of this you adduce excellent proofs; and he on the other hand says There is no many; and on behalf of this he offers overwhelming evidence. You affirm unity. He denies plurality. And so you deceive the world into believing that you are saying different things when really you are saying much the same.'

It is true that the conclusions of Zeno's and Parmenides' arguments come to the same thing. But it is important to recognize how new, and how different from Parmenides' arguments, were the pieces of reasoning Zeno made use of in supporting various Parmenidean theses. The important difference in the argumentation of the two thinkers lies in the difference in the basic concepts around which their reasoning revolves. The concept of *nothing*, which has played such an important role in the thinking of existentialist philosophers in the last decades, was central to Parmenides' arguments. If a thesis implies the existence of not-being, so the reasoning ran, then the thesis is false. Zeno's argumentation revolved about the concept of the infinite. If a thesis implies the existence of an infinity of things, then the thesis is untenable. Parmenides used the concept of *nothing* to discredit the world of sense, Zeno the concept of *infinity*. What was not grasped in the Platonic dialogue was the differentiating feature of Zeno's argumentation, his basic tenet that an infinite whole, that is, a *consummated* infinite, is impossible.

This thesis, that the number of members in an actual assemblage must be finite, is central to each of his arguments in defense of various of the Parmenidean claims. It is supported by the apparently simple considera- tion that if there are many things there must be exactly as many as there are, that is, a definite, and therefore finite, number. It will be some number which can be used to name the sum of terms in an actual collection, that is, some number in the series 1, 2, 3, 4, ... etc. Now Zeno argued also that if there are many things they must be infinite in number, his intention being to show the hypothesis that there is more than one thing to be self- contradictory. As there cannot be less than one thing, since then there would be nothing, his defense of Parmenides' hypothesis of the being of the One would then be complete. The contradiction he sought to elicit in the notion of a collection of things follows only for a collection of more than one thing. The arguments for the two propositions, that a multipli- city of things is finite, and that it is infinite, are, in Zeno's words, as follows:

'If things are a many, there must be just as many as there are, and neither more nor less. Now if these are as many as there are they will be finite in number' (*Fragment* 3, in: Nahm, 1947, p. 122).

'If things are a many, they will be infinite in number; for there will always be other things between them, and others again between them. And so things are infinite in number' (*Ibid.*, p. 122).

Of these two arguments the important one is the first, which does not depend on the Parmenidean thesis about non-being, as does the second. Its conclusion, that the number of existing things cannot be infinite, that is, that there cannot be an actual infinite totality, is derived from a consideration which is deceptively simple and which itself rests on com- plex ideas some of which need to be made explicit. Consider the series 1, 2, 3, 4, ... etc. Galileo pointed out a strange fact about this array, which is that a part only of the array considered as a totality has no fewer members than the whole. This becomes clear when we notice that every number has a square and every square is the square of a number. There thus cannot be more numbers than there are squares, else there would be some numbers which had no squares. And there cannot be more squares than there are numbers else some squares would be the squares of no numbers. Hence the members of the following two series can be exactly paired without remainder:

K_1: 1, 2, 3, 4, 5, ...

K_2: 1^2, 2^2, 3^2, 4^2, 5^2, ...

It will be obvious that the elements of K_2 are some only out of the set K_1 and yet are no fewer than the elements of K_1 since the elements of the two sets are 1–1 correlatable with each other. Galileo's conclusion was that 'the attributes "equal", "greater", and "less" are not applicable to infinite, but only to finite, quantities' (1914, pp. 32–33). This would imply that we cannot intelligibly say that there are fewer squares than numbers, or no fewer squares than numbers, and thus we can say nothing whatever about what is shown by his consideration. This certainly leaves the notion of an infinite set a mystery.

Leibniz came to a different conclusion. In 1698, in a letter to Bernouilli he wrote: 'In fact many years ago I proved that the number or sum of all numbers involves a contradiction (the whole would equal the part) ...' The proof he referred to was the following: '...the number of all numbers implies a contradiction, which I show thus: To any number there is a corresponding number equal to its double. Therefore the number of all numbers is not greater than the number of even numbers, i.e., the whole is not greater than its part.' (1951a, p. 99)

In opposition to the views of Galileo and Leibniz, Cantor maintained the applicability of the terms 'equal', 'greater', and 'less' to infinite sets. And far from admitting it to be self-contradictory that the whole of an infinite set should be equal to a part, he took 1–1 correlatability of an infinite set with a proper sub-set of it as a *defining* characteristic. The three positions with regard to infinite sets nevertheless remain, despite the existence of the theory of transfinite numbers as a present part of mathematics. It might be thought that only a failure to see the logical incompatibility between the existence of transfinite arithmetic and Galileo's and Leibniz's positions was responsible for the hold these latter positions continue to have. But if Leibniz's view, for example, were correct, this need not imply that transfinite arithmetic must be jettisoned. It may imply no more than that this arithmetic needs to be reinterpreted.

6

We may digress here to remark that what the mathematician does is all right but that what his terminology leads us to think he does may be all wrong. Transfinite arithmetic creates the idea of a super-huge, and a huge that is still greater than the super-huge – of an inexhaustible that is even more inexhaustible than an inexhaustible. But all this may be a fiction created by the mathematician's vocabulary, which carries with it ideas appropriate only to talk about finite quantities. '$\aleph_0$', the symbol which Cantor used to denote the number of all cardinal numbers, is naturally associated with the idea of a number which is enormously larger than any of the finite cardinals. The difference between a finite and an infinite class is considered, by those who think in terms of extensions, as a difference in magnitude. Against this Wittgenstein remarked that when one says 'The alphabet is a, b, c, d, and so on' the 'and so on' is an abbreviation; but when one says 'The cardinals are 1, 2, 3, 4, and so on' this phrase is not an abbreviation. The 'and so on' used when one talks of generating the integers by adding 1 plays a different role. To say that a person has learned how to do $\aleph_0$ additions is not to say he has learned to encompass an enormous task, but merely that he has learned to continue adding indefinitely. To learn to add up to 100,000,000 is analogous to learning to add indefinitely, but the analogy is not given by saying that in the first case one has learned a process which gets one nearer to infinity. As Wittgenstein put it, 'Infinity has nothing to do with size' (Lecture notes, taken by Alice Ambrose, 1934–35), though the way we have learned the term 'infinite' is responsible for our supposing that it does. It should not be concluded, however, that the irrelevance of this idea of a huge number makes it improper to use the term. We can talk of infinities without supposing we are talking of the very large or the very small.

An infinite set is usually represented as a totality having odd properties, and the expression 'infinite number' as denoting a number which behaves in strange ways, for example, as not being decreased by the subtraction of any finite number and as not being increased by addition of or multiplication by any finite number. Zeno, on the contrary, thought of it as denoting an impossible number, not a queer one. And his position is not without its defenses. Some philosophers have thought that difficulties felt about the notion of an infinite collection, a notion whose legitimacy is nevertheless supported by its use in mathematics, are simply due to the finitude of our own minds. As Galileo said, they are 'difficulties which arise from Discourses which our finite understanding makes about Infinities' (1914, p. 31), the suggestion being that although finite minds cannot comprehend an infinite totality an infinite mind could. But this begs the question regarding the possibility of there being an infinite totality. And the concept of an infinite totality has to be investigated without regard to psychological considerations. Leibniz declared that 'the infinite cannot be a true whole' (1916, pp. 163–164), implying that there cannot be an infinite *totality* of things, and Aristotle implies the same thing by his words, 'Nothing is complete which has no end' (*Physica*, Bk. III, 207^a). The underlying idea is that there is an incompatibility between being a totality and being endless, so that the concept of a consummated infinite is the self-contradictory concept of an endless collection which has an end. The argument that a plurality of things must have a determinate number contains the implication that an infinite totality is logically impossible, not merely something that is beyond the grasp of our mind. Concretely, the infinite geometrical series $\frac{1}{2} + \frac{1}{4} + \frac{1}{8} + \dots$ would according to Zeno's position not be an entity too vast for the mind to comprehend; rather, it is a series which cannot exist as a whole.

With regard to this series, whose sum is said to be 1, one mathematician has written: 'What does the mathematician mean when he says that the "sum" of this halving series is 1? Clearly it is not a sum in the sense that one speaks of the sum of a finite series. There is no way to sum an infinite series in the usual sense of the word because there is no end to the terms that must be added' (Gardner, 1964, p. 126). And another mathematician wrote: 'This is a new idea of "sum". Heretofore a sum has been obtained by adding a definite number of addends. But clearly the terms of an infinite series can never be completely added' (Lennes, 1928, p. 113). These two sets of remarks indicate that the reason for there being no way of arriving at the sum of an infinite geometrical series in the usual sense of 'sum' is that there is no 'definite number' of addends. And there is no definite number of addends because there is no end to them. The 'sum' of the series is not the sum of arithmetic addition. In the arithmetic sense the series has no sum. It is not that the terms of the series can never *humanly* be completely added together; they cannot in principle be completely added. Not even Divinity could sum up an unending series of terms, because that would mean coming to the end of that which has no end. The logical impossibility of summing up the series implies that the series has no sum in the arithmetic sense, and this in turn implies that the series does not exist as an entirety. Russell has said that people make 'the mistak-

6*

en supposition that there cannot be anything beyond the whole of an infinite series, which can be seen to be false by observing that 1 is beyond the whole of the infinite series $\frac{1}{2}, \frac{3}{4}, \frac{7}{8}, \frac{15}{16}, \ldots$' (1929 p. 188). And he also said, 'the first infinite number [$\varkappa$0] is, in fact, beyond the whole unending series of finite numbers' (*Ibid*, p. 196). But Russell assumes the existence of a collection the possibility of which is in question, without meeting the contention that if a series is endless it cannot exist as a consummated whole.

To return to Zeno's basic thesis that whatever is shown to imply an infinite totality is thereby shown to be impossible. Zeno used this thesis in a number of his arguments, particularly in his attacks on the common-sense beliefs that motion occurs and that space exists. Against the reality of motion and in defense of the static universe he devised a number of acute and powerful arguments. We shall give these arguments against motion, presenting in some detail the two which relate to space rather than time, together with one further argument against the reality of space. The so-called dichotomy argument goes as follows: 'You cannot get to the end of the race-course ... You must traverse the half of any given distance before you traverse the whole, and the half of that again before you can traverse it. This goes on *ad infinitum* ...' (Burnet, 1920, p. 318). In other words, for a body to move through any distance, regardless of how large or how small, it must complete an infinite number of decreasing sub-distances, which is to say it must finish a non-ending series of acts of moving from one position to another. To *finish* its trip it must bring to an end the series $\frac{1}{2} + \frac{1}{4} + \frac{1}{8} + \ldots$ Motion is therefore impossible, and to use Aristotle's expression, 'can have no part in reality'. We may now supplement the argument by showing that the supposedly moving body cannot leave its original position. To leave a position is to arrive at a new one, and this could be effected only by going through an unending number of acts of traversing sub-distances. So we may conclude that wherever a thing is, there it must remain, unalterably stationary.

The second argument against motion, the so-called Achilles and the tortoise paradox, is more persuasive to some people, but does not actually differ in any essential respect from the dichotomy paradox. A paraphrase of this argument is as follows: 'Achilles will never overtake the tortoise. He must first reach the place from which the tortoise started. By that time the tortoise will have gone some way ahead. Achilles must then make up that, and again the tortoise will be ahead. He is always coming nearer, but ne never makes up to it' (*Ibid*). Now let us state the

Achilles argument without reference to the tortoise, which was introduced for color: Given a distance d half of which by hypothesis has been traversed. Half of the remaining distance, $\frac{d}{2}$, will have to be traversed before $\frac{d}{2}$ is traversed, and supposing again its first half to have been traversed, there remains half of the remaining half yet to be traversed, *ad infinitum*. In other words, no matter how many half-distances have been covered, there always remains an infinite number of further sub-journeys to make, which implies that the total distance can never be completed. We can now extend this reasoning, as in the case of the dichotomy, to show that the supposedly moving thing cannot leave its point or origin. For the first half of the distance which by hypothesis has been covered is subject to the same consideration. If we allow that half of it has been covered and again half of the remainder, etc., there always remains an infinite number of further sub-distances to be covered. And this applies to any part of the total distance, however small. Achilles can never leave his original position, because in doing so he would be embarked on a logically impossible task.

Zeno's third argument against motion, which is linked with the dichotomy and the Achilles, is in brief as follows: A moving object, for example, an arrow in flight, is at any moment of time *at a place*, and therefore at that moment will be at rest. This applies to all the moments of time at which the arrow is said to be in flight. Consequently it is always at rest.

Several objections to Zeno's paradoxes have been raised, and need to be examined, if only briefly. Some interpreters have claimed the arguments rest on a false idea of space, the idea, namely, that it consists of points, in consequence of which motion is erroneously thought of as a process of passing points distributed on a line. According to this criticism space cannot consist of points and therefore motion does not consist of passing points. It is not difficult to see that Zeno's arguments against motion do not rest on this idea of space. They make use only of the notion of a distance, or length, the crucial thesis being that to traverse a length an infinite number of sub-lengths will have to be traversed. The arguments need not be framed by reference to geometrical points.

A second objection has been that Zeno's argumentation rests on the false idea that traversing a distance would take an infinite amount of time, his argument implying that since each sub-distance requires some amount of time, an infinite number of sub-distances would require an infinite amount of time. It is pointed out that the time-intervals decrease with the decreasing distances and thus that the sum of the time-intervals will be the finite sum of a geometrical series of time-intervals. Motion, then, is held not to imply a temporally unending task. Two observations may be made. One is that the dichotomy (as well as the Achilles) needs make use only of the notion of an infinite number of acts of traversing distances, without regard to time. The other observation is that the same consideration applies to the notion of an infinite number of time-intervals as to an infinite number of space-intervals. Neither can have an arithmetic sum. Considered as a geometric series of time-intervals, a minute can no more come to an end than an infinite series of space-intervals can be passed through. Zeno's dichotomy argument gives no comfort to those philosophers who have pointed out the 'mistake'. Russell writes that it is only medically rather than logically impossible to write down all the integers (1936, p. 143) because it is theoretically possible to write each succeeding number in half the time taken to write the preceding one, so that at the end of two minutes (allowing one minute for the first operation) all of them will have been written down. But this begs the question. He proves the possibility of the impossible, that is, finishing an infinite number of tasks, by assuming the possibility of the impossible, coming to an end of an unending series of time-intervals. (For a fuller discussion of this, see Ambrose, 1966, pp. 59–65.)

A last objection has been made, not against Zeno's reasoning, but against his conclusion, namely, that motion does not exist. Some philosophical mathematicians have interpreted the reasoning, particularly in the arrow paradox (though it also applies to the other two), as showing, not that motion does not exist, but instead, what motion consists in: Motion is just a succession of 'static states of rest'. Russell, for example, concluded from Zeno's reasoning that '...we must entirely reject the notion of a *state* of motion. Motion consists *merely* in the occupation of different places at different times ... There is no transition from place to place...' (1938, p. 473). But this interpretation is only a subtler way of denying reality to motion. In effect it says that what appears to be a case of a thing moving from one place to another is really a case of a thing being at a series of places without being in transition from one to another. Giving up the notion of a 'state of motion' is giving up the possibility of motion. Being in motion entails being in transit; and if Zeno's reasoning shows that the possibility of being in transit must be rejected, then it shows that the reality of motion must be rejected. As one scholar put it, motion cannot be built out of a series of immobilities. The claim that

Zeno's reasoning shows what motion consists in is, despite its semantic appearance to the contrary, equivalent to the conclusion naturally drawn from the reasoning, namely, that motion does not exist.

A final example of Zeno's refutation of a hypothesis by showing it to imply an actual infinity is his argument against the reality of space. 'If there is such a thing as space', he says, 'it will be in something, for all being is in something, and that which is in something is in space. So space will be in space, and so on *ad infinitum*. Accordingly, there is no such thing as space'. (*Fragment* 4, in: Nahm, 1947, p. 122) This argument against space rests on the thesis that a multiplicity must be a finite multiplicity. The thesis may be summed up in the proposition that being actual entails being finite. But by its very nature space is such that the existence of one space entails the existence of an infinite number of spaces, the argument being that any space is embedded in a more inclusive space. Parenthetically, the argument could equally be that any space encloses an infinite number of smaller spaces, which also collides with the thesis of finitism.

A further consideration which makes use of Zeno's notion that every space is included in a greater space brings out the following contradiction: If space exists then the space that exists will be all the space that there is. It will exist as an entirety, S, which will be the whole of space. Every actual space will then be either a part of this whole space S or identical with it. But S cannot be all the space there is. For S, like any of its parts, will itself have to be included in a space S' where S' is neither identical with S nor a part of S, which by hypothesis was the whole of space. This shows that space cannot exist as a whole. The hypothesis that space exists implies a contradiction. It cannot therefore have real existence.

It will be recalled that Zeno's arguments were directed to defending the Parmenidean hypothesis of the One, and that Parmenides held the One to be a spatial magnitude. But there is an obvious inconsistency between the argument against space and the thesis that the One has body. For whatever has body must be in space. If one were asked to give the defining properties of a body one would undoubtedly include in one's list a property Moore singled out: 'occupation of space' (1953 p. 131). From the thesis that the Real is a magnitude the existence of space follows. Zeno's critique of space was a boomerang which destroyed the position it was intended to protect. But more important than this, it initiated a remarkable transformation in the conception of the Real. By implication, and apparently unwittingly, Zeno undermined his master's thesis that Being is a corporeal magnitude. Melissos, another pupil of Parmenides, went much further, explicitly denying that Being could be both one and have body. His grounds were that 'if it should have thickness, it would have parts and would no longer be a unity' (*Fragment 9*, in: Nahm, 1947, p. 267), or as Leibniz put it in his letter to De Volder of June 23, 1699: 'Matter is not *a* substance, but a plurality of *substances*' (1951c, p. 164). A being 'cannot be both material and perfectly indivisible or endowed with a true unity' (1951b, p. 107). The natural conclusion is that the Real must be of the nature of mind. Interestingly enough, this conclusion foreshadows the pluralistic metaphysics of Leibniz, aecording to whchi a substance without parts 'must be conceived in imitation of the idea we have of souls' (*Ibid*, 1951b).

The thesis that reality is of the nature of mind is central in the monistic metaphysics of Bradley. There it is argued explicitly that the Real is to be identified with experience. We have already referred to the experiment in thought by which Bradley sought to establish this. We are asked to 'find any piece of existence, and then judge if it does not consist in sentient experience ... When the experiment is made strictly', he writes, 'I can myself conceive of nothing else than the experienced' (1925, p. 145). Because anything else is inconceivable the conclusion is that 'sentient experience ... is reality, and what is not this is not real' (*Ibid*, p. 144). But the experience which is the same as reality is nevertheless not the experience encountered in everyday life. Ordinary experience is constituted of a plurality and diversity of experiences occurring in time, whereas the Real is nontemporal. To justify this claim about reality it is argued that an analytical scrutiny of time exposes it as unreal.

In developing the immaterial monism which evolves so naturally from the monism of Parmenides, the pattern of demonstration he followed might well be repeated here: First to establish the existence of the real and then to demonstrate its properties. In the present case what first has to be established is the existence of experience. This follows from the inconceivability of anything other than experience coupled with the undeniable existence of appearances – appearances of there being material things, selves, relations, space, and time. If appearances exist and only experience is conceivable, then experience exists. But there is a plurality of appearances, of diverse kinds, and it has now to be demonstrated that the Real in its ultimate nature cannot be characterized by the attributes we find in the appearances. As against everyday experience, the Real, it is argued, is an experience not in time (and hence incapable of change), is a single experience rather than a succession of individual psychical occurrences, and is non-relational and undifferentiated.

That the real is nontemporal is argued from the premises that the real must be consistent and that time is self-contradictory. To demonstrate the contradictoriness of time we are asked to consider the stream of time, past, present, and future, as a succession in which the present becomes the past and the future the present. Consider now the present which, being present, can contain no part of the past and no part of the future. Were it to contain part of the past, what is past would be present, and were it to contain part of the future, what does not yet exist would exist now. Yet any interval of time, and hence any present interval – what Aristotle called 'the now' – because it has duration, must contain within it both a before and an after. For no interval in time's passage, however small, is indivisible. As Bradley says, 'Time in fact is "before" and "after" in one' (1925, p. 39). But this commits us to a *present* past and a *present* future. Only a now which is a durationless instant will fail to contain a succession. But duration cannot be constituted of what is durationless. Beginning from time as it presents itself in our experience, it is thus argued that it cannot be a character of the real. The real transcends time.

Bradley in one place observed that 'motion implies that what is moved is in two places in one time' (*Ibid*, p. 44). This contradiction rests on a contradiction which shows up in the conception of time: It will be clear that whatever happens happens in the present. It is obviously absurd to say that something is happening in the past or is happening in the future. It will also be clear that time present, the now, cannot contain any part of the past nor any part of the future. Consider now any occurrence, such as change of position, taking place in the present. Let the following diagram depict the change of position of a particle α moving from x to y in the now.

the now

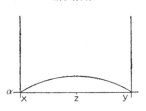

It will be clear that α will effect the first half of its transition xz before effecting the second half zy. xz will precede zy, so that with respect to xz, *zy* will be future, and with respect to *zy*, *xz* will be past. But both parts of the change of position will occur in the now, and both of the sub-intervals of time will have to be temporally co-present. Hence a moving particle will be in two places simultaneously. But the more important consequence, with respect to time, is that part of the past will be in the present, and part of the future as well. In other words, the present contains within itself what it cannot possibly contain and hence cannot be real. The conclusion can be summarized somewhat differently in the following way: The present must be exhaustively constituted by past and future, which between them leave no ontological room for the present: 'As a solid part of time the "now" does not exist' (*Ibid*, p. 41). But if the present cannot exist as a reality, neither can time.

As a corollary, the experience constituting reality will not be experience as we know it, a succession of separate occurrences. Instead it will be a single psychical entity, of quite a different sort from the succession of transitory perceptions Hume described a mind as being. That the real is one, and cannot be more than one, is maintained on the basis of a doctrine crucial to this form of idealism, namely, that all relations are internal. Proceeding again from appearances as presented in our experience, it will be admitted that relations appear to be of two kinds, external and internal, as they are usually called. Things are said to be externally related when the relation between them could fail to hold and the things be what they are. Objects adjacent to each other, or contemporaneous with each other, are examples of things usually considered to be externally related: *x* could fail to be next to *y*, or to be contemporaneous with it, and be what it is. Things are said to be internally related when their natures determine that the relation must hold, and the things could not be what they are outside of that relation. 'l greater than' is such a relation between 6 and 5. Being what they are 6 and 5 must be so related, and terms not standing in that relation could not be 6 and 5. Any putative change in an internal relation carries with it a change in the nature of the terms. On the position under discussion, all relations, regardless of appearances, are internal. 'Every relation essentially penetrates the being of its terms.' (*Ibid*, p. 392). Relations 'qualify or modify or make a difference to the terms between which they hold', and at the same time the relations a thing has are 'grounded in its nature' (Joachim, 1906, p. 12). Something in its nature, some complexity, determines its relations to other things.

Several arguments can be given in support of this doctrine. One, formulated by Prof. Brand Blanshard, and attributed to Hegel and the

Cambridge philosopher, Ellis McTaggart, is as follows. Consider the relation of difference, which clearly holds between any two things, say a ballet dancer and an Iowa farmer. This relation is held to be internal, on the ground that 'if the relation of difference between farmer and ballet dancer were removed, one or the other would not be what he is. Indeed neither could be what he is, for if the relation of difference were removed they would be identical with each other, which is something neither is now. And if this argument is valid at all, it is valid of every pair of differing things in the universe. That seems to carry with it at once the conclusion that everything is internally related to everything else' (1967, p. 229).

Another argument for the internality of relations can be discovered in what underlies a statement made by Russell, which in turn echoes remarks made by Bradley. In the course of a discussion Russell once said that to know everything about Russell one would need to know everything about the universe. In Bradley's words: '...to know perfectly his own nature would be..to pass in knowledge endlessly beyond himself' (1925, p. 581). If one had perfect knowledge 'one could start internally from any character in the Universe ... and from that pass to the rest' (*Ibid*, p. 580). The same idea was poetically expressed by Tennyson in his 'Flower in the crannied wall'. It is clear of course that the remark holds not only for Russell and the flower, but for the smallest grain of sand. To know everything about it is to know everything about the cosmos. What underlies this claim is a consideration which can be brought in support of the position that all relations are internal. This is the following. Take any truth about a relation in which Russell stands to anything else, for example, a droplet of water in the Pacific. This will be a truth about Russell. It will tell us something about what he is, his nature. And this implies that relational facts enter into his total nature. In other words, things apparently external to Russell must in their correct perspective be viewed as constitutive of his nature and therefore cannot be externally related to him. Their true relation to him must be intrinsic.

Now inasmuch as everything is related to everything else, and the nature of a thing is constituted by such a cosmic network of relations, the conclusion to be drawn is that, underneath, all things are really one and the same – Russell, the grain of sand, and the universe. The consequence of saying that to know everything about any one thing one must know everything about the cosmos is that in its ultimate nature that thing and the cosmos are identical. To express this in a formula, letting Tx be total knowledge of x and TU be total knowledge of the universe, if $Tx = TU$ then $x = U$. And as this formula holds for every apparent thing $a_1, a_2, \ldots$ $\ldots a_n$ into which x specifies, $a_1 = a_2 = \ldots = a_n$ since each will be identical with U. Despite apparent plurality, there will be but one thing: U. And U is 'not the sum of things' (*Ibid*, p. 487–488). The argument from the internality of relations shows at the very least that reality is not a mere collection, a sum of disparate entities, but instead forms a whole the parts of which are really integral to each other. Reality at a logical minimum must be an organic unity.

One further important feature of the Real remains to be demonstrated, namely, that the single experience which constitutes it is completely undifferentiated. It is maintained that in the Real, or as Bradley calls it, the Absolute, differences which present themselves in ordinary experience as qualities, terms, and relations are completely merged and cancelled out. Indeed, it is the divisive power of thought which is responsible for breaking up the wholeness of reality into this multiplicity of categories. Things within these categories which common sense takes to make up realiy, are the products of 'our vicious abstraction' (*Ibid*, p. 573). 'It is a very common and most ruinous superstition', said Bradley, 'to suppose that analysis is not alteration' (1922, Vol. I, p. 95). It is interesting to compare Bradley and Bergson on this point. Bergson held that the intellect, in the service of man's practical needs, breaks up experience into manageable elements, but that far from giving a true picture of reality, it effects a distortion. The intellect 'spatializes' the continuous flow of experience into discrete units. Difficulties which arise when we think, say, about time are merely the product of the falsifying intellect, for example, the contradiction which was elicited in the concept of time with the help of a spatial diagram. Looking at time through spatial spectacles misrepresents the continuous as being discrete. Similarly, according to Bradley, by viewing reality through intellectual spectacles which break it up and make it conform to such categories as things in relation and substances and their attributes , thought represents the undivided wholeness of the One as a multiplicity containing qualitative difference.

That an undifferentiated wholeness is the condition of reality prior to thought's supervention is, however, a claim which needs to be substantiated. Bradley defends this claim by arguing against the possibility of any sort of diversification. That the Absolute cannot be a whole constituted of terms in relation, i.e., that it must be a non-relational whole, is supported by the argument that relations imply a contradiction. This is his means of showing that 'relations do not and cannot exist in the Absolute' (1925, p. 528). The unreality of relational phenomena of the sense world, like that of other phenomena, is demonstrated by a *reductio ad absurdum* form of proof. First, it will be clear that if there are two or more terms, they will stand in some relation to each other, say, of similarity or dissimilarity, to cite two possibilities. Regardless of whether the relation holding between two particular terms x and y can be specified, there must be some relation, R, between them. But the relation R is not nothing. It also is something and must count as a term. Now by its nature a term cannot stand outside of all relations to other terms. It in turn must be related to them. Thus the term R, 'being something itself' (p. 32), must stand in some relation, R_1, to the term x and in some relation, R_2, to the term y. But both R_1 and R_2 will have to count as terms, and must in turn stand in relations to their terms; and this proliferation continues *ad infinitum:* '. . .we are hurried off into the eddy of a hopeless process, since we are forced to go on finding new relations without end. The links are united by a link, and this bond of union is a link which also has two ends; and these require each a fresh link to connect them with the old.' (p. 33). The proposition that R relates x and y implies the existence of an infinite number of relations, and as an infinite totality is impossible, the proposition must be false. In other words, the existence of distinct terms implies a relation between them, which nevertheless cannot relate them: It implies that they must be related and cannot be. On the other side, a relation is something which must relate terms and cannot relate them. This shows that the concept of the relational is self-contradictory and cannot apply to reality.

Ultimate reality is thus a whole in which all differences disappear, a higher experience which 'contains and transforms all relations' (p. 528). But since 'appearance must belong to reality . . . the bewildering mass of phenomenal diversity must somehow be at unity and self-consistent' (p. 140). 'The apparent discordance . . . is overruled into harmony' (p. 488), and contradiction 'is removed . . . by the whole which transcends it' (pp. 571–572). These words do little to convey a clear idea of the Real. Like the Platonic sojourner who returns to the cave, the metaphysician of the undifferentiated One must experience difficulty in communicating his vision of reality. Perhaps it can be communicated only to those who are endowed with special refinements of perception. And this may find expression in a tendency satirically attributed by Timon to Xenophanes, whom he reported as saying: 'Wherever I turn my mind, everything resolves itself into a single Unity.' It may be that only those of a mystical temperament are privileged to get a glimpse of what Bradley called the Absolute.

It will be interesting and instructive to consider briefly one rival metaphysical system, Leibniz's monadism. Although, like Bradley's monistic system, it can be classified as a form of idealism, it differs in being pluralistic. Here we shall develop a variant of the Leibnizian system, introducing a small number of innovations whose implications can be left to the reader to work out. The picture of reality given us in the *Monadology*, a picture current through the Middle Ages and into the eighteenth century, was that of a 'great chain of being', constituted in the Leibnizian view by a continuum of minds hierarchically ordered and differing from each other only in degree. The chain extends from the lowest order of entities, those making up inanimate matter, through the various higher forms of phenomena in nature, including plants, animals, and human beings, up to the highest possible being, God. The extreme limit at one end of the scale is the perfect monad, at the other end Parmenidean non-being, a hierarchy described by the poet James Thomson in 'The Seasons' as 'the mighty chain of being, lessening down from Infinite Perfection to the brink of dreary nothing, desolate abyss!'

It is not the present purpose to give an abbreviated description of Leibniz's picture of the universe, but it is germane to the central problem his system was constructed to cope with to note the occurrence of the same problem in antiquity. Leibniz himself declared that anyone who wished to understand him 'must understand Democritus, Plato, and Aristotle'. It is probably fair to say that Democritean atomism came about from puzzles about infinity and continuity made explicit by Parmenides and Zeno. Democritus' demonstration of the impossibility of a cone would seem to show this. The general problem is, 'How can what is continuous consist of indivisible elements?' In connection with the cone, Democritus' conception of it as built up of innumerable thin layers tapering off to the vertex presented the puzzle of how a solid whose sides had slope could be constituted. If the layers were unequal, 'they will make the cone irregular as having many indentations, like steps, and unevennesses; but, if they are equal, the ... cone will appear to have the property of the cylinder, and to be made up of equal, not unequal circles, which is very absurd' (Turnbull, 1961, p. 25). Here we have a graphic illustration of the problem centering on the divisibility of matter. Democritus did not, of course, solve the problem of infinitesimals, but it is evident that he was interested in the notion of infinite divisibility.

In the background, it would seem, the problem at work was the application of Zeno's reasoning to what might be called the Parmenidean conception of matter as a plenum occupying space. Democritean atoms can be viewed as the result of fragmenting Parmenidean Being into an indefinite number of micro-beings, ultimate particles answering to the Pythagorean notion of a point with bulk. Melissos had argued that anything having body and therefore thickness must consist of parts, and hence that the Parmenidean macro-atom is not a true unity. If Being is in space it will be a collection or aggregate of parts, and according to Democritus these parts will be micro-bodies each of which is a plenum with the essential property of being indivisible.

How the rudiments of Leibnizian theory derived from Greek materialism may be gleaned from the antithetical positions of Anaxagoras and Democritus with respect to the divisibility of matter. Democritus maintained that there is a least of that which is small, and this is the indivisible, material atom. According to one classical scholar, without a least all matter would be annihilated. On the other side Anaxagoras had declared that 'there is no least of what is small, but there is always a less' (in: Nahm, p. 151). The two alternatives have support in arguments that present us with an antinomy: Matter, as something which by its nature is composite, cannot consist of ultimate parts, and yet it must. On the one hand, it is argued that there can no more be least constituents of what is extended than there can be smallest spaces. Any ultimate *spatial* part α will itself occupy some space, however small, and will thus consist of mutually external parts each of which occupies a fraction of the space occupied by α. On the other hand, it is argued that if the original extension is to exist it must consist of ultimate parts. To argue this side of the antinomy as Kant did, any parts of a spatial composite, like bricks in a wall, will stand in some sort of arrangement and could in principle have a different arrangement. If there were no ultimate parts – if, instead, every part were an arrangement of parts, etc., then if the *total* arrangement were thought away nothing would remain to enter into a new arrangement.

Leibniz starts from the proposition that matter is composite, and accepts the thesis that what is composite must consist of simples. But he escapes between the horns of the dilemma by maintaining that these simple parts are immaterial. They are of the nature of minds, 'animated points' as he called them, and to these the property of extension is inapplicable. The line of reasoning by which he arrived at this conclusion may have been the following. A piece of matter, being an extended substance, is a composite and must consist of terminal parts arrived at by a process of division, whether finite or not. With respect to any one of these parts there will be three possibilities, that it is (1) an extended and divisible substance; (2) an extended and indivisible substance, and (3) a non-extended and indivisible substance. The first alternative is immediately eliminated inasmuch as an extended and divisible substance cannot be a terminal part. The second alternative is eliminated as self-contradictory, for being extended entails being divisible. Only the third alternative remains, that the final parts of an extended substance are substances to which the concept of divisibility is inapplicable. Inasmuch as the only conceivable substances other than matter are minds, these must be minds. Leibniz denies that they can be geometrical points: 'A multitude can derive its reality only from genuine units ... which are quite other than mathematical points ... of which it is certain the continuum cannot be composed' (1951b, p. 107).

We may summarize the argument in the proposition that the existence of matter entails the existence of simple sentient substances, the monads. This plainly is not a proof of the existence of monads. To establish their existence it would seem necessary first to establish the existence of matter. Russell said of Leibniz that he started 'from the common-sense belief in the reality of matter' (1900, p. 74), but that 'the question: Does matter exist? is ... one which Leibniz never thoroughly faced' (p. 70). It would be interesting to explore the possibility of demonstrating the existence of monads without facing this question. In what follows we shall contribute an argument for their existence which does not assume the existence of matter and which at the same time does not require the existence of God. How such a non-theological proof affects the details of Leibnizian monadology we shall not undertake to examine.

The argument for the proposition that the existence of matter entails the existence of simple immaterial substances rests on the axiom that nothing can be a substance which is neither simple nor composite. The dichotomy *simple-composite* categorizes all possible substances. It is exhaustive of the possibilities, and the two sub-categories, *simple* and *composite*, are mutually exclusive. At times Leibniz characterizes the composite as 'not a substance properly speaking', so that it remains for simples to count as substances. Being simple they have neither causal 'inlets' nor causal 'outlets'. Nothing can enter into them from the outside, nor can anything leave them from within. 'The monads have no windows through which anything can enter or depart.' This holds for *all* monads without exception. Now Leibniz distinguishes between the created monads and the uncreated, necessarily existing supreme monad, God. But an argument can be given to show that every monad, regardless of its degree of approximation to perfection, is uncreated and exists necessarily.

That monads cannot be created, and hence cannot be created by God, follows simply from their fundamental properties. God is a substance, and since He cannot be composite He must be simple. By his very nature, then, He will have no inlets or outlets. Like any other monad He will be hermetically sealed with respect to causation; He can suffer nothing within Himself from the outside nor create anything outside Himself. Such creativity could not flow from his perfection, as it would be incompatible with his nature as a monad. Hence, even though the supreme monad exists, the existence of other monads could not be laid at his door, as, jocularly speaking, he has no door. Leibniz produced the celebrated ontological argument for the existence of God conceived of as an absolutely perfect being (to be considered in a later chapter). But this is not pertinent to the present task of showing that all monads exist necessarily in virtue of being monads. An argument to show this will of course apply equally to all monads, perfect and imperfect.

Let us begin with the axiom that a monad could possibly exist and make the supposition that it does not. Then by a straightforward line of reasoning it can be shown to follow from this supposition that it could not exist, which contradicts our axiom. The supposition that it does not exist will therefore have to be rejected, and the necessary consequence will be that it does exist. The line of reasoning is this: No monad can be brought into existence by another monad since no monad is capable of acting outside itself. Hence if a monad did not exist it could not be brought into existence by any other thing. That is, if it did not exist it could not come into existence by causation. But as there is no other way in which a substance could be brought into existence, it could not exist. This goes against the admitted possibility of its existing, and the conclusion therefore is that it exists. But the existence of a thing which can be deduced from its *possible* existence is necessary existence. Hence all monads constituting the great chain of being exist by necessity in virtue of being monads. For the argument applies to every conceivable, and therefore possible, monad.

No more can be said here about the metaphysics of the monad, but it is

7

interesting to notice a difference in the way the world looks through the monistic spectacles of absolute idealism and the pluralistic spectacles of monadistic idealism. According to the former all (apparent) relations between things are internal, so that things merge into each other and lose their differentiation in the whole. On the monadistic view we are presented with a collection of substances which remain distinct from each other and are externally related only. Relations in which simple substances stand to each other cannot, because monads are simple, make a difference to them. In addition to this important difference between the two idealistic metaphysics, there is a further point of important difference, and also a point of similarity. These have to do with the ontological status of space and time. The view that matter is composed of monads implies that that which is in space is composed of elements none of which is in space. The problem posed by this reduction of material substance to a multiplicity of unextended, nonmaterial substances is resolved by the view that space is 'a confused perception'. Space, Leibniz maintains, is imaginary, s wholly mental thing. As in the metaphysics of absolute idealism, it has the status of a mere, or delusive, appearance.

The point of important dissimilarity between the two metaphysical positions concerns the status of time. A monad, although simple, experiences natural changes of various sorts, in perception, desire, volition, etc. And these can occur only if time is real. Although Leibniz is not unequivocal on this point, it is clear that the existence of a monad requires the reality of time. Even though its inner changes had, as Bradley would hold, the status of appearances, time would be real. This type of consideration can be directed against the Bradleian position, but more important, it can be used to protect Leibniz's position. It will be recalled that appearances, for example, of change taking place, were declared to exist even though unreal. Although it seems possible to deny the existence of material things, motion, qualitative change, etc., it takes more than philosophical boldness to deny that motion and change appear to occur and that material things appear to exist. The sensible appearances are undeniable. Now for an appearance to occur there must be time for it to occur in. Without time there can be no appearance of succession, for example; for the appearance of succession itself contains succession. And this could not take place if time were unreal. On the Leibnizian view space is not required for the existence of the monad, but time is required for the plurality and succession of psychical states which the simple is capable of experiencing. To revert to the distinction made early in this chapter between two types of metaphysics, the monadistic theory is not a metaphysics of complete transcendence, whereas absolute idealism, in placing the real beyond both space and time, is.

DOUBTS AND QUERIES

1. In Chapter 3 important use was made of the claim that no term has a descriptive function if its antithesis has no use to describe a theoretically possible circumstance. What does this claim imply with regard to the Parmenidean theses that motion, plurality, etc. are inconceivable and that being stationary and one are real? Put differently, if no theoretical room is left for one sort of phenomenon, or no 'logical space' for it, to use Wittgenstein's expression, is the necessary space required for antithetical phenomena precluded? For instance, does the claim that unoccupied, or empty, space is inconceivable imply that occupied space is also inconceivable? In other words, does our being able to think of an occupied space involve knowing what it would be like for that space not to be occupied?

2. In the *Phaedo* Socrates declared that nothing could be slow which had not previously been swift, nor swift which had not previously been slow, his claim being an instance of the general thesis that opposites pass into each other. On the Parmenidean view the One could not have become what it is from a prior state of being many, and Being could not have become what it is from a prior state of being nothing. How does this square with the Socratic assertion? It would seem clear that a thing cannot *become* φ without first having been not-φ. Can a thing *be* φ without the possibility of there being a thing which is not-φ?

3. The Parmenidean position is that not only could Being not have come from nothing but that Being has no conceivable antithesis: Being is, and not-Being is inconceivable. Is it possible for Being to be conceivable if not-Being is inconceivable? Some recent existentialists have claimed that not only is not-Being, or nothing, conceivable but also that it exists. How is this sort of opinion with respect to not-Being to be explained?

Parmenides said that non-Being is inconceivable and unutterable. If his statement is intelligible, i.e., tells us something about what he is talking about, then it would seem that non-Being is conceivable and is capable of being referred to by means of language. If it is not intelligible, then his words tell us nothing. How would a Parmenidean deal with this dilemma?

7*

4. Zeno's dichotomy argument is an analysis of the concept *motion*, eliciting entailments embedded in the concept of a moving object. It is of the form: Being in motion entails traversing a distance; traversing a distance entails traversing half the distance first, etc., etc., *ad infinitum*. The argument, in other words, consists solely of a series of putative entailments. But the conclusion that motion does not exist appears to be about a phenomenon, about what occurs or does not occur. If the argument against motion is *a priori*, then the proposition that motion does not exist cannot be empirical (Ch. 2). Can a proposition be empirical, make a claim about what does or does not exist, and rest on *a priori* premises? If it cannot, can it be about reality? Leibniz held that a necessary truth makes a declaration about all possible universes. Does this imply that Zeno's proposition tells us about what cannot occur in any possible universe?

5. The conceivability criterion of Parmenides and the consistency criterion of Bradley imply that whatever is conceivable or self-consistent is true, and that what is self-inconsistent, or implies a contradiction, is false. These principles together with considerations professing to show that phenomena of everyday experience such as change and the like are self-contradictory and hence mere appearance, imply that the real is not encountered in everyday experience, and that the appearances do not picture a possible reality. The implication with regard to the appearances is that their corresponding realities would be self-contradictory. Can there be appearances of what is self-contradictory? Does the appearance of anything which, if it existed, would imply a contradiction, imply that the appearance itself is self-contradictory? If the appearance of a self-contradictory state is itself self-contradictory, then by the consistency principle it cannot exist as a reality, and if it does exist it cannot be self-contradictory and hence must picture a conceivable reality. For example, the sensible appearances of there being a dagger on the table or a water mirage in the desert pictures what could conceivably be the case, an actual dagger on the table and a body of water in the desert. If the existence of sensible appearances does imply the conceivability of the corresponding reality, what is the implication of this when coupled with the conceivability or consistency criterion of reality? Do the common-sense phenomena that were argued out of existence as being self-contradictory appearances spring back into existence?

6. What does it mean to say that everything we can think of has being? What is the difference between existence and subsistence? The claim that thought must have an object, strengthened by the argument that

thinking of a unicorn is different from thinking of a griffin and both of these are different from thinking of the Empire State building, are taken by some philosophers to imply that a griffin, a unicorn, and the Empire State building are different objects present to thought, all of which have being. Does the difference between the first two and the third lie in the first two subsisting and the third existing? Is a griffin which subsists an actual griffin, a flesh-and-blood creature which does not exist? Does the difference between subsistence and existence refer to different ways in which the same thing can have being, such that a griffin which only subsists can acquire existence and the Empire State building can lose its existence and become subsistent? Could a thing be half-existent and half-subsistent, and if so, what would be the difference between the half that exists and the half that only subsists? Some philosophers have claimed that there is no difference between subsistence and existence, and that a thing either exists or just does not exist. Supposing this to be correct, does the conceivability criterion joined to the argument formulated by Moore imply that at least one thing of every conceivable kind exists – does it imply the overpopulated universe?

If we attempt to keep the distinction between subsistence and existence, what criterion will distinguish between them? Could there be a criterion distinguishing the existence of an even number between 5 and 7 from its subsistence? In the case of this example what is conceivable exists. One would not wish to hold this for the conceivable unicorn. Yet the conceivable unicorn and the conceivable even number between 5 and 7 are alike in that neither is in space and time.

7. A great deal of what Zeno, Parmenides, and Bradley held hangs on the thesis that the actual infinite is impossible. Zeno's basic argument, which is presupposed by many philosophical propositions, is that a number of things must always be a definite and therefore finite number. The indefiniteness of the number of a collection is always an indefiniteness in our knowledge of the exact number and never in the collection itself. The Zeno-Leibniz claim can be summed up in the formula, Every number is a finite number. Does this proposition imply that the concepts *number* and *finite number* are identical? If they are, then does it follow that 'Every number is a finite number' reduces to the true but empty statement that every number is a number? Does preventing this reduction, which would seem to require preserving a distinction between the concepts *number* and *finite number*, imply the possible existence of an infinite number, that is, of the actual infinite?

8. It would seem possible to suppose a thing to enter successively into various relations. How would an advocate of the doctrine that these relations are all internal respond to the following critical comment by Russell: 'The doctrine in question holds that a thing is so modified by its relations that it cannot be the same in one relation as in another. Hence, if this doctrine is true there never can be more than one fact concerning any one thing' (1914, p. 150). Furthermore, can an advocate of this doctrine consistently hold that a new relation 'modifies' or 'makes a difference to' *that* thing? Bradley was explicit in holding change to be impossible, on the ground that for a thing A to change there must be something which remains identifiably the same, but if A changes, A becomes A_1, A_2, . . ., and A no longer exists. Russell may not have had in mind the application of his consideration to relations into which one and the same thing enters successively. But it applies to these as well as to relations it may have simultaneously to other things.

Limiting consideration to a plurality of relations holding simultaneously, note the difficulty posed for the doctrine of internal relations: If a given thing A which stands in relation R to B at the same time stands in a relation R' to C, then it would have to be identically the same thing which stands in two different relations. It would therefore have to have an identity of its own, apart from its relations. But this would seem to imply that the relations in which it stands to B and C are external to it, or at any rate, that not more than one of its relations could be internal.

9. On the doctrine of internal relations, according to which a given thing has the relations it has in virtue of its nature, what is the status of a true proposition about that thing? If this doctrine is correct, will the classifications of propositions, 'analytic' and 'synthetic', have the same function they now have in the language?

10. It will be remembered that Bradley professed to show that only sentient experience is real by making what appeared to be an experiment in thought. The outcome of the thought experiment was that only experience is conceivable. Does this statement violate what may be called Wittgenstein's dictum that a term has no application if its antithesis has none? It might be claimed that it does violate it, for the following reason. The implication of the statement is that non-experiential reality is inconceivable and thus that the expression 'non-experiential reality' (and equivalent expressions) denotes no concept. If that is the case then the statement that every conceivable reality is experience would imply that the concept *experience* does not have a use to distinguish between

conceivable realities. Hence 'every conceivable reality is experience' would reduce to the uninformative truth that every conceivable reality is a conceivable reality. Could Bradley's claim about experience issue from a thought experiment? We can make the thought experiment of doing a complicated sum or of trying to picture in imagination a polygon with a million sides, but can we make a thought experiment of trying to conceive the inconceivable, for example, a blue patch which is uniformly red?

11. In the Bradleian demonstration of the unreality of relations, consider the first step in generating the infinite regress, namely, that the relation assumed to hold between terms x and y, say, color difference, must itself be related by new relations R_1 and R_2 to x and y, resp. Does specifying R_1 and R_2 present a difficulty which has a bearing on the validity of the demonstration?

12. Does Leibniz' view, according to which the ultimate parts of matter are nonmaterial, imply that there is no material least, and does this in turn imply the annihilation of matter?

Leibniz holds that space is a confused perception. Does this imply the unreality of space and therefore the nonexistence of matter? Leibniz's inference of monads from matter may be stated in the form: If matter exists, monads exist. Is this equivalent to an inference about the nature of what might exist from the nature of what cannot exist?

REFERENCES

Recommended reading:
   G. W. Leibniz, *The monadology*.
Further readings:
   F. H. Bradley (1925), *Appearance and reality*, Chs. 3, 4, 13.
   Plato, *Republic*, Bk. VI, section 507 to end
   of Book; Bk. VII, sections 514 to 519.
   –, *Phaedrus*, sections 246 to 252.
   –, *Phaedo*, sections 73 to 77.
   Benedict de Spinoza (1901a), *Ethics*.

5. Philosophical Theology

The idea of God plays an important role in the mental life of everyone, atheist, agnostic, and believer alike, and its consequences for the development of civilization have been fundamental. It perhaps is not an overstatement to say that without the idea of a divine overseer of the universe who sets moral standards and metes out rewards and punishments in accordance with man's moral dues, civilization would not have evolved. The myth Plato ascribed to Protagoras concerning how mankind acquired justice from the hand of Zeus parallels the Biblical account of the divine origin of the ten commandments. Both accounts tell us the same thing, that man pulled himself out of primal anarchy with the help of the concept of a divine lawgiver.

In one place Freud describes the feeling of helplessness induced in us by an overwhelmingly vast and impersonal universe; and about religion he said that 'its ultimate basis is the helplessness of mankind'. This is perhaps what we glimpse behind F. P. Ramsey's brave words: 'I don't feel the least bit humble before the vastness of the heavens. The stars may be large but they cannot think or love; and these are qualities that impress me far more than size does' (1931, p. 291). The same feeling about the non-human world around us undoubtedly is behind poetry which in various ways humanizes Nature. Voltaire said that if there were no god man would have had to invent one, and indeed, psychoanalysis tells us that God is an unconscious invention: He is the magnified image of the human father projected into the cosmos as the Heavenly Father. We may also guess that if there were no evidence for God's existence this too would have had to be invented. 'Knowledge' which springs from need has a function to console much more than to satisfy scientific curiosity; and it is the same with religious evidence, and reported visions and miracles, which are used to bolster such claimed knowledge.

In philosophy as in religion the concept of the divine is of central importance. It permeates nearly all, if not all, metaphysical systems. Here our concern is to present and examine evidence for the existence of a transcendent being, but in the form of arguments available to the scrutiny of everyone, atheist, agnostic, and believer. Unlike experiments conducted in the laboratory, miracles cannot be repeated; and visions, and mystical experiences in general, cannot be made publicly accessible. But a philosophical argument, and the analysis of a concept, are public pieces of evidence, can be presented on request, and can be assessed with relative objectivity. Philosophical theology attempts to explicate the idea of a transcendent god, lay out the lines of reasoning for and against the existence of such a being, and establish its relation to the universe, particularly to the existence of evil.

Philosophy provides us with a number of different though related pictures of a transcendent god, several of which may be mentioned briefly. Xenophanes gives us the following remarkable, nonanthropomorphic description: 'God is one, supreme among gods and men, and not like mortals in body or mind'. 'The whole [of God] sees, the whole perceives, the whole hears'. 'But without effort he sets in motion all things by mind and thought'. 'It [i.e., being] always abides in the same place, not moved at all, nor is it fitting that it should move from one place to another'. (in: Nahm, 1947, p. 109) In Aristotle we find the narcissistic conception of God as the object of universal love and the only object worthy of his own contemplation since he is 'the most excellent of things'. Wittgenstein remarked that 'when I move something, I move'. By contrast, when God, according to Aristotle's conception, moves something, he himself is unmoved: He is the Unmoved Mover.

In traditional philosophical theology there are three major arguments for the existence of God, the teleological, cosmological, and ontological arguments; and each of these is associated with a special picture. The teleological argument links up with the image of God as the master architect-builder who gives form to matter according to a prior world-plan. The cosmological argument is associated with the idea of God as a super-magician who creates matter itself, the stuff of which the universe is formed, out of nothing. Finally, the ontological argument, which deduces God's existence from his nature alone brings up the picture of an aloof being of inconceivable grandeur. All three pictures are linked with the idea of perfection: the perfect designer, the perfect creator, the perfect being. Kant said there are only three possible proofs for the existence of God, the major proofs just mentioned. But in fact other proofs exist in the literature, including one by Kant himself. Two of these may be touched on before taking up the major arguments.

Leibniz gives an interesting if curious proof of God's existence, which may be called the argument from eternal truths. Truths, as we have seen (Ch. 2), are of at least two kinds. Some truths. such as 'it is raining', are contingent, that is, not necessarily always true, while others, such as '2+2 = 4', are true necessarily, that is, such that they could never have been false and could never be false. Leibniz called such truths eternal. The proof to be given here rests on the so-called conceptualist view that the components of propositions are thoughts. Propositions, which on this view are made up of thoughts, will require a mind in order to exist. Without a mind which holds them in existence there could be no truths. Hence if any proposition is an eternal truth – true for all times, past and future as well as present – there will be an eternal thought and consequently an eternal mind whose thought it is. 'If there were no eternal substance', said Leibniz, 'there would be no eternal truths' (1900, p. 288). And this substance, to use Aquinas' words, 'men call God'. It is of some interest that Russell held that the concepts entering into a contingent proposition are brought together by the relating activity of the mind, which implies that the proposition would not exist independently of a mind. On this view the concepts *Desdemona*, *loves*, and *Iago*, for example, are combined by the mind into the proposition 'Desdemona loves Iago'. (Its falsehood, however, is determined by a fact external both to the proposition and the mind.)

Book Λ of Aristotle's *Metaphysics*, from which the material at the end of this chapter is taken, is the fountainhead of later philosophical theology. Elements of his discourses on Divine Substance have found their way into both the cosmological and ontological arguments. Here we shall try to distil from these considerations a demonstration of the necessary existence of God which is not classifiable as belonging to either of these types. This is the demonstration of an Unmoved Mover, which is not a cosmological argument although it is taken to be such by a number of commentators. It proceeds from the necessary existence of time, rather than from the existence of a contingent thing, and by a series of entailments arrives at the existence of an eternal substance. The argument begins with a distinction between perishable and imperishable things, time belonging to the latter category. Unlike contingent things, which might or might not exist, time not only exists but exists necessarily. The argument for its necessary existence is as follows: Time can have neither beginning nor end, for to do so would imply a contradiction. To have had a beginning implies a time at which it began and before which there was no time; and to have an end implies a time at which it ends, after which there is no time. Nothing which can have no beginning can begin to be. Now if time did not exist it could not begin to be. It could not come into existence and hence could not exist. This goes against the fact that time does exist, but more important for the argument, it goes against the fact that it *could* exist. Therefore time does exist; and anything whose possible existence implies its actual existence exists necessarily. Hence time has necessary existence and is therefore eternal. It can similarly be argued that time exists continuously. Were it to exist intermittently there would have to be times during which there is no time, which is absurd.

Now a time empty of all change, in which nothing whatever happens, is impossible. So if time continuously exists, continuous change must occur. Time could not be continuous and change discontinuous. Aristotle specifies the continuous change as motion in a circle, but it is not necessary for the argument that the change be change of position, or motion. Then since time is eternal, motion also is eternal. Now motion must have a cause, not a cause which creates it (inasmuch as being eternal, it is uncreated), but a cause which sustains it. And the cause of eternal and continuous motion must be an eternal continuous cause. Since only substance, an individual thing, can be a cause, the Eternal Cause of motion must be an Eternal Substance. (For a similar claim, see Berkeley.)

This Substance has been called the Prime Mover, but care should be taken not to interpret 'Prime Mover' as a being prior in time to motion, as its initiator. The Aristotelian argument makes it impossible for there to be a time prior to which motion did not exist, and prior to which the Prime Mover did not exist. Divine Substance, motion, and time are coeval. Furthermore, this Substance could not have originated motion, since the existence of motion, which is implied by the necessary existence of time, is not only eternal but necessary. That the Prime Mover sustains motion without originating it raises a question about how this is brought about. Aristotle distinguishes between what he calls efficient and final causation. When an efficient cause is operative it must itself undergo a change in order to bring about its effect, as when a bat sets a ball in motion, and a player sets the bat in motion. An efficient cause, in bringing about a motion, itself moves, and in turn requires an efficient cause, which in bringing about a motion also moves, etc., *ad infinitum*. Hence the Divine Substance in sustaining motion could not itself move or change, as that would imply an infinite and therefore impossible number of causes going back in time. Divine Substance is not an efficient cause of motion, nor is it subject to efficient causation. It is the Unmoved Mover.

But if this Mover is not the efficient cause of continuing motion in virtue of some activity in itself, then another sort of causation – final causation – must be operative. The difference between efficient and final causation seems to be the same as the distinction to be found in the philosophical literature between mechanical and teleological causation, or perhaps the same as that to be found in Wittgenstein between cause and reason. A final cause is that for the sake of which something is done. The Divine Substance, which brings about its effect without *doing* anything, is this kind of cause. The world revolves around Divine Substance because of what it is, not because of what it does. In Aristotle it is the ultimate object of desire, or love. Like the *Mona Lisa*, which without any effort on its part draws people to it, Divine Substance keeps the universe in motion by being the universal object of striving. In Aristotle's words, 'the final cause ... produces motion by being loved, but all other things move by being moved' (*Metaphysics*, 1072^b).

There are two different concepts of God which need to be separated out before we can proceed to the traditional arguments. One, which might be called the Michelangelo conception and is the folk image behind most religious thinking, is that of a magnified human figure, a Titan who is ruler of the cosmos. The other conception is that of a transcendent being, a being that is not representable in sense or imagination, who combines in himself all possible perfections. Philosophical theology concerns itself only with the second concept. Thus, the argument linked with the notion of an architect-builder of the universe establishes, if it establishes anything at all, the existence of a transcendent architect, one who gives form to the matter in space in accordance with a plan, and is himself not in space. What all three of the traditional arguments are intended to establish is the existence of an absolutely perfect being, than which a greater is inconceivable. Of such a being pictorial representation is impossible. If it exists, it unites in itself all desirable attributes to their limiting degree: It is all-knowing, all-wise, all-powerful, all-good, etc. Nothing less than this could count as the supreme being, for nothing less than this would be a being 'without defect'.

The teleological argument, or the so-called argument from design, proceeds to the existence of a supreme being by inference from evidence of purpose in the world. We normally distinguish between artifacts and natural objects, an artifact, like a shoe or a watch, being a contrivance made for a purpose. Archdeacon Paley (1813) asks us to consider what we would think if we came upon a watch on a heath. Our unhesitating inference would be that it had been manufactured, and subsequently lost there. Suppose that the first people to scale Mt. Everest found a watch on top, still ticking and showing the correct time. This of course did not happen, and that it should happen would be enormously unlikely. But it is theoretically possible, so let us suppose it to have happened. What would be a reasonable inference? One possibility, the one that would naturally occur to us, is that it was an artifact rather than a natural object and had somehow been transported to the mountain top. Another is that molecules of matter in the area had by mere chance come together to form a watch that was still ticking. As between these two possibilities there can be no question regarding which is the reasonable one to infer. The improbability of molecules coming together to form the watch is astronomical, in fact so staggering that even though there were no evidence of another human being having been there, including the Abominable Snowman, and no evidence turning up in the future of anyone's having been there, the inference that it was not there by an accident of nature would be incomparably the more reasonable.

Consider now the physical universe with its intricate and stupendous complexity. In the large as well as the small the visible universe with its systems of stars and planets and its biological and botanical organisms gives us overwhelming evidence of design. The universe as a whole presents itself to us as being a cosmic artifact. The probability of its having come into existence by chance and its continuing to operate in regular ways by chance is infinitesimal. If we think that the existence of a watch implies the overwhelming likelihood of its having had a designer, how much greater is the likelihood that the cosmos had a designer. The teleological argument is, of course, an argument by analogy with human artifacts and human designers. But nevertheless an inference which is reasonable in one sort of case would seem to be reasonable in the other, the difference being primarily in the nature of the kind of designer inferred. In the one case there is the theoretical possibility of checking the inference by independent verification procedures in sense experience. In the other case this is ruled out, as the inference is to a transcendent being, to an artificer who is not himself in space and therefore is not open to direct sense tests.

This argument may be characterized as wholly empirical and as proceeding by probable reasoning. We might distinguish between the Aristotelian demonstration and the teleological argument by saying that the latter proceeds from a premise that could be true, the specific claim being that it is probably true, whereas the Aristotelian demonstration proceeds from a premise that is put forward as a necessary truth. The teleological argument maintains that it is vastly probable that the cosmos is an artifact and therefore vastly probable that it has an artificer. The theoretical possibility remains open, of course, that the cosmos acquired and retains its structure by mere chance, and hence that it is not logically certain that there is a supreme contriver.

A number of objections have been raised against the teleological argument, several of which may be gone into here. This argument professes to establish the likely existence of a single architect-builder. But the inference could with equal plausibility be to a number of artificers working in cooperation. It leads to a polytheistic conclusion at least as readily as to a monotheistic conclusion. We might even say it leads with greater plausibility to a polytheistic conclusion, for as experience has shown over and over again, large-scale endeavors are the results of cooperation among a number of builders rather than of a single builder. Even such a relatively small thing as a watch is the product of many different craftsmen and designers. Hence, since the teleological argument is an argument by analogy with what is encountered in experience, seemingly the more plausible conclusion is that the universe was made by a number of planners rather than by one only. Against this consideration it has been urged that the over-all unity of the cosmos, which suggests a single unified scheme of things, attests to a single designer. There is some force in this objection, it must be admitted, but nevertheless there is no question but that a single unified plan can issue from the cooperative efforts of a number of planners, each contributing his share to the total plan agreed on by all.

Another objection, which can be mentioned only briefly here as it will be gone into later, is that the teleological argument does not permit the conclusion that the ultimate craftsman is benevolent. To many people nature presents a horrifying spectacle of torment and suffering, which is difficult to duplicate in the most dreadful of nightmares. With regard to horror in the world, fact far outruns fiction. Every entrancing scene nature presents hides the agony of living creatures, who feed and are fed upon. The romantic poets who invest nature with so much beauty ignore the facts to which Hume calls attention: 'A perpetual war is kindled among all living creatures. Necessity, hunger, want, stimulate the strong and courageous; fear, anxiety, terror, agitate the weak and the infirm ... On every hand animals are surrounded with enemies which cause their misery and seek their destruction' (1947, Pt. X). Bradley maintained that there is a balance of pleasure over pain in the world, but this would seem to be a reassurance formula, which can work only for someone with a talent for blinding himself. For if we open our eyes and look around us, just the opposite would seem to be the case: Suffering far exceeds pleasure. However, supposing that in fact pleasure outweighs pain, this fact could nevertheless not be used to justify the massive existence of pain. And if we are to be faithful to the argument from analogy, it must be admitted that the physical evils besetting living creatures suggest a certain amount of malevolence in Deity. Ernest Jones reports the following comment from a conversation among doctors concerning a youth 'who had just died from a massive sarcoma that enveloped his thigh bone like a malignant mushroom . . . : "If I ever get to heaven I should like to ask the principal Person there what He has to say about this".' (1959, p. 102).

At most, the argument from design would seem to permit the inference of a being with *limited* benevolence. And it would seem also to permit only the inference of a being with limited existence in time, that is, a being that is not eternal. Many artifacts outlast their makers. There are watches and clocks still in existence long after their makers have died, and many edifices that have outlasted their architects. The pyramids have endured many times the life spans of their builders. So the present existence of a contrivance is not a guarantee of the existence of its contriver. A number of present day theologians have declared that God is dead, and although their evidence may not entitle them to make an outright declaration, the argument from design certainly leaves open the possibility that the maker of the universe no longer exists. To sum up, the argument from design is based on an analogy with perishable artifacts made from prior existing material by artisans who themselves came into existence and eventually passed away. Within the bounds of the analogy the inference from a cosmic contrivance differing from an ordinary contrivance merely in having a longer duration can only be to a craftsman who also has a limited existence in time or in any case is not necessarily eternal. It may well be probable that He (and his possible collaborators) at one time existed, but He may no longer exist even though his work remains. And it is an open possibility that the cosmic artifact which like other artifacts was brought into existence may like them eventually revert to a primal state of unstructured matter.

The teleological argument, which is based on analogies with what is encountered in experience, has as its underlying idea the notion of prior existing materials which place limitations on the craftsman. The argument permits only the inference to a limited craftsman, one who is restricted by the materials at hand and hence who is not a being without defect in respect of power, span of existence, and even perhaps in respect of moral goodness. It does not permit us to infer the existence of a perfect architect or designer. Nevertheless, we naturally make an inferential leap to the perfect designer. If now we ask ourselves how it is that we unhesitatingly go beyond the permissible inference from evidence of design in nature to a perfect craftsman who is not limited by the material at hand, we find that all along we have been operating on the premise that the creator of the universe is also the creator of the substance of the universe. He is not a being whose workmanship is in any way hampered by pre-existing material. In other words, the teleological argument makes covert employment of the idea that God is the creator of matter. And in doing this it rests on the cosmological argument for the existence of God. This is a form of argument which professes to demonstrate the existence of an ultimate cause of matter itself. Not only does he imprint his design on matter, but out of nothing he creates it. In the Babylonian creation myth Marduk sits on his rush mat and from the surrounding mud creates man. The god of rational theology is also the creator of the substance from which man is made.

The most general and natural form of the cosmological argument may be stated in a series of propositions.

1. Something exists, as a mere matter of fact.

2. Whatever exists must have a cause which brought it into existence.

3. There cannot be an infinite number of causes going back in time.

As for (1), it makes no difference to the argument what it is that exists, whether a mote of dust, a planet, a constellation of stars, or a human being. This is an empirical premise which sense experience establishes. Locke, Leibniz, and Descartes begin with their own existence as an incontrovertible fact of experience. But the premise used need not be the existence of oneself; it could be anything whatever. Proposition (2) is the medieval dictum *'ex nihilo nihil'*. Nothing cannot be a cause, or a productive source, of what is. In Leibniz's words, 'nothing cannot produce a Being' (1916, Bk. IV, Ch. 10, p. 501) and in Locke's, 'non-entity cannot produce any real being' (1928, Bk. IV, Ch. 10). Behind this pronounce-ment lies a *Gedankenexperiment*. Try to conceive of something coming into existence just by itself, without any cause. Suppose a piece of chalk, shown by chemical tests to be a calcium compound and nothing else, leaves a tracing of gold particles when used to write, or that an ordinary light bulb remains lighted when unscrewed from its socket. These are clearly imaginable occurrences. But what we cannot think is that the bulb is an ordinary bulb that remains lighted without cause, and that the piece of chalk is an ordinary piece of chalk which behaves in an unaccountable way. Suppose tests had been made under laboratory conditions which disclosed nothing in the chalk or the bulb to account for the difference in behavior. We should nevertheless say that there must be a cause which science has been unable to discover. We should continue to say this no matter how long the tests continued. That there must be a cause is, as Hume said in expounding the view opposed to his own, 'one of those maxims, which tho' they may be deny'd with the lips, 'tis impossible for men in their hearts really to doubt of' (1888, Pt. III, Sec. 3). We might amend Hume's words to say that it is impossible also to doubt this with their minds. An uncaused occurrence can no more be conceived than a valley without a mountain.

Of proposition (3), namely, that there cannot be an infinity of causes for any existent, Descartes said, 'It is perfectly manifest that ... there can be no regression into infinity' (*Meditation* III). Any chain of causes proceeding backwards in time from a present existent must have a termi-nus which will be the first cause of that series. And since a first cause can have no cause, this first cause will be an eternal being. This is the con-sequence of propositions (1), (2), and (3). Given the empirical premise that something exists and the two *a priori* propositions that whatever exists has a cause and every sequence of causes must have an end, it follows that there must be a first cause which will be the source of all that exists.

This argument has widespread appeal and has won the assent of many theological thinkers. Unfortunately, however, as it stands it contains a contradiction. The second proposition is in flagrant contradiction to the conclusion. If everything that exists must have a cause then plainly the putative first cause will itself have to have a cause, which implies the contradictory proposition that the first cause is not the first. A curious and nihilistic consequence follows from propositions (2) and (3), a con-sequence which goes against the empirical premise as well as the conclu-

8

sion: It is that nothing whatever exists. If whatever exists must have a cause and there cannot be an infinite number of causes of causes, then the existence of anything would imply a contradiction, namely, that something has a cause and yet cannot have one. The conclusion must therefore be that nothing exists. As Leibniz remarks, '. . . we ourselves should not be, which is contrary to the first truth of experience' (1916, p. 501).

A second version of the cosmological argument avoids the contradiction in the first, although it may contain difficulties of its own. The corrected version distinguishes between contingent things and non-contingent things. A contingent thing is one the nonexistence of which is conceivable, such that its existence implies a cause. A thing like a tree or a granite mountain is something the nonexistence of which is conceivable, and hence if it exists it must have been brought into existence by something else. Even one's own nonexistence is conceivable. Thus, when Descartes poses to himself the question as to the cause of his existence he implies that there was a time when he did not exist. He thus implies that he is a thing the nonexistence of which is conceivable. The reasoning now proceeds almost as before. The empirical premise is that a contingent thing exists. The causal axioms now are that every contingent thing must have a cause and that there cannot be an infinitely long chain of causes. The conclusion is that there must be a first cause. But the two axioms imply that the first cause cannot be contingent. The first cause must be a necessary being, one whose nonexistence, unlike that of a contingent thing, is inconceivable and whose existence does not imply a cause. The force of this argument may be summed up in the classical formula: The contingent is grounded in the necessary. This we might say is the essence of the Lockeian proposition that if anything exists, something has existed from eternity: 'If therefore we knew that there is some real being, and that non-entity cannot produce any real being, it is an evident demonstration, that from eternity there has been something' (1928, Bk. IV, Ch. 10). To sum up, the existence of anything which has a beginning in time implies the existence of something which has neither a beginning nor an end in time, and the existence of a caused being implies the necessary existence of an uncaused being. To use the words of Aquinas, 'and this men call God'.

If, however, we ask ourselves what entitles us to call such a being by the exalted name 'God', that is, what entitles us to characterize it as a perfect being, we find ourselves falling back on the ontological argument. The logical link between the conception of a necessary being and that of an absolutely perfect being than which no greater is conceivable is that the only substance which has necessary existence is a perfect substance. The ontological argument attempts to demonstrate that the very conception of a perfect being, unlike the conception of one that is less than perfect, implies the existence of a being answering to the concept. Before going into several variants of the ontological argument, one point needs to be made clear. The idea of necessary existence is not in all cases connected with the idea of perfection, which is to say that existing necessarily does not entail being perfect. The entailment holds, if it holds at all, between the notion of a *substance* that has necessary existence and its perfection. One example will make the point clear. It is easily demonstrated that there necessarily exists a prime number greater than 7^{100}. But it obviously is nonsense to say that its having necessary existence implies that it is perfect. To refer again to Aquinas' phrase, 'and this men call God', we are constrained to call a necessarily existing substance God because our idea is that amongst possible *things* only to one which has necessary existence can we attribute the conceptual content of perfection. And this is because only that which is perfect is such that from its nature alone its existence can be demonstrated *a priori*. Thus, to illustrate, a chair or a shoe is something whose nature does not imply its existence, whereas in the case of a perfect being the force of the ontological argument is to establish that its nature entails its own existence. This argument has no application to anything less than perfect.

The ontological argument has a number of variants, but all of them proceed by reasoning on concepts alone, without recourse to anything empirical. Two well-known classical formulations will be given here, the one taken from St. Anselm, its inventor, the other from Descartes and Leibniz. First of all it has to be recognized that we do have the concept of an absolutely perfect being, a being such that in respect of power, knowledge, etc. a greater is inconceivable. This fact has already been remarked before but it is important that it be noted. Very briefly, it may be argued that since we have the idea of a being less than perfect we have the idea of something perfect, which it falls short of. To put the matter verbally, in order to know what the term 'perfect being' does not apply to we must understand the term itself and thus have a concept of the kind of thing it would apply to. It will be remembered that one of Descartes' arguments for the existence of God centers on the claim that we have an idea of an infinite being and this is an idea a finite mind could not by itself alone frame. His claim, in part, was that since he could not

8*

be the author of the idea it must have an Infinite Author who implanted it in his mind. Furthermore, Descartes said, and his observation is to be taken as quite general and not merely as applying to himself: 'It is the nature of the infinite that my nature, which is finite and limited, should not comprehend it' (*Meditation* III). The objection to this is that no one can have an idea which he does not comprehend, any more than he could have a pain that he does not feel. A concept which a person cannot, to use Descartes' phrase, 'reach by thought', is a concept which he does not have. We can entertain a phrase without knowing what it means but we cannot understand a phrase without knowing what it means. To suppose that we have an idea which we do not comprehend is like supposing that we understand a phrase the meaning of which we do not know. Descartes' argument for an Infinite Author founders on this point. His claim that the idea of a perfect being is clear and distinct but that we do not comprehend it implies a contradiction. Furthermore, it is easy to see that we can have no idea of the imperfect without having the idea of the perfect, and conversely. If we took seriously Descartes' claim that we have the idea of perfection without comprehending it, we should have to say that we also have the idea of imperfection (of the not-perfect) without comprehending it. The logical outcome would be that we have neither idea, which is absurd.

Suppose now that there is the concept of a being than which a greater cannot be conceived. Anselm argues that regardless of how we acquired this concept, it is such that it must be realized. Concerning the sceptic, who denies that God exists, Anselm points out that his very denial shows that he has the idea of God. This applies equally of course to the agnostic. The agnostic who says that he does not know whether there is anything answering to the concept of a perfect being and the sceptic who denies that there is something answering to the concept, equally with the true believer, have the concept in their understanding. Given this, his famous argument is, in brief, the following. There is the concept of a being than which a greater is inconceivable. But a being which exists only in conception, or only as a thought in the understanding, is one than which a greater could be conceived, namely, one which exists in reality as well as in conception. Now, if a being than which a greater is inconceivable existed only in conception, as an idea in the understanding, then a greater could be conceived, namely, one which existed in reality as well. Hence the idea of a being than which a greater is inconceivable existing only in conception implies a contradiction. It implies that a being than which a greater is inconceivable is such that it would be greater if it existed in reality as well. It thus implies the self-contradictory concept of a being greater than the greatest conceivable being.

Anselm's own statement is as follows: 'It is one thing for an object to be in the understanding, and another to understand that the object exists. When a painter first conceives of what he will afterwards perform, he has it in his understanding, but he does not yet understand it to be, because he has not yet performed it. But after he has made the painting, he both has it in his understanding, and he understands that it exists, because he has made it. Hence, even the fool is convinced that something exists in the understanding, at least, than which nothing greater can be conceived. For, when he hears of this, he understands it. And whatever is understood, exists in the understanding. And assuredly that, than which nothing greater can be conceived, cannot exist in the understanding alone. For, suppose it exists in the understanding alone: Then it can be conceived to exist in reality; which is greater. Therefore, if that, than which nothing greater can be conceived, exists in the understanding alone, the very being, than which nothing greater can be conceived, is one, than which a greater can be conceived. But obviously this is impossible. Hence, there is no doubt that there exists a being, than which nothing greater can be conceived, and it exists both in the understanding and in reality' (*Proslogium*, Ch. 2).

This argument is difficult to evaluate because it contains an equivocation. The equivocation itself is not easily detected because apparently there is a widespread and natural tendency to succumb to it. Nevertheless, it beclouds Anselm's argument, which has to be freed from it before the force of the argument can be seen clearly and its validity assessed. The equivocation lies in the surreptitious identification of the concept of a thing with the thing itself, or, more accurately, it consists of identifying the phrases 'concept of a thing' and 'the thing conceived'. Thus, Anselm speaks of the artist's painting as existing only in the understanding before its execution and as existing both in the understanding and in reality after its execution. The suggestion is that there are two ways for a thing, such as a painting or a centaur, to exist, in thought and in reality: A centaur exists only in thought, a horse and a painting both in thought and in reality.

But a thing which is said to exist *only* in thought just does not exist, although the idea of it does. How should we understand a person who tells us that he has a million dollars, but only in his mind, not in his bank account? We should certainly not think that he was wealthy, nor try to borrow any of the money he has in his mind. It would only be a cynical witticism to advise him to take the money which is in his mind and put it in his bank account. Imagined wealth is not wealth, and the *idea* of a painting which is to be executed is not itself the painting. Thus when Anselm speaks of an absolutely perfect being existing in the understanding he commits an equivocal identification of 'the concept of an absolutely perfect being' with 'a perfect being'. What he should have said is, not that a perfect being exists in the understanding, but that there is a *concept* of such a being. The latter of course cannot be identified with the being answering to it. Anselm gives the erroneous impression of trying to demonstrate the existence of a being which already exists, or perhaps of trying to demonstrate two modes of existence of one and the same thing. Obviously if a perfect being were identical with the concept of such a being then Anselm need not have strained his intelligence to devise a proof. He could have gone straight to the existence of the being from the mere presence of the concept, and he could have urged that the sceptic who has the idea in his mind but denies the existence of a being corresponding to it commits the contradiction of allowing both that he has the idea and that it does not exist.

It would seem plain that, despite his equivocation, Anselm would not charge the sceptic with committing himself to this kind of transparent contradiction. Anselm's argument is to be understood as an attempt to demonstrate the existence of a being exemplifying the concept of perfection. It is, in other words, put forward as a demonstration of the existence of something in addition to the concept, through an analysis of what the concept entails. The Cartesian-Leibnizian version makes this entirely clear. Freed from the Anselmic equivocation, what emerges in the ontological proof is that existence is thought of as a characteristic of things, the possession of which, like the attribute of power, augments their nature. Existence is taken to contribute to the perfection of a thing, and its lack to constitute an imperfection.

The Leibnizian-Cartesian form of the ontological argument is the following: 'God is the greatest or (as Descartes says) the most perfect of beings, or rather a being of supreme grandeur and perfection, including all degrees thereof. That is the notion of God. See now how existence follows from this notion. To exist is something more than not to exist, or rather, existence adds a degree to grandeur and perfection, and as Descartes states it, existence is itself a perfection. Therefore this degree of grandeur and perfection, or rather this perfection which consists in existence, is in this supreme all-great, all-perfect being: for otherwise some degree would be wanting to it, contrary to its definition. Consequently this supreme being exists' (1916, p. 502). This formulation brings out clearly what the intended force of the Anselmic demonstration is, namely, to establish existence of a being from examination of mere concepts, and not to establish an added mode of existence of something which already exists. Restated in Anselm's language, Leibniz's formulation becomes the following. The concept of an absolutely perfect being, than which a greater is inconceivable, is that of a being which lacks no possible perfection and is therefore a being without defect. Now the supposition that an absolutely perfect being does not exist involves the concept of a being which is absolutely perfect but which nevertheless lacks a perfection possible to it, that is, of a being without conceivable defect which nevertheless suffers from one. It thus implies the self-contradictory concept of a greatest conceivable being than which a greater is conceivable. To assert that the concept of a nonexistent absolutely perfect being is internally inconsistent is to say in other words that being perfect is incompatible with not existing, and thus to say that the concept of an absolutely perfect being entails the existence of the corresponding reality. The supposition that God exists is not only a possible supposition but is a necessary truth.

One further variant may be added to the store of ontological arguments for the existence of God. The concept of a perfect being implies the concept of a being which is everything it can be. It is a being with no unrealized potentialities, which means that it has every attribute its nature is capable of possessing. And this implies that its actual properties coincide precisely with its possible properties. Every property which is possible to a perfect being it possesses. If it lacked a property it could have it would thereby fall short of what it could be, and thus would contain a defect in its actual nature. Now amongst the properties it could have is the property *existence*. It follows directly that existence is a property which it does have. Thus by the necessity of its own nature a perfect being is an existent being, just as it is an all-great being.

The ontological argument, which attempts to demonstrate existence, has been subjected to criticism from Anselm's own day on. The demonstration has had an interesting history of decline and revival. It may be likened to the phoenix which arises from its own ashes. By many it has been thought to have been demolished, but it has been revived time and again in somewhat different form by important philosophers up to the present day. (See Hartshorne, 1962, and Malcolm 1963). Kant was thought to have delivered the *coup de grâce* to the argument, and the monk Gaunilo in Anselm's time presented a consideration which, in anticipation of Kant's point, threw the Anselmic argument into a curious paradoxical light. Gaunilo asks us to consider the concept of a perfect island, and urges that by parallel reasoning its existence can be demonstrated. Let us suppose this island to be a veritable Garden of Eden, a wondrous place that abounds with everything desirable and in which evil has no place. Suppose it to be a perfect garden, than which a more perfect is inconceivable, that is, lacking no perfection a garden could have. Gaunilo urges that in accordance with Anselm's reasoning this superlative garden-island must exist, for it could not lack existence without being less perfect than it might be. A nonexistent perfect garden is a perfect garden that is less than perfect. If we are to avoid contradiction we must accept the consequence that such a garden exists. Gaunilo's own formulation is the following: 'You can no longer doubt that this island which is more excellent than all lands exists somewhere, since you have no doubt that it is in your understanding. And since it is more excellent not to be in the understanding alone, but to exist both in the understanding and in reality, for this reason it must exist. For if it does not exist, any land which really exists will be more excellent than it; and so the island already understood by you to be more excellent will not be more excellent' (1939, p. 151)

Gaunilo's point has not been sufficiently appreciated by philosophers, and it is important enough to bring its force out as clearly as possible. A major criticism of Gaunilo's objection has been that the ontological argument does not hold for concepts or objects drawn 'from the finite world'. It has been maintained that only with regard to the concept of an absolutely perfect being can existence be deduced, and that existence cannot be deduced from the concept of a finite thing that is perfect of its kind. But this is only to protect an argument behind an intellectual cloud. For in fact the argument applies with equal cogency to the concept of a perfect thing regardless of whether it is a finite thing or an infinite being. The idea behind the objection to Gaunilo is that nothing finite can be perfect, and that the ontological argument applies only to that which is perfect. But if we can have the idea of an unlimited perfect being we can unquestionably have the idea of a limited perfect being, that is to say, a perfect thing of its kind. We can have the concept of a perfect orchid, than which a more perfect is inconceivable, a perfect detective, one who can solve every conceivable crime, and so on. Given this, the ontological form of reasoning applies to the concept of perfect finite things with the same force precisely that it applies to an unlimited perfect being.

The key presupposition of the ontological argument is the thesis that existence is an attribute the possession of which lends a degree of perfection to a thing and the lack of which constitutes a defect. Now the argument in the case of the perfect garden-island, or of a perfect anything, proceeds as before. Gaunilo's island, *qua* island, will be less perfect than it could be if it lacks existence. The concept of a nonexistent perfect island is the self-contradictory concept of a perfect thing of its kind, than which a more perfect thing of its kind is inconceivable, which at the same time, because it lacks existence, is such that a more perfect thing of its kind is conceivable. This is no less valid than the argument that the concept of an absolutely perfect being which lacks existence is the concept of an absolutely perfect being than which a more perfect is conceivable. If the one is valid, then so is the other. The concept of a finite perfect thing will be the concept of something which must have, among the properties contributing to its perfection, the property of existence. What Gaunilo shows about the ontological argument is that it has a bizarre, unacceptable consequence. Accepting it requires our accepting the proposition that at least one perfect thing of every conceivable kind exists. The world becomes overpopulated with perfect things. Think of anything whatever, no matter how exotic or fantastic, and by means of the ontological argument it can be shown that a perfect thing of that kind exists. Perfection becomes a drug on the cosmic market.

Gaunilo does not show what is wrong with the Anselmic argument. He only elicits a consequence which anyone with sobriety of mind and a well-preserved sense of reality would reject. It has been argued above that if the ontological argument is valid for the concept of an absolutely perfect being it is also valid for the concept of a perfect limited being. Hence, by *modus tollens*, if the second is rejected as invalid the first must be rejected also, although, of course, rejecting a proposition as false is not the same as showing that it is false. Kant, who was anticipated by Hume, professed to *show* what specifically the mistake in the Anselmic argument is. He went to the crux of the matter and subjected to an analysis the claim that existence is a characterizing property, the possession of which adds to the nature of a thing and the lack of which takes away from its nature. Some philosophers, notably Bertrand Russell, have maintained that existence is not an attribute of things at all. And Kant seems to have held this in asserting that '"*being*" is obviously not a real predicate', but not in any clear-cut way. The conclusion he clearly came to is that existence is not a characterizing property and therefore not a property the possession or lack of which would have an effect on the nature of a thing, on what it is. If this is correct, then the ontological argument is invalid, as it makes use of the proposition, without which it cannot do its work, that a thing which lacks existence lacks a perfection. An attribute cannot be a perfection without being a characterizing property the possession of which in some way contributes to the nature of the thing.

Kant has the following to say on this point: 'By whatever and by however many predicates we may think a thing – even if we completely determine it – we do not make the least addition to the thing when we further declare that this thing *is*. Otherwise, it would not be exactly the same thing that exists, but something more than we had thought in the concept; and we could not, therefore, say that the exact object of my concept exists. If we think in a thing every feature of reality except one, the missing reality is not added by my saying that this defective thing exists. On the contrary, it exists with the same defect with which I have thought it, since otherwise what exists would be something different from what I thought. When, therefore, I think a being as the supreme reality, without any defect, the question still remains whether it exists of not' (1929, Ch. 3, Sec. 4. p. 505). Hume put the matter more simply as follows: 'It is ... evident, that the idea of existence is nothing different from the idea of any object, and that when after the simple conception of anything we would conceive of it as existent, we in reality make no addition to or alteration on our first idea ... When I think of God, when I think of him as existent, and when I believe him to be existent, my idea of him neither increases nor diminishes' (1888., Bk. I, Pt. III, Sec. 7).

It is interesting as well as instructive to compare the Humeian-Kantian view with regard to existence with Moore's position concerning such attributes as 'being beautiful', 'being hideous', and the like, attributes Moore called 'non-natural'. The importance of the comparison will be seen by the light it throws on the Kantian assertion that 'all existential propositions are synthetic', which implies of course that the proposition that a perfect being exists is synthetic and cannot be established by an *a priori* argument. Kant's explicit position against Anselm's is that the proposition 'a perfect being does not exist' is not self-contradictory and thus that the proposition that a perfect being exists is not analytic. But it seems plain enough that he also wished to maintain that it is not synthetic *a priori* either. In saying that existential propositions are synthetic

Kant is to be understood as implying that they are empirical, in the sense of having either of two possible truth-values, neither of which belongs to them 'by inner necessity'. An existential proposition, according to Hume and Kant, can have no *a priori* demonstration, and in particular, that a perfect being exists can have none.

To come back to Moore's theory that some attributes are non-natural. His position is that a property like 'being beautiful' is just as much a property of things as is the property 'being round', but that unlike the property 'being round' it has no descriptive force. In principle it is possible to describe an object completely in respect of color distribution, shape, etc., if it is a visual object, or of tonal qualities if it is a sound sequence, without using any term denoting a property like 'beautiful', 'hideous', 'pleasant', 'entrancing', and so on. In other words, according to Moore, terms standing for non-natural properties, unlike terms referring to naturalistic properties, do not enter into the description of an object. To say a gem has such-and-such a shape, such-and-such a color and brilliance is to describe the gem; but to add 'and it is beautiful' is not to augment the description of it. Equally, to say 'but it is not beautiful' is to subtract not a whit from its description. It should be pointed out that according to the so-called emotivist theory terms which are said to denote non-natural properties do not stand for properties and instead have only an emotive function in the language, that is, a use which, like 'ouch!' and 'bah!', gives vent to feelings.

Be this as it may, Moore's view is that value terms do stand for special properties, properties which are such that in knowing that things have them we know nothing about the descriptions the things fall under. The proposition that the *Mona Lisa*, for example, is beautiful ascribes a property to the *Mona Lisa*, as does the proposition that the *Mona Lisa* is a picture of a woman with a mysterious smile. But if we knew the first only we should know nothing about the visual properties of the picture. And if we knew both that the *Mona Lisa* is the picture of a smiling woman *and* beautiful we should have no better idea of the visual appearance of the *Mona Lisa* than is given by the proposition that it is a picture of a smiling woman. (One of his arguments for this is that it is possible for people to disagree over whether a thing is beautiful or not. At least one of the opinions must be false, which implies that statements using value terms have truth-values and thus that the value terms must stand for properties. The pair of statements, 'The *Mona Lisa* is beautiful', 'The *Mona Lisa* is not beautiful', contradict each other, and hence one must be a truth about the *Mona Lisa* and the other a falsity.) Moore's own words are: '... intrinsic properties seem to *describe* the intrinsic nature of what possesses them in a sense in which predicates of value never do. If you could enumerate *all* the intrinsic properties a given thing possessed, you would have given a *complete* description of it, and would not need to mention any predicates of value it possessed; whereas no description of a given thing could be *complete* which omitted any intrinsic property' (1922, p. 274).

It is to be noted that the conjunction of the complete naturalistic description of the *Mona Lisa* with the phrase 'but it is not beautiful' is not a contradiction, and the negation of the conjunction (which will be an implicative proposition) is not a tautology, or to use Leibniz's phrase, not an identical proposition. That is, the implicative proposition in which the complete naturalistic description of the *Mona Lisa* occurs as antecedent and in which 'it is beautiful' occurs as consequent is not a tautology of the form $p.q. \supset .p$. But it is according to Moore a necessary truth. The consequent, or the predicate, is *entailed*, not analytically but synthetically, by the complex of attributes characterizing the *Mona Lisa*. It is not a conjunctive part of the antecedent and cannot be obtained 'by dissection' of the concepts entering into the antecedent, but is nevertheless entailed by it. The proposition is to be counted as synthetic *a priori*. A value predicate is entailed by naturalistic properties without itself being a naturalistic property or any conjunction of naturalistic properties.

Existence, on Kant's account of it, bears a resemblance to non-natural properties. Like them it has no descriptive force. To say that the *Mona Lisa* exists is no more to describe Leonardo's painting than to say that it is enthralling. The term 'exists' no more enters into the description of a thing than such a term as 'beautiful'. But the difference between the terms is that whereas the second according to Moore is entailed by a set of descriptive properties, the first is not. Existence is neither part of the description of a thing nor is it entailed by any description, and hence not by the description of a perfect being. Thus the existential statement 'an absolutely perfect being exists' is synthetic without being *a priori*.

A great deal of controversy has revolved around the ontological argument, and some philosophers continue to think the form of argument presented here is valid. Other philosophers, who have rejected it as invalid, have, however, attempted to save the general form of the argument which professes to deduce God's existence from his nature by distinguishing between two different ontological arguments to be found in Anselm.

The contention is that one argument, which uses the notion that existence is a perfection, is invalid, and that a second argument, which uses the notion of *necessary* existence is a perfection, is valid. In the third chapter of his *Proslogium* Anselm argues that 'it is possible to conceive of a being which cannot be conceived not to exist; and this is greater than one which can be conceived not to exist'. Necessary existence is viewed as a characterizing attribute which lends a degree of perfection to whatever possesses it. Restated in terms of the notion of necessary existence Leibniz's argument becomes something like this: To exist necessarily is something more than to exist contingently. Therefore the perfection of existing necessarily could not be lacking to a 'supreme all-great, all-perfect being', than which a greater is inconceivable. The conclusion is that God exists and that his existence is not contingent.

The distinction here, as will readily be seen, harks back to the second cosmological argument which distinguishes between contingent and non-contingent things. A being that exists contingently is one which, no matter how great, could conceivably perish and pass out of existence. But a being that has necessary existence obviously could never perish. Descartes reassured himself against the possibility that he was being deceived by an evil genius by demonstrating that God could not be a deceiver. And some people feel reassured by the thought that they will never be left helpless in an overwhelming cosmos by the death of God. Thus Spinoza seemed to require what might be called ultimate, i.e., logical, assurance against loss of a perfect being the love of which is human blessedness. The love of contingent things, he says, is accompanied by sadness if they perish, and by fear of loss while they exist. 'But love toward a thing eternal and infinite feeds the mind wholly with joy, and is itself unmingled with any sadness, wherefore it is greatly to be desired and sought for with all our strength' (1901, p. 4). This is to say that noncontingent existence is counted as a perfection in a loved thing, and it is an imperfection in a thing that it can pass away and leave us alone in a cosmic void. Achilles would have been more perfect had he been made wholly invulnerable, and divine substance would be less than perfect if it were vulnerable to nonexistence.

The second version of the ontological argument is linked with the rejection of the Kantian-Humeian thesis that all existential propositions are contingent, a thesis which if true rules out of court any attempt to demonstrate the existence of a thing from mere concepts. An example of the kind of proposition which is brought against this thesis is the proposition 'There exists a prime number greater than 7^{100}'. This plainly is existential and it is *a priori* true. Euclid proved *a priori* that there could not be a greatest prime, which makes necessary the existential proposition that there is a prime greater than 7^{100}. The fact that there are such propositions is used to protect the ontological argument against the view that existence cannot be deduced from concepts. But the defense will not do. It is plain that philosophers like Kant and Hume who make the general statement that no existential proposition is necessary have in mind existential propositions about things, about what Locke called real being, not propositions about numbers and other abstractions. These philosophers certainly were aware of existential propositions in mathematics and could not have maintained that their demonstrations were in principle invalid. It is certainly to be supposed that they allowed the necessary truth of such propositions and the possibility of demonstrating them *a priori*, and intended their own generalization to cover only existential propositions about things, whether imperfect or perfect. Kant's statement is easily corrected by the addition of two words: 'All existential propositions *about things* are synthetic.' The second version of the ontological argument, which attempts to prove the necessary existence of a thing, as against abstract entities like numbers, properties, propositions, and the like, requires that a special logical place be given one proposition amongst propositions which state the existence of things. What has to be determined is whether the proposition 'There necessarily exists a perfect being' can be an exception to the general rule about propositions referring to things.

One thing that goes against its being an exception is that it is possible to 'prove', paralleling Gaunilo's reasoning against Anselm, that at least one perfect thing of every conceivable kind has necessary existence. If necessary being counts as a perfection in a thing and its lack an imperfection, then the notion of a perfect Garden of Eden than which a more perfect is inconceivable will be the notion of a necessarily existing garden. Now, a Garden of Eden which necessarily exists will be superior to a Garden of Eden which has only contingent existence, one which could wither away. And a garden which is perfect in every particular but is perishable is less excellent than it would be if it were imperishable. Hence the notion of a contingently existing perfect garden is self-contradictory: The conception of a perfect garden entails its non-contingent existence. It follows in general that at least one perfect thing of every imaginable kind has necessary existence. As an ironical paradox it also follows that if

God is the creator of things he could have created only those things in the world which are less than perfect. For that which has necessary existence can at no time have failed to exist and therefore could not have been brought into existence by an act of creation, divine or otherwise. It would surely be a paradox to suppose that God existed in the presence of a perfect world of things, to which he decided to add a realm of imperfection.

The bizarre consequence which follows from the second form of the ontological argument shows that something is wrong with it and it is not difficult to see what the mistake is. The term 'necessary existence' denotes a characterizing property of *things* or substances no more than the term 'existence', and thus does not denote a property which could confer a degree of excellence on anything. If, to refer back to Kant, 'we do not make the least addition to the thing when we further declare that this thing *is*', then we make no descriptive addition to a thing when we declare it to exist necessarily. If 'existence' is not descriptive of a thing, then 'necessary existence' is not descriptive of a thing either. What prevents philosophers from seeing this is an association of ideas in the back of their minds where it is not clearly perceived. A *psychological* identification is made between the terms 'necessary existence' and 'everlasting and indestructible being'. Or better, as an addition to its logical sense, the sense of *everlasting and indestructible* is imported into the term 'necessary existence'. It is this importation which blinds some philosophers to the logical realities of the argument. The words 'everlasting and indestructible' in their usual connotation have the sense in which the Great Pyramid or the stars are said to be everlasting and indestructible. Necessary existence has nothing to do with existence in time; it has nothing to do with duration, whether short or long or even eternal. An object which is eternal exists in time and is such that its existence could be conceived of as coming to an end in time even though that never happens. The statement '2+2 = 4' has been called, by Leibniz for example, an eternal truth. But by this could only be meant a statement which possesses its truth-value by logical necessity, one which could not be false, not one which could *never* be false. It is an absurdity of language to say that yesterday 2+2 equalled 4 and that next year it will still equal 4, and it is an impropriety of some sort to say that 2+2 always has been, is, and will be equal to 4. '2+2 = 4' is a non-temporal truth, not a temporal truth which is forever true. There is no 'forever' which is not a temporal forever. And anything temporal could in principle have an end in time. Russell somewhere said that $2+2$ will equal 4 even far out in space, and this is as misleading as to say $2+2$ will equal 4 even far into the future. The arithmetical proposition is no more temporal than it is geographical.

It may throw the second ontological argument into a more intelligible light to point out that there is no real difference between it and the first argument. Supposing for the moment that the first argument is valid, then it is easy to see that *necessary existence* is just existence which is deduced from the concept of a thing. Obviously, the existence of a thing which is entailed by the conception of that thing is necessary existence: Being entailed by the conception is what is meant by 'necessary existence'. And those who maintain that *necessary existence* rather than *existence* is a perfection are counting the entailment itself as a perfection. Anselm's contention that 'a being which cannot be conceived not to exist is greater than one which can be conceived not to exist' is only another way of saying that a thing whose existence is entailed by its concept is superior to a thing whose existence is not entailed by its concept. This is to say nothing more than that entailed existence is superior to existence which is not entailed. There is no difference between necessary existence and entailed existence, and indeed the ontological argument is an attempt to show that in the case of one concept *existence* is entailed. This is all that is meant by the claim that a perfect being has necessary existence. The statement 'An absolutely perfect being has necessary existence' reduces to the statement 'An absolutely perfect being is one whose existence is entailed by its concept'. To say that a thing has necessary existence is only to repeat in more mystifying words that the thing's existence is deducible from its concept. It will be clear that *existence* that is entailed is not different from *existence* which is not entailed. The difference is only in how existence is related to a concept. Hence, in general, if existence is not a perfection it cannot count as a perfection in the ontological argument, which thus founders on this point.

To return to Kant's original contention that there can be no purely *a priori* demonstration of the existence of a perfect being, and to the more general thesis that a proposition declaring the existence of a thing is contingent. From these we may conclude that like any ordinary thing, a perfect being is a being that might not exist. The theological proposition 'God exists', like the proposition 'Betelgeuse has a satellite', may be true, but could be false. The denial of the one is a contradiction no more than the denial of the other; and if the fool to whom Anselm refers denies the existence of a perfect being, he does not in so doing embrace the contradictory concept of a greatest conceivable being than which a greater is conceivable. The theological proposition is in a peculiar position. It is not *a priori* true, and there would seem to be no possible empirical evidence for it. It thus appears to fall under the razor of logical positivism, which excises from intelligible discourse indicative statements which express neither an *a priori* proposition nor one which can be established or rendered probable to a degree by empirical evidence. Without going into the positivist criterion here, it can be seen that two sorts of difficulties stand in the way of accepting the theological proposition. One is what might be called an external difficulty, namely, that the proposition is such that there is genuine empirical evidence against it. The other difficulty is an internal one in the concept figuring in it, namely, the concept of a greatest being which combines in itself the attributes of power, knowledge, and goodness to their limiting degree.

The internal difficulty can only be touched on briefly here, but it is the kind of difficulty that should make the wary reader doubt whether the concept is *genuine*, that is, whether the phrase 'absolutely perfect being than which a greater is inconceivable' denotes a concept at all. Whether a being could be all powerful was debated by medieval thinkers in the form of the picturesque question whether an all powerful being could make a stone too heavy for him to lift. A being of limited power could, in principle, make an object so heavy that even though his power were titanic he could not raise it. Now an omnipotent being could certainly do what a being with limited power could do. But to suppose that an omnipotent being could make such a stone produces an obvious contradiction. For if he can, there will be something he cannot do, namely, lift it; and if he cannot make such an object there will again be something which goes against his omnipotence. The important question raised by this colorful paradox is whether there is any such idea as power than which no greater power is conceivable. Whether there can be a thing whose power is so great that none greater is conceivable is comparable to the question whether there can be a number so great that no greater is conceivable. This of course is connected with the Cantorian notion of a consummated infinite discussed in Chapter 4. It may be that the concepts of infinite realized power, infinite actualized knowledge, etc. are spurious. If they are, then the notion of 'a greatest, than which a greater is inconceivable' likewise will be spurious. And the Anselmic description of God will be a semantic counterfeit which passes for real

9

linguistic currency only because people are blinded by their religious needs.

As an aside, it may be observed that the notion of the consummated infinite which was rejected as impossible in one connection, that is, in connection with the series of causes going back in time, seems to be accepted as possible in connection with such attributes as power and knowledge attributed to a perfect thing. If the concept of an actual infinite aggregate, say, of causes, or the concept of a being infinite in respect of power or of knowledge, is logically impossible, then it will be logically impossible for the concept to be exemplified. The notion of such a being will not be merely the notion of something which might not exist, but will be the notion of something which could not exist. Leibniz attempted to show that the concept of such a being 'is possible, and implies no contradiction' (1916, p. 504). And it is important to determine whether the concept is possible: Whether it is such that the nonexistence of a perfect being is deducible from it, or whether neither the existence nor the nonexistence of such a being is deducible from it.

Assuming the latter alternative to be the case, empirical evidence is at hand which goes against the existence of an all powerful, all good being. It is plain that evidence that does this will go against the existence of a greatest conceivable being. An ancient piece of reasoning, attributed to Epicurus, on the relation between Deity and the existence of evil brings out a consideration which tells against His existence. The following passage from Hume sums it up: 'The questions asked by Epicurus, of old, are yet unanswered. Is Deity willing to prevent evil, but not able? Then He is impotent. Is He able, but not willing? Then He is malevolent. Is He both able and willing? Then whence cometh evil? Is He neither able nor willing? Then why call Him Deity?' (1947, pt. X). Natural evil on a vast scale exists, and it is only to treat evasive philosophical denials and explanations of it with a respect they do not deserve to take them seriously and to examine them at any length. Evil does exist, and it is plainly possible to conceive of its not existing, and certainly to conceive of there being less of it than there is. Moreover, it would be better for evil not to exist than to exist. A universe free from evil, in which no agonizing pain is suffered, in sum, a universe which has no place for the four horsemen of the Apocalypse, is far better than one in which evil flourishes. Clearly then, an all good being would be morally revolted by its existence and would wish to exorcise it from reality, and an all powerful being would be able to destroy it. Hence, since evil exists the inescapable consequence is that a being who both wishes to eradicate it and has the power to do so does not exist. Some philosophers have argued that the existence of evil does not go against the all-goodness of God, but rather that it shows him not to be all-powerful: He is infinite in respect of goodness and limited in respect of power. It could equally well be argued that the existence of evil does not show a limitation in God's power, but instead shows that he is not all good. Regardless, however, of which of these alternative conclusions one finds compatible with one's religious needs, the important fact implied by the existence of evil is that there does not exist a being who is *both* all-powerful *and* all-good, and therefore that there does not exist a supremely perfect being.

Some philosophers have maintained that evil is a necessary prerequisite for good and that its existence is incompatible with neither God's goodness nor his power. Leibniz took the position that this is the best possible of all worlds, the reason being that a supreme being would not countenance less than this. The implication of this position would seem to be that the discovery of anaesthetics could not improve the world and thus that some philosophers are able to stand on their heads and with the greatest cleverness demonstrate that they are right side up. F. H. Bradley consoled himself with the belief that, in a universe which in order to contain good must contain evil, there is a preponderance of good over evil. But this proposition, apart from the myopia its acceptance requires, could only issue from savagery that is covered over by a veneer of civilization and morals. Only a compromise between savagery and the demands of civilization would permit a cultivated person to find acceptable the pleasures of some balancing the agony of others. And a being who weighed pains and pleasures in this way we should hardly think either benevolent or moral. Bradley, as will be remembered, held a metaphysical view according to which the appearances were resolved in a higher unity where no differences existed. The implication with regard to evil is that it too is 'absorbed' into a whole where it is transfigured. About this one can only say that despite its being absorbed into a higher harmony it exists *here* to plague us and other living creatures. And it would be better for *us* if it did not exist here. Evil is something the nonexistence of which is conceivable and is certainly something which could be conceived as being less in quantity and intensity. The magnitude of evil in the universe, not to speak of its mere existence, is sufficient evidence to disprove the existence of a supremely perfect being.

Evil has been distinguished into two kinds, natural and moral. Natural

9*

evil cannot be attributed to man's doing, whereas the blame for moral evil is placed on man himself. Having free will, he receives moral credit for his good deeds and moral demerits for his wicked deeds. The evil brought about voluntarily by him is to be laid at his door, rather than at God's. Unlike natural evil, moral evil is man's responsibility. And it would seem that he has much indeed to answer for. Without going into the ins and outs of evil in relation to man's free will we may permit ourselves the observation that a free will united with a morally good nature will issue in freely willed good acts and joined to a morally corrupt character will issue in freely willed evil acts. Satan voluntarily dedicated himself to evil, which he would not have done if his character had been different. It would seem plain that in giving man free will an all-good, all-powerful, all-wise being would have given him also a good nature to go with it. The inference to be drawn from the existence of man himself is that a supremely perfect being does not exist!

We turn now to the second cosmological argument, which professes to establish the existence of a necessary being as the cause of contingent things. The formula corresponding to this version of the cosmological argument is that the contingent is grounded in the necessary. It is natural to fill in the notion of a necessary being with the conceptual content ascribed to God and to proceed to the conclusion that a necessary being is absolutely perfect. But the inference from necessary being to perfection is an inference which may be unwarranted. Kant maintained that the cosmological argument depends on the ontological argument, and the teleological argument in turn upon the cosmological, and that in order to show the invalidity of these two it was only required to show the ontological argument to be invalid. He may be said to have held a 'dominoe theory' with respect to the three proofs; when the first falls the others fall with it. By showing that existence cannot be deduced from the concept of a perfect being he thought that he had also shown the impossibility of demonstrating the existence of the magical creator of matter and of the master-designer of the universe. As in his view there are only three possible arguments for the existence of a divine being, he claimed to have shown the impossibility of demonstrating its existence. Against Kant's contention about the logical relationship between the three traditional arguments, it is to be maintained here that the three arguments are entirely independent and revolve on three different concepts. The concept of a first cause which the cosmological argument employs is not the same as the concept of a perfect being which the ontological argument employs, and the concept of the fashioner of the universe, who impresses form on matter, is different from both. It is possible for the creator of matter not to be a perfect being and it is possible for the architect of the universe not to be the creator of matter.

The cosmological argument can at most demonstrate the existence of a creator of the substance of the universe, and it cannot go beyond this to demonstrate the existence of a being without defect. The identification of the cause of matter with a perfect being goes beyond what the cosmological argument, if valid, could establish. The inference that the cause of matter is a perfect being is without logical foundation. Kant may have had this in mind when he maintained that he had shown the impossibility of demonstrating the existence of a perfect being. Since neither the cosmological nor the teleological argument could demonstrate the existence of such a being, it was sufficient to show the invalidity of the ontological argument to demonstrate that *no argument* could do this. The validity of the cosmological and teleological arguments in no way hangs on the ontological argument, nor does the validity of the teleological argument hang on the validity of the cosmological argument. The two arguments have to be dealt with separately.

To come now to the non-contradictory variant of the cosmological argument. In essence it maintains that the existence of contingent things can only be explained in terms of necessary existence, or that nothing can exist unless a necessary being exists. The argument appears to make use of the empirical premise that a contingent thing exists, and by means of the propositions that every contingent thing must have a cause and that there cannot be an infinity of causes, arrives at the conclusion that an uncaused and therefore necessary being exists. Kant described this argument as a nest of sophisms, which indeed it is. Here the discussion of it will be confined to making a small number of points. For one thing, it can be shown that the cosmological argument, which to all appearances makes use of three premises to arrive at its conclusion, in fact uses none of them. Their only function is to give an empirical deductive facade to an argument which makes use only of a conceptual distinction, the distinction between the mere concept of a contingent thing and the mere concept of a non-contingent thing. The concept of the contingent logically requires the antithetical concept of the non-contingent, and if this pair of concepts has possible application to things it is easily shown that independently of whether a contingent thing exists or not, a non-contingent thing does exist. The existence of a non-contingent thing follows from the distinction itself, and indeed from the concept of a non-contingent thing alone. For the conception of a non-contingent thing, as opposed to that of a contingent thing, is the conception of a thing the nonexistence of which is inconceivable. That is, it is the conception of a thing the nonexistence of which is an impossibility of concepts, and the existence of which therefore is necessary. It is easily seen that neither the existence of a contingent thing nor the thesis that every contingent thing must have a cause, nor yet the proposition that there cannot be an infinite totality of causes plays any logical role whatever in the demonstration of the existence of a necessary being. The existence of such a being follows from mere concepts.

The argument thus is ontological in character, but it is not the ontological argument of Anselm and Descartes. These philosophers held that the existence of a perfect being was implied by the concept of such a being. Here it has been reasoned that the existence of a necessary being is implied by the concept of a non-contingent thing, with nothing else requisite for the implication to hold. If we recall the claim that no existential propositions about things can be *a priori* we may indeed think that a paralogism of some sort is buried in this non-Anselmic piece of reasoning. For we seem to have here a proof of God's existence if only the notion of a perfect being and that of a necessary one are identified. Aquinas in his third argument for the existence of God, which proceeded from the existence of contingent things to a thing which exists necessarily, made this identification when he said 'This all men speak of as God'. One may justifiably ask how this identification is arrived at, for the idea of an entity which has necessary existence carries with it no suggestion whatever as to its nature, as to *what* it is that has necessary existence. The concept of necessary existence, like the concept of existence, is contentless. The reason behind the tempting identification, when brought into the open, seems to be that only a *perfect* being can have necessary existence, that is, existence by the necessity of its nature. But this does not stand up to scrutiny, for it implies that numbers and the like do not have necessary existence, inasmuch as it makes no sense to speak, for example, of a prime number lying within a certain range of numbers being either perfect or imperfect.

The reader can begin to see for himself that the notion of a non-contingent entity has no application to things to which the word 'substance' correctly applies. The pair of antithetical terms 'contingent thing the nonexistence of which is conceivable' and 'necessary thing the nonexistence of which is inconceivable' have mutually exclusive ranges of application, the elements in each range belonging to logically different types. Consider now the conception of God as an entity perfect in its nature. If the concept is such that its instance belongs to one type, it cannot belong to the other type. And if the instance is a *substance*, related in various ways, for example as creator, to the world of contingent things, it will itself belong to their type and be such that its nonexistence is conceivable. The notion of God as something which has necessary existence places God in the class of entities such as numbers, attributes, and the like, which is absurd.

To return now to the cosmological argument from the existence of a contingent thing to the existence of a necessary being. Since a thing whose nonexistence is inconceivable must exist regardless of whether there is a contingent thing, we concluded that the existence of a necessary being is not demonstrable from the premise that a contingent thing exists. Equivalently, it may be shown that the existence of a contingent thing does not logically depend on the existence of a necessary thing. To put the matter somewhat differently, it may be shown that the contingent is not logically grounded in the necessary. Letting C stand for 'contingent' and N for 'necessary', the thesis that the contingent is grounded in the necessary may be expressed as:

$$(\exists x)Cx \rightarrow (\exists y)Ny.$$

The denial of this putative entailment will be a logical impossibility. In the notation of modal logic, where $\lozenge$ stands for possible, the entailment expression is restatable as

$$\sim \lozenge [(\exists x)Cx \cdot \sim (\exists y)Ny].$$

This is to the effect that it is not possible for a contingent thing to exist and a necessary thing not to exist. And this formulation makes it look as though an existential statement referring to a contingent thing cannot, because of its logical relationship to the denial of an existential statement referring to a non-contingent thing, be true jointly with it. But it can easily be seen that the reason why a statement of the first sort cannot be true jointly with the denial of an existential statement of the second sort is not that there is a logical incompatibility between the two, but that a statement of the second sort is in itself not logically open to denial. The logical impossibility of the *conjunction* vanishes into the logical impossibility of the second conjunct, $\sim (\exists y)Ny$, i.e., into

$$\sim \lozenge [\sim (\exists y)Ny].$$

This statement is to the effect that it is impossible for there not to be a necessary thing, which is to say it is impossible for there to fail to be a thing the nonexistence of which is inconceivable. And this is just the tautologous statement 'There necessarily exists a thing which has necessary existence':

$$\sim \Diamond \sim (\exists y)Ny.$$

The philosophical proposition $(\exists x)Cx \rightarrow (\exists y)Ny$, instead of being a genuine entailment is, we may say, made true vacuously by the putative fact that the consequent itself is a necessary proposition. This consequent is such that it is implied by every proposition, simply because it is necessary, and for no other reason.

It may be of some use to distinguish between two kinds of implication: those the denials of which yield a conjunction made impossible by the impossibility of one of the components, and those the denials of which give rise to conjunctions whose components are inconsistent with each other. In the one case the inconsistency is solely in one of the components; in the other it obtains *between* the components. Thus, whereas in the second kind of case there is a genuine inference from the first component to the negation of the second, there is no genuine inference in the first kind of case. The difference between the two may be described by saying that in the one case the implication is *made good* by the consequent alone, and in the other by a logical relationship in which both components figure. In this latter kind of case there is a genuine inference-bridge from the antecedent to the consequent; metaphorically speaking, the inference is supported at both ends. In the other the inference is supported only at one end and can truly be characterized as vacuous. This inference-bridge, no more than a traffic bridge with one support, can function to convey one from one side to the other.

What may be learned from this is that although the concept of the contingent is bound up with the concept of the non-contingent, the existence of a contingent thing is not logically dependent on that of a non-contingent thing. The ontological fact reflected by the logical point that there is no inconsistecy *between* the propositions $(\exists x)Cx$ and $\sim (\exists y)Ny$ is that the contingent is not grounded in the necessary. In sum, it is impossible for a contingent thing to exist and a necessary thing not to exist, not because the existence of a contingent thing *depends on* the existence of a necessary thing, but because it is impossible for a necessary thing not to exist. A contingent thing can only be grounded in another contingent thing.

To bring this into connection with the two propositions that every contingent thing must have a cause and that there cannot be an infinite totality of causes, it can be seen that at least one of these propositions has to be given up. For their combination now implies that no contingent thing could exist. Some philosophers, for example, Bertrand Russell, feel no objection to the notion of the consummated infinite and would experience no difficulty in rejecting the second proposition. A philosopher of this persuasion could then hold that the present existence of contingent things implies an infinite series of antecedent contingent things going back in time. The implication of this view is that contingent things must always have existed. The world of contingent things is eternal at least with respect to the past. Other philosophers find it difficult to accept the thesis of the consummated infinite but experience no difficulty in rejecting the proposition that every occurrence *must* have a cause. Thus Ayer has said: 'But why should it be supposed that every event must have a cause? The contrary is not unthinkable, nor is the law of universal causation a necessary presupposition of scientific thought' (1954, p. 272). On this position a contingent thing is not only something which may fail to exist but is also something which could fail to have a cause. It could be conceived of as not existing and also as having begun to exist just by itself, without having been brought into existence by something else. The world of contingent things may on this view be eternal with respect to the past, but need not be. It might have come into existence some time in the past, prior to which no contingent thing existed. Science will perhaps some day be in a position to answer this question.

In an earlier chapter the position was taken that the consummated infinite is impossible (Ch. 4, pp. 119–129). And this necessitates rejecting the proposition that every occurrence must have a cause and admitting that a contingent thing may begin to exist unaided by a cause. But then anything which is a cause of a contingent thing will itself be a contingent thing, which may or may not have a cause. The existence of things fills some people with a sense of mystery. They are thrown into wonder by the fact that there is something rather than nothing. The question, 'Why should there be something rather than nothing?', has deep roots in the minds of many people, who feel that the existence of things must have an explanation. And one explanation which resolves their wonder and apparently satisfies their curiosity is that the material world was brought into existence by an act of divine creation. But it will be plain that the cause of material existence will itself have to be a contingent thing the nonexistence of which is conceivable. Thus, the mystery of existence which is removed from the material world by this explanation is transferred to the existence of God, where apparently it creates no uneasiness. But the mystery of existence pertains as much to the creator of matter as to matter itself. The existence of a creator of matter rather than his nonexistence is an ultimate subject of wonder. There is no denying the possibility that matter was created by God and that God just spontaneously began to exist. But no more probability attaches to the proposition that matter was created than that it simply began to exist. The only hope of some sort of demonstration of the existence of a divine being lies in the teleological form of argument, about which Kant said, 'This proof always deserves to be mentioned with respect. It is the oldest, the clearest, and the most accordant with the common reason of mankind' (1929, Bk. II, Ch. 3, Sec. 6).

It is important to point out a difference between the cosmological argument, or rather, what is left of it, and the teleological argument. Shorn of the thesis that every contingent thing must have a cause and freed from its connection with the notion of a necessary being, the cosmological argument does not advance the attempt to explain the mystery of existence. Construed as an inference from the existence of physical reality to a cause (or causes) it transfers the mystery of contingent existence, which we wish to penetrate, to the cause itself. It leaves us with a companion to the child's troubling question, namely, 'Why is there God rather than nothing?' The teleological argument, which proceeds from an analogy with artifacts to the existence of a cosmic craftsman, does seem to take us a step froward towards satisfaying our wish to understand the world. It gives us a possible explanation, not of the existence of matter, but of structured physical reality, or how it is that materials are formed into a cosmos instead of being a chaos. The argument is graphically summed up by a character in a recent play: 'Who can believe that this entire world just happened?' Who can believe that matter just formed itself into the Parthenon, and who can believe that matter just formed itself into a cosmos?

The teleological argument has a number of obvious shortcomings and in its present form points no more to monotheism than to polytheism. The *Iliad* says: 'The rule of many is not good; one ruler let there be.' Monotheistic religion insists on the rule of One for the universe, but the teleological argument as it stands at present does not entitle us to this conclusion. The argument does possibly make probable the existence, in the past at least, of a cosmic titan, at least one, who imprinted his ideas on matter and fashioned it into a universe. However short this argument falls of the intended goal, one thing in its favor has to be noted. This is that of all the arguments to be found in rational theology it alone is bound up with a picture of God which bears a resemblance to the God of western religion. It is linked with the image of a prodigious, superhuman figure who, unlike the Anselmic God, has limitations, experiences wrath, can feel love and compassion, and can be moved by prayer. Like the Christ in Michelangelo's Last judgment, he is capable of compassionless hate, but he is also moved to sorrow by the fall of the sparrow. Freud perhaps had in mind the comparison between the ontological and teleological conceptions of God when he wrote: 'Philosophers stretch the meanings of words until they retain scarcely anything of their original sense; by calling "God" some vague abstraction which they have created for themselves, they pose as deists, as believers, before the world; they may even pride themselves on having attained a higher and purer idea of God, although their God is nothing but an insubstantial shadow and no longer the mighty personality of religious doctrine' (1943, p. 57).

DOUBTS AND QUERIES

1. Some philosophers have attempted to solve the problem of evil in relation to the existence of an ideally perfect being by urging that good and evil are not actual qualities of things or states of affairs but are wholly subjective and determined solely by our ways of looking at things. Spinoza said: 'As for the terms *Good* and *Bad*, they indicate no positive qualities in things regarded in themselves, but are merely modes of thinking, or notions which we form from the comparison of things one with another. Thus one and the same thing can at the same time be good, bad, and indifferent. For instance, music is good for him that is melancholy, bad for him that mourns; for him that is deaf it is neither good nor bad' (1901, Preface). The intent of this is to suggest that good and evil are not to be found in things and therefore do not really exist. To say that they are merely 'modes of thinking' and consequently only subjective is a way of dismissing them or denying their reality entirely. The implication is that since evil does not exist in things or states of affairs there is nothing incompatible with the existence of a perfect being. Is it a sufficient reply to this attempt to bring the existence of a perfect being

into harmony with the everyday world to say that although things like violins, orchids, and books are neither good nor bad in themselves, the mental states they produce *are* either good or bad? Is it an answer to say that the true home of evil and good, as of pain and pleasure, is sentiency, and that without sentiency there is neither good norevil? Can it be effectively argued that a philosopher like Spinoza denies the reality of good an evil because he looks in the wrong place, and failing to find them there, infers that they do not exist? If maintaining that evil exists only in sentiency, or in 'modes of thinking', is not equivalent to denying that evil exists but is only to locate it, then is the existence of evil in sentiency incompatible with the existence of a perfect, almighty, all-good being?

2. It will be remembered from Chapter 3 that antithetical concepts are related in two different ways. Some pairs are related in such a way that an instance of one could not become an instance of the other, for example, *odd* and *even* as applied to numbers. Others are so related that what exemplifies one member of the pair could change over and exemplify the other, e.g., *swift* and *slow*, *stationary* and *in motion* as applied to objects. How are *contingent existence* and *necessary existence* related to each other? Could a thing which might not exist become something which could not conceivably fail to exist, and conversely? In discussion with the Harvard logician H. M. S. Scheffer, the question arose as to whether God could change into a true mouse, where being a true mouse would prevent its changing back into God. Behind this of course was the question as to whether an all powerful necessarily existing thing could change itself into something which exists only contingently. Do the concepts of contingent existence and necessary existence have what may be called logically exclusive ranges of application in respect of type, such that if one applies to substances, occurrences, sensible appearances, etc., regardless of degree of perfection or imperfection, the other cannot?

3. The thesis that all existential statements about things are synthetic is not arrived at inductively; rather, it is an entailment claim to the effect that being a thing (or a substance, or an occurrence, or a sensible appearance, etc.) entails being such that its nonexistence is conceivable. This would imply that the antithetical concept *non-contingent existence* does not include within its possible range of application anything to which we should apply Locke's phrase 'real existence'. If this is so, then the claim that a perfect thing has necessary existence would entail an inner inconsistency and the conclusion that the first cause of things

has necessary existence would imply that this cause was itself not 'a real being'. How are such implications to be assessed?

If the concept of necessary existence cannot apply to a real being, what is wrong with the proof, Chapter 4, that monads have necessary existence?

4. Is the analogy between an artifact and the world of nature justified? What would count as a non-artifact? According to physics a droplet of water and a particle of dust are complex electrical systems. Does this mean that a particle of dust is an artifact? If so, what would count as a natural object as opposed to a crafted object? Does the teleological argument covertly deny the distinction it requires between the two kinds of objects? The following consideration makes it look as though it does deny this distinction. If the argument rests on the covertly accepted proposition that in the end all objects found in nature are artifacts, then the distinction between artifacts and natural objects vanishes and so does the analogy. For the analogy of a watch with a galaxy or an organism implies the statement that objects found in nature which are not made by human artisans are very probably artifacts. This sort of statement can only be made if the distinction between artifacts and natural objects which are not crafted by any artisan, divine or otherwise, is preserved. The statement that such-and-such an object probably was fashioned implies the possibility of the object's not having been fashioned. It thus implies the distinction between made things and things that just happened to be such-and-such. Does the teleological argument preserve the required distinction?

5. Suppose the teleological argument does preserve the required distinction between artifacts and natural objects, and that the analogy between a watch and, say, the solar system makes it probable the solar system was a cosmic artifact, that is, a system in which means were adapted to ends. What is the difference between the inference to its Designer and the inference from a violin to a violin maker? In the case of the violin it is theoretically possible to establish in the usual way the existence of a violin maker. What the existence of a violin makes probable could be independently established, for example, by finding the violin maker himself. Is this a possibility in the case of the cosmic artisan? The conclusion of an inference which is made probable by one piece of evidence could be supported by other possible pieces of evidence and is such that in principle it could be checked without recourse to further *evidence*, that is, by discovering the thing the evidence points to. Is this possible in the case of the teleological argument?

6. The teleological inference to a supreme Designer is based on an analogy with artifacts and their makers, where both the artifacts and their makers are things in the cosmos. Does the teleological inference to an architect of the world who 'exists outside the world' violate the conditions of the analogy in proceeding to the existence of a transcendent being, not to be found in space? See Kant's Fourth Antinomy. Suppose staying within the bounds of the analogy entitles us at most to infer a titanic spatial figure, something like a magnified carpenter who is in space and makes spatial objects. Would this imply that like an ordinary carpenter or watchmaker who exemplifies the adaptation of means to ends and who himself must count as an artifact, the magnified Designer also exemplifies the adaptation of means to ends and must count as an artifact? If an artifact requires a maker, are we impelled to the inference that the maker of the universe himself had a maker, etc.? Does staying within the analogy on which the teleological argument revolves imply that as in the case of the cosmological argument which does not explain the mystery of existence, the teleological argument does not advance our understanding of structured matter?

7. On Kant's account the teleological argument logically hangs on the cosmological argument, which hangs on the ontological argument, so that if the latter is invalid, all are invalid. And as these are the only possible proofs for the existence of a transcendent God, the existence of such a being lies beyond the possibility of demonstration. It is theoretically indemonstrable. Furthermore, the existence of a transcendent being cannot in principle be verified in sense experience; no sense experience could make its existence certain or probable to any degree, however small. A proposition which is theoretically indemonstrable cannot be *a priori*. Its denial deos not imply a contradiction or a logical impossibility. Furthermore, a proposition which in principle is incapable of verification in sense experience is not empirical. Hence, on Kant's own account the sentence, 'A transcendent God exists' expresses neither an empirical nor an *a priori* proposition. And thus according to the positivist criterion for literal significance, the sentence has no meaning. Is there an effective way of meeting this positivistic claim?

8. The traditional cosmological argument makes use of the notion of causation and lays down as an axiom the proposition that every contingent thing has a cause. Some philosophers, in accordance with this, have maintained that either a thing has a cause or exists necessarily. This would seem to eliminate the possibility of something being both

contingent and having no cause. The idea of a contingent existent having no cause has by many philosophers been identified with the idea of something produced by nothing. Ayer, as was pointed out, found no intellectual difficulty in the idea of a contingent thing coming into existence without a cause. Other philosophers have maintained the inconceivability of an uncaused thing. Thus Locke said, '... man knows by an intuitive certainty that bare *nothing can no more produce any real being than it can be equal to two right angles*' (1928, Bk. IV, Ch. 10, Sec. 1). And Spinoza said that 'a little reflection' shows that it 'is impossible that something should be made out of nothing' (*Ethics*, Pt. IV, note to proposition XX). What is the explanation of this disagreement between philosophers? Are we to conclude that some philosophers claim to conceive what is inconceivable or that other philosophers conceive perfectly well what they declare to be inconceivable? Is the disagreement between, for example, Ayer and Locke, to be explained by psychology, or in some other way?

Aquinas held that God created matter out of nothing, while Spinoza, as has just been seen, maintained that it is impossible for something to be made out of nothing. If, as Locke implies, the notion of something coming from nothing is a logical absurdity, then the notion of God creating matter out of nothing would be a logical absurdity, comparable to the idea of his making a four-sided triangle. How is the difference between Aquinas and Locke to be explained? Is there a difference between saying that something comes into existence without a cause, that it comes from nothing, and that it was made out of nothing by God?

9. Socrates in the *Phaedo* asks: 'From the senses then is derived the knowledge that all sensible things aim at an absolute equality of which they fall short? ... Then before we began to see or hear or perceive in any way, we must have had a knowledge of absolute equality, or we could not have referred to that standard the equals of which are derived from the senses? – for to that they all aspire, and of that they fall short.'

These questions imply that the concept of the ideal limit of a series of more and more nearly equal physical things itself has no application to physical things, the same with regard to the concept of an ideally perfect, frictionless surface and an ideally perfect straight edge. If the notion of the ideal limit of a series of approximations has no possible application to any member of the series, then the concept of the limit is not a concept which could be exemplified and is thus not the concept of a possible thing. Now if the notion of an absolutely perfect thing, than which a greater is inconceivable, involves the notion of ideal limits, which could not be exemplified in anything, the concept itself could not be the concept of a possible being. Is the concept of a being that combines in itself a number of properties capable of being possessed to a degree by things (e.g., immovability), but which it possesses to 'the highest degree', the concept of a possible being? Does it denote the unrealizable ideal of a series of possible beings approximating to it, comparable to the series of rationals approximating $\sqrt{2}$? Is this latter what Kant implied when he spoke of the concept of an ideally perfect God as not being *constitutive*, i.e., as not being the concept of an object, but as having only a *regulative* employment, comparable to that of a mathematical formula for ordering numbers in a series? (See Appendix to the 'Transcendental dialectic'. Of the 'Regulative use of the ideas of pure reason'.)

Is there a connection between the critique of the ontological argument and the view that the concept of an ideally perfect being has only regulative employment?

REFERENCES

Recommended reading:
   Aristotle, *Metaphysics*, BookΛ.
Further readings:
   St. Anselm (1939), *Proslogium*.
   Immanuel Kant (1929a), *Critique of pure reason*, 'Transcendental dialectic', Ch. 3, Sec. 3–8.
   Norman Malcolm (1963), *Knowledge and certainty*, 'Anselm's ontological arguments'.

6. Abstract Entities

Parmenidean metaphysics raised the question about the possibility of thinking of what does not exist. Parmenides himself maintained that it is impossible to think of what is not, on the grounds that thought must have an object and the nonexistent cannot be an object. Normally we should allow that it is impossible to pick a flower that does not exist but not that we cannot think of a flower that does not exist. But the implication of the Parmenidean position would seem to be that a flower that does not exist cannot be thought of. Followed through, the Parmenidean position leads to a paradoxical consequence which makes the position unacceptable. This is that it is impossible to hold a true belief, a consequence which must be too shocking even for the most extreme Parmenidean. The Parmenidean position plainly implies the impossibility of believing that something exists which in fact does not exist, or more generally, the impossibility of believing what in fact is not the case. For to believe what is not the case would imply that there was no object of thought and therefore no object with regard to which a belief was being held. It thus implies the impossibility of there being a false belief. (It may be argued that about an actual thing of which I am aware, for example, a book, I may have the false belief that it has 500 pages, in which case there would be an actual object with regard to which I am holding a false belief. Nevertheless, a Parmenidean would have to maintain, however paradoxical it may seem, that the supposed object of thought, book-having-500-pages, refers to what is not the case and so cannot be an actual object of thought.) But there cannot be a true belief if there cannot be a false one. In a related connection Austin wrote: '... talk of deception only *makes sense* against a background of general non-deception' (1962, p. 11). And we may similarly say that intelligible talk about true beliefs is possible only if in the background there are conceivably false beliefs. Spinoza asserted: 'He who has a true idea, simultaneously knows that he has a

145

true idea and cannot doubt of the truth of the thing perceived' (*Ethics*, Pt. II, Prop. 43). It is easily seen that his words imply the impossibility of having a false belief. For if when one has a true idea one knows it is true, then any idea which is not true would be recognized as such and would not be believed. It then follows that there cannot be true beliefs if there cannot be false ones, for having a true belief implies the possibility of being mistaken. It is not possible to think of what is the case if the possibility of thinking what is not the case is ruled out as logically impossible. But the possibility of there being false beliefs implies the possibility of thinking of what does not exist. Despite the Parmenidean position, there is no real question as to whether it is possible to think of what is not the case. The question is not, 'Is it possible to think of what does not exist?' There is only the question, '*How* is it possible to think of what does not exist?' What is the explanation of our being able to think of what does not exist, for example, Pegasus and blue roses?

Plato's celebrated theory of universals provides one philosophical answer. Provisionally we may distinguish between concrete things like pens and books and mental images, and concepts of things and of images. I can think of a book without seeing it and I can think of a blue mental image without having one. And when I do, what is present to my mind is a concept. As some philosophers have put it, 'We think by means of concepts'. In addition to concrete things, mental images, specific feelings of various sorts, etc., there are concepts which, unlike these, are general. And we are able to think of things in their absence, and even of things which do not exist, by means of concepts which are present to thought in their stead. When I think of the Queen of England, what is present to my thought is a concept to which she answers, and when I think of Pegasus the object of my thought is a concept to which nothing answers but to which something could conceivably answer.

It is admittedly the case that mathematicians think in the abstract, that they think, for example, of $7+5$ being equal to 12 as against 7 apples plus 5 more being equal to 12 apples. If mathematicians were unable to think in the abstract there would be no such discipline as mathematics. It is difficult to see how Parmenides could have failed to note the distinction between the abstract and its concrete instances, which would have provided him with an explanation of how it is possible to think of things in their absence and of things which do not exist. Russell said that 'classes which are infinite are given all at once by the defining property of their members' (1927, p. 170), which means that a class the members of which cannot all be given at once, and thus not given *directly*, are given indirectly by their defining property. Regardless of whether there can be an infinite class, the implication is that we can think of what is not presented to us by means of something else which is presented to us, in this case an abstract property as against the elements of the class. And similarly with regard to a property to which nothing actual answers: We can entertain a property which characterizes nothing whatever. And in this way we can think of what does not exist.

The mistaken idea on which the tenet of the inconceivability of the nonexistent rests may perhaps be explained best by reference to something like John Stuart Mill's distinction between the denotation of a term and its connotation. The denotation of a term like 'man' consists of the individual things to which the word applies. The connotation is the general idea or attribute of which the denotation is the set of instances. Thus the word 'man' can have the same connotation for people who have been acquainted with different, non-overlapping parts of its denotation. For example, what 'John Brown' names is part of the denotation of the word 'man'. It is the proper name of the person of whom 'man' is the general name. And the general name carries the same connotation for people regardless of whether they have had acquaintance with John Brown or not. Furthermore, it retains its connotation when John Brown ceases to be. It is evident then that the connotation of a word and its denotation cannot be identified.

Now it would seem that a philosopher who holds that we cannot think of what does not exist has identified the connotation of general words with their denotation. The consequence of this identification is that a word which fails to have a denotation, whether because it refers to fictitious creatures or because the elements making up its denotation have gone out of existence, fails also to have a connotation and becomes literally meaningless. And a philosopher who holds that we cannot think of what does not exist is in a different form of words saying that a term which has zero denotation also has zero connotation and carries with it no concept to be entertained by a mind. The moment we recognize the difference between the connotation of a term and its denotation we find that there are three sorts of entities and not, to use a recent dichotomy, only two sorts of entities, words and things. We find that in addition to words and things there are connotations, or to use a more familiar word, meanings, of general words like 'man' and 'blue'. The connotation of a term in addition to being distinguished from the denotation must also be distin-

10*

guished from the term itself, for different terms in the same language as well as in different languages may carry the same connotation. Thus, the word 'man' has the same connotation as the word 'homme', and the word 'blue' the same as 'azur'; and a person who understands one member of such pairs may not understand the other.

That general nouns and adjectives have a connotation whether or not they have a denotation is certain. The problem would seem to be, not one of determining whether connotations or meanings of terms exist, but only of determining the nature of the connotations, what sort of enties they are. Further questions arise. One is whether the meaning of a term depends on the existence of the term: A term preserves its connotation when it loses its denotation, but a question remaining to be investigated is whether the connotation vanishes when all the terms whose connotation it is cease to exist. Another question is whether the connotation of a term is an idea or thought, some sort of mental occurrence, which requires a mind for its existence. And there are other questions, for example, whether they are capable of change.

Russell has said: 'When we examine common words, we find that, broadly speaking, proper names stand for particulars, while other substantives, adjectives, prepositions, and verbs stand for universals (1943, p. 145). This is a view about the connotations of terms, and the particular view he took on this occasion was the Platonic theory that the connotation of a term is an abstract object and therefore not the kind of object that is given in sense experience. The most common name of this kind of entity is the word 'universal'. Russell goes on to say: 'Seeing that nearly all the words to be found in the dictionary stand for universals, it is strange that hardly anybody except students of philosophy ever realizes that there are such entities as universals' (p. 146). It is reasonable to suppose that Russell did not mean to imply that hardly anybody except students of philosophy realizes that general words have connotations. Rather, it would seem that he intended to imply that only philosophers have the idea that the connotations of such words are supersensible objects.

There are several well-known and time-honored arguments for the view that the meanings of general words are abstract entities, entities which are incapable of being perceived by any of the senses and are apprehended intellectually, as Plato put it, 'by the eye of the mind'. These he says, are 'invisible and imperceptible by any sense, and of which the contemplation is granted to intelligence only' (*Timaeus*, Sec. 52). It must be clear to everyone that a term like 'cup', 'round', 'to the left of' is applicable to each of a number of things and situations because of a property they have in common: The word 'cup' is applicable to each of a number of cups, regardless of differences between them, because of an attribute they possess, and the word 'round' to coins, balls, and a vast number of other concrete things differing from each other in many particular respects, because of an attribute they possess. It is the same with the relational term 'to the left of' which holds between many pairs of different sorts of things – people, pieces of furniture, mountains, etc. To sum this up in Plato's words, 'Whenever a number of individuals have a common name, we assume them to have also a corresponding idea or form' (*Republic*, Bk. X, Sec. 596). The existence of common names seems to imply the existence of common properties in virtue of which the words have multiple application. In other words, the meaning of a general word is a common property, which in contrast to the concrete things which share it, is an abstract entity.

This view, which may be called the Platonic theory about the nature of the meanings of general words, gives us an explanation of how we can go on to an indefinite number of new applications of a general word from a small number of initial applications, that is, how we are able to apply the terms 'cup' and 'triangle' to cups and triangles we have never before seen. What happens when we are taught a general noun like 'cup' or 'triangle' *ostensively*, that is, by being shown particular applications, and from there proceed on our own to new applications of the words, is that we abstract or isolate what the ostensively given cases have in common. The process of successfully abstracting a property enables us to identify new things, not included in the original ostensive definitions, to which the words correctly apply. The new applications have in common with the initial instances what the initial instances have in common with each other. Thus, one difference between the proper name 'John Brown' and the word 'man' is that by being introduced to John Brown we are not able to go on to identify other people having that name. Making the acquaintance of several persons to whom the name belongs does not enable us to pick out new people whose name it is. If we wish to apply the term 'denotation' to proper names, we may say that knowing some members of the denotation of the proper name 'John Brown' does not enable us to identify other members belonging to its denotation. The case is altogether different with the general name 'man'. Learning what some of the members of its denotation are makes it possible for us to go on to other members of its denotation. We can say with sense 'I have shown you enough applications of the word "man" for you to go on to new applications', but we cannot with sense say 'I have introduced you to a sufficient number of people named "John Brown" for you to find new bearers of the name'. We have now an explanation of how a term can have the same connotation for two people neither of whom is acquainted with members of the denotation of the term the other is acquainted with. The connotation is that which all the members of the denotation have in common with each other.

That which the things making up the denotation of a term have in common is itself not a concrete thing. It is not something which has in common with the things what they have in common with each other. In other words, it is itself not a thing falling within the denotation of the term. And unlike things which are presented to sense it is not itself an object of sense: '. . . neither through hearing nor yet through seeing can you apprehend that which the things have in common. . .' (Plato, *Theaetetus*, Sec. 185). The connotation, or meaning, of the general noun 'horse' and the adjective 'yellow' is given by the abstract words 'horseness' and 'yellowness', where horseness and yellowness are objects which can only be entertained by the mind. There is an ancient tale about a dispute over universals between Plato and Diogenes the Cynic that is pertinent in this connection: 'As Plato was conversing about ideas and using the nouns "tablehood" and "cuphood" (Diogenes) said: "Tables and cups I see; but your tablehood and cuphood, Plato, I can in nowise see". "That's readily accounted for", said Plato, "for you have the eyes to see the visible table and cup, but not the understanding by which tablehood and cuphood are discerned".' Disregarding the Platonic witticism, the point is that we see each of several cups but not the complex set of attributes referred to by 'cuphood' which is shared by the individual cups. The cups are tangible to the senses. What they have in common can be grasped only by the understanding.

A supporting argument for the Platonic view that there are such objects as supersensible universals derives from a consideration of what is entailed by things being similar to each other. The existence of things, occurrences, or situations which bear likenesses to each other, for example, mice, apples, colors, etc., implies the existence of a property, complex or simple, which characterizes each of the resembling things. To express the matter in the notation of logic, letting x and y be individual variables, R denote the relation of resemblance, and φ a property, this comes to the following:

$$(\exists x, y)xRy \rightarrow (\exists\varphi)\varphi x . \varphi y$$

The common property φ characterizes things which are or can be given to sense but cannot itself be given to sense. The existence of similar things implies the existence of common properties or universals; but it is not necessary to assume the actual existence of similar things to prove the existence of common properties. In other words, it is not necessary to argue on the basis of an empirical premise for the existence of universals. No more is necessary for the demonstration than the possibility of there being resembling things. Whether or not there are such things, the theoretical possibility of such things exists, and this implies the existence of common properties. For example, the mere possibility of there being two things which are mice implies the possibility of the property 'being a mouse' having instances, and this in turn implies the actual existence of the property. Expressed symbolically with the help of the symbol $\Diamond$ for logical possibility, this comes to the following:

$$\Diamond(\exists x, y)xRy \rightarrow (\exists\varphi)\varphi x . \varphi y$$

Thus, even though there were in fact no similar things, the logical possibility of there being such things implies, not the possible existence of a universal, but its actual existence.

In the recommended reading from H. H. Price, reference is made to a special argument by Russell for the existence of universals. This rests on a different sort of consideration from the one presented here. The existence of cases of things resembling each other, regardless of how different the cases are, implies that they all have a property in common; it implies that they are all instances of the universal *resemblance*. Russell's own way of putting the matter is as follows: 'If we wish to avoid the universals *whiteness* and *triangularity*, we shall choose some particular patch of white or some particular triangle, and say that anything is white or a triangle if it has the right sort of resemblance to our chosen particular. But then the resemblance required will have to be a universal. Since there are many white things, the resemblance must hold between many pairs of particular white things; and this is the characteristic of a universal. It will be useless to say that there is a different resemblance for each pair, for then we shall have to say that these resemblances resemble each other, and thus at last we shall be forced to admit resemblance as a universal.

The relation of resemblance, therefore, must be a true universal.' (1943, pp. 150–151) Again, it is not necessary to assume the actual existence of cases of resembling things. Regardless of whether there are actual cases of resembling things, there is the possibility of there being such cases. This implies that there could be instances of the universal *resemblance*, which thus exists. In other words, it is not necessary to look at the world of things in order to infer the existence of universals.

Russell, as will be remembered, observed that most words to be found in the dictionary 'stand for universals' and went on to express surprise that hardly anyone except students of philosophy know that there are such things as universals. Surprising as this may be, the even more striking fact is that philosophers disagree over whether there are universals. Both the layman's unawareness of universals and philosophers' disagreement over their existence require an explanation, and part of the explanation may be that they are due to an erroneous idea about the connection between the meaning of a word and the word which bears the meaning. Some people have the idea that the meaning of a word cannot exist apart from the word and hence that the meaning is not *something* in addition to the word itself. Thus, Wittgenstein invites us to make the *Gedankenexperiment* of trying to think of the meaning of a word without at the same time thinking of any word which has it. Wittgenstein's own conclusion, in consequence of performing the experiment, is that though we can think of a word without thinking of its meaning we cannot think of the meaning without thinking of a word. Some philosophers have held that a word and its meaning are given by psychological contiguity, the one given to some one of the senses and the other to the mind. But against this and in accordance with his mental experiment Wittgenstein asserted: 'When I think in language, there aren't "meanings" going through my mind in addition to the verbal expressions.' (1953, p. 107. Wittgenstein makes his point in connection with the meanings of sentences, but the same thing applies to the meanings of general words.) The idea that many people would seem to have is that the meaning of a word cannot exist apart from some word or other and therefore is not an entity in its own right. This may be part of the explanation of why it is that people come to overlook universals. They overlook them in consequence of having a certain idea about the phrase 'meaning of *w*'. In a metaphor, they have the idea that the meaning of a word is related to the word in the way in which a smile is related to a face. The meaning of a word can no more exist apart from the word than a smile apart from the face.

Now a person who is unaware of universals is not unaware of the fact that general words have meanings. Rather, we may say, the unawareness consists of looking at universals in a special way, as being linguistically dependent and therefore as not being entities in their own right. To put the matter somewhat differently, the idea that universals are linguistically dependent, that is, dependent for their existence on symbolization, results from the identification of 'universal' with 'meaning of a general word'. If in addition to holding that the meaning of a general word is a universal we think, as indeed might seem natural, that a universal is the meaning of a general word, then it will follow that a universal can exist only as the meaning of a word and cannot exist independently of some expression or other. It will follow, if a universal φ, for example whiteness, exists, that φ is the meaning of a word; and therefore it will follow that a word exists.

There are a number of powerful reasons, however, against identifying universals with the meaning of words. These do not, of course, upset the view that the meaning of a word is a universal. They are only reasons against the converse of this proposition, namely, that to be a universal is necessarily to be the meaning of a general word. One reason which comes to mind immediately is the following. It undoubtedly is a fact that there was a time prior to which no language, however rudimentary, existed. And there can be no doubt that before that time there existed many groups of similar things, that is, things similar to each other in regard to shape, or size, or texture, etc., and that there were many cases of one thing being between other things, which is to say that there were instances of *betweenness*, and also of other relational concepts. It follows from the fact that there were similar things prior to the existence of language that there were common properties prior to the existence of words whose meanings they now are. This of course implies that common properties, properties which are at present the meanings of such words as 'white', 'between', 'mouse', have an existence independently of the existence of language. It follows thus that the meaning of a general word can exist apart from a word which happens to symbolize it. We may say that the meaning of a word is as independent of the word as the word of the meaning.

This argument uses an empirical premise to establish that universals are independent of language, the premise, namely, that there were similar things before there was language. But it is easily seen that the empirical premise can be dispensed with and the same consequence obtained from the nonempirical proposition that there could, theoretically, have been similar things prior to language. The logical possibility of there being similar things prior to language implies the logical possibility of there being common properties prior to the existence of any words which may later acquire them as their meanings; and this is sufficient to establish the independence of the meaning of a general word from the general word. The logical possibility of unsymbolized existence implies the independence of a universal from any sort of symbolization. Later an argument will be given for the view that in addition to being intelligible objects universals are also eternal. As can readily be seen, if the argument for the eternality of universals is correct it will follow that universals can exist unsymbolized. The eternality of universals is equivalent to their having necessary existence, and since no language has necessary existence the consequence is that being a universal cannot entail the existence of language. The logical ground for this is that which is necessary, and cannot fail to exist, cannot imply anything contingent, that is, anything which could fail to exist. To put the matter somewhat more formally, if the argument for the eternality of universals is correct, the proposition that universals exist will be necessarily true; and since the proposition that language exists is contingent, such that it could possibly be false, the proposition that universals exist cannot imply the proposition that language exists.

One further argument may be added for the independent existence of universals, an argument deriving from considerations to be found in Moore's *Commonplace book* (1962). There the argument was directed to the independent existence of propositions. Here our concern is with universals, which, however, belong to the same class of entities that propositions belong to, i.e., abstract entities. As will be remembered, a version of Moore's argument has already been given in Chapter 1, but it is worthwhile restating it in a somewhat expanded form, as the existence of propositions, as well as that of universals, is at present under extensive discussion and debate. Moore distinguishes between an indicative sentence and a proposition, which he identifies as its literal meaning, or as what it says. He points out not only that different sentences can express one and the same proposition, which implies that a proposition cannot be identified with a sentence, but also that the terms 'true' and 'false' are correctly applicable only to propositions and not to sentences. The following consideration can easily be seen to lead to an argument which shows that propositions do not depend for their existence on the existence of sentences or any other linguistic unit: 'Every proposition which is true, except propositions about sentences, *could* have been true, even if there had been no sentences: From the fact that it is true that the sun is shining it does not follow that there are any sentences, since if the sun *is* shining, it follows that it is true that it is, and it obviously does not follow that there are any sentences' (1962, p. 359). Moore's argument suggests a further argument for the independent existence of propositions. Consider the proposition which is expressed by the words 'No language exists'. This proposition is of course false, not only because languages do exist but also because it is brought to attention by the English sentence used to express it. But the proposition is false only as a matter of fact, and is such that it could theoretically be true. If the proposition were true the sentence used to introduce it would of course not exist; and there would then exist one proposition not expressed in any language. The fact that the proposition *could* be true implies that the existence of a proposition does not depend on its being linguistically expressed. And since every proposition involves at least one component which is a universal it follows that universals do not require for their existence the existence of any symbol. We may say that a general name cannot exist without a corresponding universal, but a universal can exist without having a name.

It may be urged that although a proposition cannot be identified with a sentence in any particular language it is not something over and above and in addition to sentences and has to be identified with a class of sentences. Thus, according to Moore (1962, p. 359), F. P. Ramsey has advocated the view that '. . . a proposition is a class of sentences, grouped together as having the same meaning' And A. J. Ayer in a similar vein has said: '. . . we may define a proposition as a class of sentences which have the same intensional significance for anyone who understands them. Thus, the sentences: *I am ill, Ich bin krank, Je suis malade*, are all elements of the proposition *I am ill*' (1951, p. 88). This sort of view undoubtedly appeals to those who are opposed to committing themselves to 'the metaphysical doctrine that propositions are real entities' (*Ibid.*), but the argument which establishes the possibility of a proposition existing though unexpressed in words applies with equal force to the view which represents a proposition as being a class of synonymous sentences. The proposition that no language exists implies the proposition that no synonymous sentences exist, and since the proposition that no synonymous sentences exist could be true there would be at least one proposition even though there were no synonymous sentences. The plain consequence is that a proposition cannnot be identified with a class of sentences, nor a universal with a class of words having the same meaning.

Universals have a number of important features, amongst which is the Parmenidean feature of being incapable of change. Unlike concrete things which can change their color, shape, etc., that is, can exchange some of their properties for other properties, universals are not subject to change. A green apple can become red and a cube of wax can become spherical, but the property *greenness* cannot change into the property *redness*, nor the property of being a cube into the property of being a sphere. To consider another example, a group of seven things can lose one of its members and become six, but the number 7, which characterizes the original group, cannot itself change into the number 6, which characterizes the altered group. A mouse can be imagined to become a horse, and a pumpkin a carriage, but the universal whose instances are mice cannot change into the universal whose instances are horses; and the universal whose instances are pumpkins cannot change into a universal whose instances are carriages.

A further Parmenidean feature is that they are incapable of motion. We can speak of whiteness being at a place, which is to say that the attribute *being white* characterizes something at a given place, but it makes no sense to speak of whiteness moving from one place to another, although, of course, it is perfectly intelligible to speak of a thing characterized by whiteness moving from one place to another, e.g., a falling snowflake. Aquinas thought that angels changed place without being in a state of transition from one to the other. An angel is at various places without going from one to the others. We may say that like angels universals are at different places without getting to those places.

Universals are also said to be capable of being in many places at one time, which of course makes them unlike concrete things which can be at one place only at any time. The property a universal has of being capable of being many places at once, or to use a more recent phrase, the feature of being in local separation from itself, puzzled Plato and philosophers after him. But it will be clear that there can be a number of things each of which has a given property φ and that if φ itself must count as an entity, φ will be where the things are which it characterizes. It will also be possible for φ to exist and be *nowhere*: This will be the case when there are no things characterized by φ.

Several further features require discussion: These are that they are eternal objects which have their eternality in virtue of having necessary existence, and that they are objects which are capable of being entertained in thought but are such that their existence does not depend on their being thought. A further feature requiring discussion is that the existence of a universal does not imply the existence of instances. A philosopher who holds that a universal can exist uninstantiated is said to hold the theory of the abstract universal, as against the theory of the concrete universal attributed to Aristotle.

To argue first for the eternality of universals. If the argument is correct it will show that unlike ordinary things which come into existence, endure for a time, and pass away, universals neither come into existence nor pass out of existence. The line of reasoning is simple and direct. Take for example the universal *man*, which quite certainly failed to have instances at some time in the past and probably will cease to have instances at some time in the future. For any time t, regardless of how remote, it is, however, logically possible for there to have been a man, that is, for there to have been instances of the universal *man*. It is thus implied that at that time the universal *man* existed. The logical possibility of there being instances of a certain kind does not, of course, imply that there are or were instances; but it does imply the actual existence of the universal, which could be instantiated. This conclusion applies to all times, not only to the past and present but to the future. The plain consequence is that the universal *man* exists at all times, which is to say that it has eternal existence.

Not only this, it follows also that the universal *man* has necessary existence: At no time is it conceivable for it not to exist. The fact that a universal has necessary existence can perhaps be made more perspicuous in the following way. It is intelligible to assign a date to an instance of a universal, to say such a thing as '3000 years ago a man existed', but it is not intelligible to assign a date to a universal. A date could be assigned to a universal only if it made sense to speak of a universal coming into existence at that date. But talk about a universal coming into existence implies the possibility of its not existing, which our argument has ruled out. We may say that like the arithmetic equation $3+5 = 8$, which is a nontemporal truth, a universal is a nontemporal entity. Its existence at all times differs in an important logical respect from that of a contingent thing which exists at all times. Some philosophers, for example Aquinas, have the idea that a contingent thing is one that must have have a beginning in time and must come to an end in time, which implies that a contingent thing could not exist eternally. But the objection to this is that a contingent thing could conceivably exist at those times when in point of fact it does not. It therefore could in principle exist at all times, which is to say, eternally. The supposition that no contingent thing has eternal existence is an empirical hypothesis, which could be false. There is no contradiction in the proposition that there is a contingent thing which has always existed and will always continue to exist, although of course throughout its existence it will be such that it could cease to be. By contrast, the existence of a universal is necessary to it: At no time could it be conceived of as not existing. Universals have necessary eternality.

It needs to be shown now that although universals are possible objects of thought they are capable of existing unthought. In the Platonic dialogue *Parmenides* the view that universals are thoughts is examined and rejected because of certain grotesque consequences. The view that universals are thoughts goes by the name of conceptualism, which has had many distinguished advocates. For the present, however, it is important to see what evidence can be brought for the view that universals are not to be identified with thoughts. Before proceeding to the argument it should be pointed out that the view that universals are possible objects of thought but do not depend for their existence on being thought by anyone conforms to our ordinary modes of speech. We say, for example, that two people can think of the same number or the same attribute of a thing, and this implies that there are two private mental events, which consist in thinking about the same entity. The object of the two acts of thinking is the same, and is common and public as opposed to the mental occurrences which are private to the individual minds. Ordinary language suggests that the number 7, for example, can be thought by many different people, that it is not private to any one of them, and that it continues to exist even when not thought by anyone. If all thinking creatures went to sleep, the number 7 would remain as a possible object of thought. It would seem true, furthermore, that there are many numbers which have been thought of by no one. It is true, for example, that there is some number greater than any so far thought of.

The great mathematician Kronecker declared that God created the integers and man made the rest. It is not certain whether he meant this literally, but in any case a possible suggestion of his words would seem to be that the integers are God's thoughts which educated mankind is privileged to share. God's mind holds them in continuous existence as, according to Berkeley, God's mind holds physical things in continuous existence. It will be recalled that according to Leibniz the existence of eternal truths requires the existence of an eternal contemplator. The point of calling attention to this is that orinary language, which suggests the objective existence of universals, as common and independent objects of thought, is silent on the question as to whether universals depend for their existence on a divine thinker. A special argument therefore is required to show, if indeed it can be shown, that universals have an existence which is independent of contemplation by an eternal mind. It has already been argued that universals are necessary existents, objects which in principle and by their very nature cannot fail to exist. This makes it easy to show that God could not have created the integers, for that which cannot fail to exist could not have been created. Creation implies the coming into existence of a thing and a time prior to which it did not exist. It is also now a simple thing to show that universals do not depend for their existence on being thought. For that which exists in virtue of what it is could not depend for its existence on anything other than itself. Universals are necessary objects which may be eternally contemplated by a cosmic Mind, but the fact that they are constantly contemplated is a fact that is external to their own existence.

From the eternal and necessary existence of universals nothing can be inferred about the existence of an eternal mind. And neither can the existence of instances be inferred, which is to say that from the existence of universals the existence of nothing either supernatural or natural can be inferred. The latter can be seen to follow directly from the necessary existence of universals. In contrast to a universal, c.g., the universal *horse*, a natural object corresponding to it, that is, one of its instances, has only contingent existence. It is plain that what is contingent and could fail to exist cannot be inferred from that which has necessary existence. Expressed in terms of propositions, this comes to saying that a necessary proposition cannot imply a contingent one; for if the antecedent of an entailment is necessarily true, that is, has but one possible truth-value, and its consequent such that it could possibly be false, we should have the logical absurdity of there being no possible condition under which a contingent proposition could be false.

This can be seen from the following consideration. To suppose an entailment to hold between a necessary proposition p and a contingent proposition q is equivalent to supposing the impossibility of p being true jointly with the falsity of q:

$$\sim \Diamond (p \boldsymbol{.} \sim q)$$

The necessary truth of p eliminates p from making the conjunction impossible, so that it must be $\sim q$ that makes the conjunction impossible. But this means that, contrary to hypothesis, $\sim q$ is impossible, or alternatively, that q is necessarily true. So we have as a consequence that q, which by hypothesis is contingent, can under no condition be false. To express this in the notation used in Chapter 1:

$$\sim \Diamond (p . \sim q)$$
$$\sim \Diamond (\sim p)$$
$$\therefore \; \sim \Diamond (\sim q)$$

We now apply this consideration to the question whether the existence of a universal implies the existence of an instance of it. The proposition that universals have necessary existence implies the proposition that there necessarily are universals:

$$\sim \Diamond \sim (\exists \varphi) U \varphi$$

The proposition that the instances of universals like *horse* and *yellow* have contingent or non-necessary existence implies the proposition that it is possibly false that there are such instances:

$$\Diamond \sim (\exists x) \varphi x$$

It follows directly that the proposition $(\exists \varphi) U \varphi$ does not imply the corresponding proposition $(\exists x) \varphi x$. The general proposition, $(\varphi)(\exists x) \varphi x$, is contingent and cannot be inferred from the existence of universals. The doctrine that universals exist independently of instances was given the Latin tag, '*ante res*'.

The view developed here regarding the nature of the meanings of general words is essentially Platonic and has been advocated by a line of important thinkers up to the present day. It is important to realize that Plato used his theory to construct a special metaphysics about the nature of physical reality. The world of sense-given objects, as opposed to the supersensible realm of universals, is conceived of as an inferior copy of the world in which perfection resides. It may be useful to remark here that Plato's metaphysical thinking brings together the picture of the world as depicted by Heraclitus and that depicted by Parmenides, the ever-flowing and the changeless. In the *Timaeus* (Sec. 52) Plato says, '... there is one kind of being which is always the same, uncreated and indestructible ... invisible and imperceptible by any sense ... And there is another nature of the same name with it, and like to it, perceived by sense, created, always in motion, becoming in place and again vanishing out of place, which is apprehended by opinion and sense'. Of the latter there can be opinion only, but of the former, exact knowledge. (It is noteworthy that the Platonic theory which assigns opinion to the world of sense is embedded in the sophisticated doctrines of such philosophers as A. J. Ayer and Hans Reichenbach, according to whom knowledge of the existence of things necessarily falls short of cerrtainty, our beliefs with regard to things being at most probable hypotheses.) Some mathematicians have described their work as reporting discoveries in the kind of being that is always the same. Thus, G. H. Hardy represents the mathematician as a cartographer of the realm of eternal and intelligible objects, the realm of abstract entities: 'I have myself always thought of a mathematician as in the first instance an *observer*, a man who gazes at a distant range of mountains and notes down his observations. His job is simply to distinguish clearly and notify to others as many different peaks as he can...' (1929, p. 18).

It is worth pointing out that Plato held two special theories about the nature of universals and their relationship to particular things. These theories require some discussion, not so much because of their historical importance as because they are still very much alive in the minds of contemporary philosophers. They are theories which are not only about the nature of universals but also about the nature of predication. Before embarking on an explanation of the two theories, the ideal-copy theory and the essence-participation theory – both of these theories are expounded and subjected to a subtle critique in the *Parmenides* – it needs to be pointed out that no important difference is to be marked between universals which are designated by general nouns, or substantives, and those designated by adjectives. The basic point of identity between them is that each kind of universal is capable of having instances, which is to say that universals of each type can count as common properties, properties which can characterize a plurality of things. A universal which is capable of having instances is said to characterize its instances: Thus, the universal *man* characterizes Alcibiades and Russell, which instantiate it, and the universal *cerise* characterizes color patches, which instantiate it. To say that there are three men is to say there are three things characterized by the common property *being a man*, and to say that there are three cerise things is to say there are three things characterized by the common property *being cerise*.

The most famous and controversial of the two special theories about

11

universals is the so-called Ideal theory according to which universals are ideally perfect things of their kind. On this view the universal *man* is an ideally perfect man and the universal *horse* an ideally perfect horse. And to characterize a thing as being a man or a horse is to assert a likeness to the exemplar: For a thing to be characterized by the attribute *horse* is for that thing to resemble the perfect horse in the Platonic pantheon of universals. The other theory represents a universal as being an essence the presence of which in a thing gives it its specific character. An essence may be viewed as a sort of ingredient, which when present in a thing contributes to its nature. Thus, the nature of a concrete thing is constituted by a set of essences, and the ascription of an attribute to a thing is viewed as the attribute's being in some way present in the thing. Wittgenstein compared the relationship holding, according to Plato, between a property of things and the things it characterizes with the relationship of alcohol to wine, beer, and the like (1958, p. 17). Like alcohol which can exist in a pure state, an essence can exist without being present in anything, and it can be an 'ingredient' in a number of different things. It has to be understood, of course, that an essence, which is an abstract entity, is not present in a thing in the way in which a physical ingredient is. Each of the two special Platonic theories poses difficulties, particularly the Ideal theory.

The Ideal theory carries with it poetic appeal, but does not seem to withstand criticism. An ancient refutation which Plato himself stated – this is thought to have been first formulated by a Sophist named Bryson – was the so-called argument of the third man. This argument purports to show that the Ideal-copy theory implies the existence of an infinite number of things, ideally perfect, of any given kind. The statement 'Socrates is a man' is on this theory equivalent to 'Socrates resembles the ideally perfect man'. Now two things resemble each other in virtue of having a common property. In the case of the resemblance between Socrates and the ideal man this is the property *man*, the resemblance implying both that Socrates is a man and that the ideal man is a man. This further property *man* has to be viewed as itself a second ideal man which both Socrates and the first ideal man resemble, etc. *ad infinitum*. The Ideal theory according to the argument of the third man overpopulates the cosmos with ideal things. Depending on whether one rejects the notion of the actual infinite or not, this argument will seem to be conclusive or not wholly conclusive, although admittedly the consequence is bizarre.

The important consequence which may be drawn from the Ideal theory has never been stated in a clear way, and it constitutes an overwhelming objection which is independent of the objection that the theory generates an infinite number of things of any given kind. This objection, instead of showing the Ideal theory to imply that an infinite number of things must exist, shows it to imply that nothing exists. It will be clear to begin with that according to the Ideal theory the property designated by a general word will be a thing in the same way in which a member of the denotation of the word is a thing, differing only in respect of perfection. The Ideal theory has been discussed in connection with the general question as to whether a property can be a predicate of itself. Without going into this general question, it can be seen that if a property is self-predicating the property itself will fall into the range of its own instances. If the attribute *man* is self-predicating then it will be a man regardless of particular ways in which it differs from ordinary men. It will be an instance along with whatever other instances there are. To refer back to the Mill distinction between the connotation and the denotation of a general word, the connotation of a word, on the Ideal theory, becomes a member of its denotation, with the consequence that general words have only a denotation. This consequence is unacceptable because without having a connotation a general word cannot have a denotation. Put differently, the conclusion forced upon us by the Ideal theory is that there can be no things, whether imperfect or perfect. For the theory implies that there are *no properties:* Every property on this theory becomes a thing of the kind to which things having that property belong. But if every property is a particular thing, there will be no properties. If the word 'man' is the general name of each of a number of things, one of which is the property the word supposedly stands for, then the term designates no property and it has no connotation. The property becomes a particular amongst the things in the denotation of the term and cannot itself be that which is common to all of them. The further implication is that there can be no things – no horses, men, red roses, etc. – because without properties there can be no things. To suppose that things exist in the absence of properties is to embrace the absurdity that things are propertyless. The notion of a propertyless thing is nothing but a conceptual blank. To be a concrete thing is to be characterized by properties. In general we may say that to be a thing is to be an instance of a universal. This is the ontological correlate of the thesis that a general word cannot have a denotation without a connotation.

The essence-participation theory contains a number of difficulties, and

11*

it undoubtedly stands in need of clarification. Wittgenstein's analogy of an essence with a pure substance which can be a physical ingredient in other substances shows that there is a tendency to think of Platonic universals, or abstract entities, as being physical objects which are capable of entering into combinations with other physical objects. In this vein a philosophical logician has written: 'It is convenient ... to regard such general terms ['wise', 'city'] as names on the same footing as "Socrates" and "Paris", names each of a single specific entity, though a less tangible entity than the man Socrates or the town Boston.' (Quine 1965, p. 119). Now abstract entities are not physical objects, and it should be pointed out that they are not *less* tangible than physical objects. They are intangible entities, capabl of being grasped only by the intelligence. This is the nature of an *abstract* entity, that which is itself not concrete but can be shared by many concrete particular things. To refer back to the legendary exchange between Diogenes and Plato, the unkind comment about Diogenes' inability to see cuphood, that it showed only that he had not the understanding to discern universals, brings out the point that universals are discerned by the mind. To put the matter somewhat differently, the connotation of a general word is grasped by the understanding, and serves as a guide for the correct application of a general word, but unlike either the word which has that connotation or the things constituting its denotation it is intangible to the senses.

The Platonic view that universals characterize things but can exist in the absence of things implies the view that properties can exist even when in fact they are not the common properties of things. This view, which bears the label *ante res*, was opposed by Aristotle who held what is called the theory of the concrete universal – the theory that universals are *in res*. On this view 'no universal exists apart from its individuals' (*Metaphysics*, Bk. Z, 16). Russell has given the following account of Aristotle's position: 'Suppose I say "there is such a thing as the game of football", most people would regard the remark as a truism. But if I were to infer that football could exist without football-players, I should rightly be held to be talking nonsense. Similarly, it would be held, there is such a thing as parenthood, but only because there are parents; there is such a thing as sweetness, but only because there are sweet things; and there is redness, but only because there are red things. And this dependence is thought to be not reciprocal: The men who play football would still exist even if they never played football; things which are usually sweet may turn sour... (1945, p. 163).

Aristotle's view of universals is that they are properties which may have a multiplicity of instances, that is, be common properties, but which require for their own existence at least one instance. One philosopher has asked the question whether we *need* universals without instances, and Aristotle's answer to this question might well have been that there can be no need for that which is inconceivable. The theory of the concrete universal is that it is logically impossible for there to be an unexemplified universal. It should be pointed out that Aristotle rejects the Ideal theory which implies that a universal is a substance, something which has independent existence. And his primary objection to the essence theory seems to be that it too represents a universal as being a substance. Descartes said that substance is something 'which requires nothing but itself to exist', and in accordance with this account of substance, the Platonic essence view implies that a universal is a substance, just as alcohol is a substance on a footing with liquids in which it is an ingredient. To many thinkers the view that a universal is a kind of entity seems to be a flight of metaphysics, and the Aristotelian view which maintains that universals are common features of things seems down to earth and appeals to common sense.

The background objection against viewing a universal as having substantive existence may be the result of a *Gedankenexperiment*. As will be remembered, Wittgenstein invites us to try to think of the meaning of a word without thinking of the word. The implied outcome is that nothing remains to be thought, that the meaning of a word cannot be thought apart from the word. A comparable *Gedankenexperiment* of trying to think of an attribute without at the same time thinking of particular instances would seem to have a similar result. Diogenes' complaint may very well have been a witty way of saying that universals cannot be thought apart from things: Cuphood can only be thought of in terms of specific cups and not by itself. What in a general way can be inferred from this *Gedankenexperiment* is not at all clear, but it would seem to show that it is *psychologically* impossible for some people to think of a universal without representing to themselves instances. However, the fact that this is psychologically impossible for some and perhaps even all people does not show a logical impossibility. It does not show that a universal cannot in principle exist apart from instances. Russell has given the following explanation of how people come to overlook universals: 'We do not naturally dwell upon those words in a sentence which do not stand for particulars; and if we are forced to dwell upon a word which stands for a universal, we naturally think of it as standing for some one of the particulars that come under the universal. When, for example, we hear the sentence, "Charles I's head was cut off", we may naturally enough think of Charles I, of Charles I's head, and of the operation of cutting off *his* head, which are all particulars; but we do not naturally dwell upon what is meant by the word "head", or the word "cut", which is a universal' (1943, pp. 146–147).

This may very well explain why Diogenes could think of cups but not of cuphood, but whether or not it is the correct explanation, a simple consideration shows that a universal can exist apart from its individuals, regardless of whether people can entertain it independently. The Aristotelian view can be reformulated in the following way. The meaning of a general word like 'horse' or 'yellow' is a feature common to all those things to which the word is correctly applicable. Its meaning is, in other words, a property, and the implication of the view that a property cannot exist without being a property of something is that a general word loses its literal meaning when its denotation becomes null. In order for 'horse' or 'yellow' to have a meaning there must be at least one thing to which it correctly applies: 'No property without instances' is paralleled by 'no literally significant general word without a denotation'. The consequence of this view is logically unacceptable. It follows that such a sentence as 'There is at least one horse', which is normally taken to express a contingent proposition, one which could be false, expresses instead a necessarily true proposition. And the sentence 'There are no horses', instead of expressing a false empirical proposition, expresses one which is logically impossible. In order for the first sentence to express a proposition the term 'horse' must have a meaning, that is, must stand for a property, and on the Aristotelian view there must be things characterized by the property. Hence the proposition expressed by the sentence will have to be true: To assert that there are horses is to assert that what must have an instance has one. The second sentence, which denies the existence of horses, will, if it expresses a proposition, express one which implies a contradiction: The attribute will imply the existence of an individual which the proposition denies. On the Aristotelian view the sentence 'There are no dinosaurs' will either be devoid of literal intelligibility, that is, express no proposition at all, or express a self-contradictory proposition.

As an additional point, it is to be remarked that mathematics goes against the traditional Aristotelian doctrine, as the following consideration indicates. The particles constituting the sum total of reality will answer to some number, and however great this number is there will be a greater. The latter number will be unexemplified – a universal *ante res*. Again, it is to be noted that the empirical premise asserting the existence of a number of actual particles is not required for the conclusion. It is only required that it be possible for the total number of particles to answer to some number. There will then be some number greater than it. To put the matter somewhat differently, the number of possible things is greater than the number of actual things, and this number will be an unexemplified universal.

It is an interesting thing that the Aristotelian view which is represented by many philosophers as appealing to common sense is a kind of hidden return to the Parmenidean thesis: One cannot think of what does not exist. It is also interesting to note the accord between the Aristotelian theory and the so-called traditional square of opposition. It can be demonstrated from the square that at least one thing of every conceivable kind exists. Classical logic, which was given its original formulation by Aristotle, makes possible the demonstration of the proposition

$$(\varphi)(\exists x)\varphi x$$

For discussion of this, see Ambrose and Lazerowitz, 1962, pp. 191–5, and for a contrary view, see Hart, 1951.) Some philosophers have rejected the general theory that there are such entities as universals, both in the form given it by Plato and in the form given it by Aristotle, and have attempted to explain what it is for a general word to have a meaning without invoking them. It may be observed immediately, even before stating the various alternative theories, that the arguments *for* the general theory concerning abstract entities are also arguments against alternative theories. It is important, however, to state the various alternative theories, for their intrinsic interest amongst other things, and it is important also to see what special critiques they can be subjected to. It will have been noticed that the argument against the Aristotelian theory was not included in the arguments presented for the general theory of the abstract universal.

There are four major alternative theories which need to be considered. One of these, which is inspired by an attempt to avoid universals, will be recognized as the theory which H. H. Price calls the Philosophy of Resemblance. Russell has described the attempt in the following passage: 'If we wish to avoid the universals "whiteness" and "triangularity", we shall choose some particular patch of white and some particular triangle, and say that anything is white or a triangle if it has the right sort of resemblance to our chosen particular' (1943, p. 150). Another, related theory holds that what is normally taken, in conformity with everyday usage, to be a common property, that is, one property shared by a number of distinct particulars, is a group of entities as particular and individual as the things it is said to characterize, the relation of resemblance holding between the particular characteristics as well as between the things of which they are the characteristics. The resemblance between things will be derivative from the resemblance between their particular characteristics: 'Two things resemble each other in a certain respect' will mean on this account that each is characterized by an individual characteristic which is like the individual characteristic possessed by the other.

This type of view has sometimes been held in association with a position called nominalism. Hobbes held that particulars are called by the same name because of a resemblance between them, and declared that there is 'nothing in the world universal but names; for the things named are every one of them individual and singular' (1909, Ch. 4, p. 26). The extreme form of nominalism, which sets it off from any resemblance view regarding the meanings of general words, asserts that all that is common to a group of particulars falling under a common name is the name. On this view to say that things have a common property is equivalent to saying that they are called by the same name.

A further view, called conceptualism, which might seem to be more consonant with common sense than extreme nominalism, maintains that the meanings of words are thoughts, or to use Locke's colorful expression, 'creatures of the understanding'. A somewhat extended passage from his *Essay concerning human understanding* gives as clear a statement of the general position as is to be found in the literature: 'Words are general, as has been said, when used for signs of general ideas; and so are applicable indifferently to many particular things: and ideas are general when they are set up as the representatives of many particular things: but universality belongs not to things themselves, which are all of them particular in their existence, even those words and ideas which in their signification are general. When therefore we quit particulars, the generals that rest are only creatures of our own making, their general nature being nothing but the capacity they are put into by the understanding, of signifying or representing many particulars. For the signification they have is nothing but a relation that by the mind of man is added to them' (Bk. III, Ch. 3).

To take up the first of the resemblance theories, according to which a general word applies to each of a number of things because of a resemblance they bear to an initially chosen thing, or to use Price's term, an exemplar. A background reason for this view is the equivalence between the notion of things having a common property and the notion of their being similar to each other in some way or other. To say that x and y have a common property φ is to imply that x and y are similar in a certain respect, and to say x and y are similar is to imply that they have a property in common. It will be remembered that the argument of the third man made use of the notion that resembling things share a common property. The equivalence between possession by things of a common property and resemblance between them is taken to show that the fact that a number of things have a property in common is nothing over and above the fact that they resemble each other in a certain respect. It is, in other words, taken to show that having a common property *reduces* to the things being similar to each other. Some philosophers have fortified this reduction thesis with the claim that things that fall under a common designation may be more or less similar without a discernible thread of identity running through them. Thus, Wittgenstein invites us to inspect the various things that are called games: 'What is common to them all? [board-games, card-games, ball-games, Olympic games] – Don't say "There *must* be something common, or they would not be called 'games' " – but *look and see* whether there is anything common to all. – For if you look at them you will not see something that is common to *all*, but similarities, relationships, and a whole series of them at that' (1953, p. 31). Even in those cases in which things are exactly similar, a philosopher who holds to the resemblance theory would maintain that their having a common property in virtue of which they exactly resemble each other vanishes into their resembling each other. There are things and there are resemblances between things, and there are no entities which are the common possession of the things. As Price put it, 'There are just particular objects, and there is nothing non-particular which is "in" them, in the way that a universal is supposed to be "in" the particulars which are its instances' (1953, p. 22).

One implication of this view would seem clear: A general word, whether an adjective or a class nam, eapplies to each of a number of things in virtue of their resembling each other. Now since a resemblance between things cannot, on the theory, exist apart from things, it will follow that in order for a general word to have a meaning there must be things to which it applies. And no general word would have a meaning, or connotation, without a denotation. The criticism that applies to the Aristotelian view of the concrete universal applies equally to the present position. The sentence, 'Nothing is cerise, neither mental images nor things', becomes on this view either meaningless or self-contradictory. If it is true to say that nothing whatever is cerise, the term 'cerise' will have to have a meaning in the sentence, and this would imply the existence of cerise things. Hence the proposition would have to be false. Better still, we might say the sentence cannot be both intelligible and express a truth. If what the sentence says is true, namely, that there are no cerise things (which certainly is conceivable), the word 'cerise' will be meaningless and the sentence unintelligible. If what it says is false, i.e., if the sentence 'there are cerise things' says what is true, this latter sentence will express a proposition which *cannot* be false, which is absurd.

The sober truth is that it is possible for nothing to be cerise and that we can give intelligible verbal expression to this fact. At this moment of writing on a white sheet of paper I am neither seeing a cerise thing nor am I having a cerise image, and the thought has just occurred to me that for all I know nothing is cerise at this moment. If this is a possible thought, which it assuredly is, then the sentence 'Nothing whatever is cerise' is both intelligible and expresses what could be the case. The implication is that color words, and all general words, are capable of having a connotation in the absence of a denotation. Berkeley, who held that everything is particular gave an explanation of general ideas which seems to deny this: '. . . an idea, which considered in itself is particular, becomes general, by being made to represent or stand for all other particular ideas of the same sort (1871, Intr., Sec. 12). It is natural, indeed, to think that when we understand a color word we have an appropriate image in our minds, that understanding a color word comes down to a mental occurrence of this sort. About this Wittgenstein has made several important observations: 'If I give someone the order "fetch me a red flower from that meadow", how is he to know what sort of flower to bring. . . ? Now the answer one might suggest first is that he went to look for a red flower carrying a red image in his mind, and comparing it with the flowers to see which of them had the colour of the image. Now there is such a way of searching . . . But this is not the only way of searching and it isn't the usual way. We go, look about us, walk up to a flower and pick it, without comparing it to anything. To see that the process of obeying the order can be of this kind, consider the order "*imagine* a red patch". You are not tempted in this case to think that *before* obeying you must have imagined a red patch to serve you as a pattern for the red patch which you were ordered to imagine' (1958, p. 3). It is of course possible to try to visualize a certain color in its absence, i.e., to try to reproduce in the imagination a color that has been seen. Undoubtedly everyone has had the experience of trying to call up a color-image corresponding to a certain word *w*; and there can be no doubt that a person who tries to call up an image to which *w* applies knows the meaning of *w* apart from any examples to which it applies. Its meaning therefore cannot be identified with any part of its denotation, which is to say, against the Berkeleian view, that a particular idea, which belongs to the denotation of a word, cannot count as its meaning by making it 'represent or stand for all other particular ideas of the same sort'.

It is permissible to conjecture what the underlying mistake is which is responsible for this view. It would seem to be that some philosophers have identified the two terms 'ostensive definition of a word' and 'meaning of a word'. Color words like 'yellow' and 'cerise' (as well as words for shapes, odors, and the like) are taught ostensively, by exhibiting a number of their applications, that is, by displaying part of their denotation. And it is perhaps natural to think that the applications of the word are its meaning. But however natural, it is mistaken. For the denotation of a term, as has been said several times over, cannot be identified with its connotation... From the fact that a given word has only an ostensive definition in the language it follows that there *have been* instances to which the word correctly applies, but it does not follow that there *are* instances to which it correctly applies. And it follows that a word like 'yellow', which in order to be taught must have a denotation, does not lose its meaning for those to whom it has been taught when its denotation becomes null.

The resemblance view just discussed appeals to many thinkers as avoiding occult entities and as being unmetaphysical. The remaining resemblance view to be discussed seems also to be, at least in part, a reaction against a metaphysical view of common properties which represents them as being abstract entities existing in their own right. Although this resemblance view does not deny that in addition to concrete things there are properties characterizing them, it does deny that there are properties which are not the properties of things. Now in conformity with the anti-metaphysical formula that everything is particular and individual, this view is to the effect that the property a thing is said to have is just as particular and individual as the thing it characterizes. A common property, for example the property of being yellow, which ordinarily would be said to belong to a number of things, e.g., a mental image, an Easter egg, and a daffodil, on this view divides into particular characteristics each of which characterizes only one thing. The yellow color which characterizes the daffodil is numerically distinct from the yellow color which characterizes the Easter egg, which in turn is numerically distinct from the yellow color which characterizes the mental image, even though all color characteristics are exactly similar. Each thing will have its own particular yellow, and there will be no fewer characteristics of a given kind than there are things. A decrease in the number of things will entail a decrease in the number of characteristics. No two things can have one and the same property. If, for example, there are three billiard balls on a pool table, one white and two yellow, there will be three numerically distinct color characteristics, two of which are similar to each other and both of which are unlike the third. This view may be summed up in the words, 'The characteristics of particular things are themselves particular and not universal'. (For a full discussion, see the symposium, 'Are the characteristics of particular things universal or particular?', by G. E. Moore, G. F. Stout, and G. Dawes Hicks, 1923.)

One thing about this view cannot fail to escape the notice of anyone, and this is that it goes against ordinary language in obvious ways. If an ordinary person unacquainted with philosophy, or for that matter, a philosopher unacquainted with this theory, were to be told that there are two sheets of paper on the table each with its own whiteness he would naturally think the two sheets differed somewhat in respect of their color. And if, further, he were told that they did not differ in color but that nevertheless each had its own whiteness, he would be at a total loss. He would not understand the language that was being used. Before this usage can be understood by someone not acquainted with the theory, the usage has to be explained. The theory does not come out of ordinary usage and in fact goes against common-property talk. There is nothing linguistically odd about saying that each of three people has his own particular billiard ball, but there is a linguistic peculiarity about saying that each billiard ball has its own particular whiteness and roundness. To bring out the same linguistic point in one further connection, there is nothing odd about saying that a certain surface is the same color all over, but there is something odd about saying that if the surface were divided into smaller sections there would be as many colors as there were sections.

Apart from considerations of language it will be clear that the objection which applies to the resemblance theory according to which possession of a common property by things *reduces* to their resembling each other in a certain way, also applies to the view according to which the things have resembling properties. A particular color characteristic cannot survive its bearer, so that the nonexistence of yellow things, for example, would entail the nonexistence of the property *yellow* itself. There are of course many yellow things, but if they were all to vanish without being replaced by other yellow things there would be no property which could serve as the meaning of the word 'yellow'. In the absence of all yellow things – yellow images, yellow daffodils, etc., the word 'yellow' loses its literal meaning. Whether the word has a meaning thus depends on whether there are elements in its denotation. The connotation of a word is nothing in addition to its denotation, and when the denotation becomes null its connotation vanishes and the word loses its function in the language. The paradox is that in order to determine whether the word has a meaning we have to examine things without knowing what to look for: Not finding appropriate instances implies that the word has no meaning, which is to say that we have no notion of what an appropriate instance would be and therefore could not intelligibly say that the things examined are not instances. A consequence already familiar emerges. A sentence such as 'Nothing is yellow', if it says what is in fact true, must be meaningless. It certainly cannot count in favor of a view that an ordinary sentence which happens to assert a falsehood but which under a certain circumstance would assert what is true would be condemned by that circumstance to be literally unintelligible.

The view suffers from a further difficulty which the first resemblance view is free from. It implies an infinite regress of characteristics comparable to the infinite regress generated by the third man argument against the Ideal theory. The usual view offered in explanation of similarities existing between things is that they have properties in common. It has been already noted that this is reflected in ordinary language. On the first resemblance view common-property talk is suppressed in favor of resemblance talk, that is, talk about resemblances between things. On the second view common-property talk is suppressed in favor of talk about individual characteristics. The second view presumably attempts to explain similarities between things in terms of their having like individual characteristics. Such a fact as that two billiard balls are similar in respect of the color yellow is explained by the similarity between their two color characteristics. The similarity between the characteristics, which are themselves particular, must, it would seem clear, have a comparable explanation. The characteristics themselves will be similar in virtue of having resembling characteristics, and these in turn will resemble each other, and thus have particular resembling characteristics, etc., *ad infinitum.*

The philosophical motivation behind both resemblance views is the wish to avoid abstract entities, entities which are not possible objects of sense. Both views presuppose the tenet that every existent is individual and particular. And its extreme outcome is the form of Nominalism according to which all that is common to the things to which a general word applies is their name; things that are called by the same name have only their general name in common. On this view the function of a general word like 'horse' contracts into the function of a proper name like 'Dobbin'. In consequence, just as being told that the proper name of each of several horses is 'Dobbin' does not enable us to go on to pick out other horses bearing that name, so being told that the general name of each of a number of things is 'horse' would not enable us to pick out new animals to which the word correctly applies. If we are told that *all* that a number of things called by a given name have in common is their name, then since the names of things are not integral to the things, we should not be able to go on to apply the word to new things which in fact fall under that name. When God paraded the animals before Adam and let him name them, the animals did not come already labelled and the labels given did not contain anything which would identify their future bearers. But if in naming the animals he were giving them proper names which functioned like his own, then each new application of the name to an animal would constitute a new arbitrary linguistic convention. This flouts known fact about the use of general terms and their difference from proper names.

The force of the tenet that everything is individual and particular is to bar from existence anything which smacks of the supersensible, anything which transcends the bounds of sense. But this anti-metaphysical recipe itself may have no more substantial foundation than preference and bias. Prof. Alonzo Church, who takes the position that there are abstract entities, has defended his position as follows:

'To those who object to the introduction of abstract entities at all I would say that I believe that there are more important criteria by which a theory should be judged. The extreme demand for a simple prohibition of abstract entities under all circumstances perhaps arises from a desire to maintain the connection between theory and observation. But the preference of (say) *seeing* over *understanding* seems to me capricious. For just as an opaque body may be seen, so a concept may be understood or grasped. And the parallel between the two cases is indeed rather close. In both cases the observation is not direct but through intermediaries – light, lens of eye or optical instrument, and retina in the case of the visible body, linguistic expressions in the case of the concept' (1951, p. 104).

One further view remains to be considered, conceptualism. Locke, perhaps its most important advocate, held that there are genuinely abstract ideas, ideas which are not, as Berkeley held, just particular ideas that are made to stand for other particular ideas of the same sort. In this respect he is in agreement with the kind of point made by Church. Abstract ideas on Locke's account are creatures of the mind; but they differ from such creatures of the mind as inventions of the imagination in not being particular. They are incapable of being given to the senses and can only be objects of the understanding. Interestingly enough, Locke developed his form of conceptualism under the ontological thesis that 'all things that exist are only particulars'. Now the view that there are abstract ideas, in conjunction with the ontological thesis that every existent thing is particular, implies, among other things, that abstract ideas do not have objective existence. And as a place had to be found for them, Locke relegated them to the mind. But as it turns out, the mind cannot house them either, for the particularity thesis bars them from existence altogether. To use an expression from Wittgenstein, the thesis leaves no 'logical space' for them. Ayer, who rejected universals on grounds comparable to those of Diogenes, remarked that a nonempirical world had to be invented to house them (1951, p. 43). Although Locke's home for abstract ideas is not an invention, his particularity thesis prevents it from offering them ontological sanctuary.

It is not difficult to see how it is that the thesis that everything that exists is particular prevents the existence of abstract ideas not only in objective reality but also in the sphere of the mental. If nothing can exist which is not particular, then nothing which is not particular can exist in a mind. The particularity thesis is incompatible with the existence of abstract ideas, regardless of domain. A modern philosophical logician in a symposium on universals wrote: 'When we know things, we frame in our minds certain images, concepts, etc. It must be stressed that those subjective entities are *real*, consequently individual, being parts of an individual mind' (Bochenski, 1956). It would seem to be a *non sequitur* to urge that a *concept* is not abstract because it is in an individual mind, but the argument that since a concept is *real* it is individual appears to make use of the particularity thesis to infer that concepts are individual. The point comes out clearly if for 'real' we substitute 'exists'. Then the philosophical claim with regard to concepts is that since they exist they are particular and not abstract. The alternative to the implication that concepts are particular is that they do not exist, and this is the conclusion one would normally come to.

The inconsistency between Locke's conceptualism and the particularity thesis should not go unnoticed, although the inconsistency by itself does not show that there are no abstract entities. If the thesis is true, the Lockeian form of conceptualism is false, but then Lockeian conceptualism may be true and the thesis false. Conceptualism has to be considered on its own merits. It is, however, pertinent to observe that the arguments for the theory of the abstract universal, if correct, upset the thesis, taken as a generalization about ontology. It will be remembered that against the literal interpretation of Kronecker's statement that God made the integers it was argued that numbers, having necessary existence, could not have been created. Numbers cannot be the creatures of a mind, whether divine or not. Their existence in a mind, or as objects of a mind, will, on this argument, also be necessary and consequently not be dependent on a mind. The same considerations hold for attributes in general.

It is not easy to get a clear view of conceptualism, but it does seem to deny that there are such things as common properties, properties which can be shared by a number of things and are not less objective than things themselves. The position ends up with abstract ideas which are shadowy substitutes for common properties. On Locke's account 'Ideas become general by separating from them the circumstances of time and place, and by any other ideas that may determine them to this or that particular existence. By this way of abstraction they are made capable of representing more individuals than one...' (1928, Bk. III, Ch. 3, Sec. 6). But the idea which represents a number of individuals is not an attribute of the individuals, that is, not a common property. Instead, it is an idea, or a concept, which is in the mind. The basic argument for Lockeian conceptualism is the so-called vagueness consideration. The point of this argument is to show that common properties which, if they existed, could be made the connotations of general words, do not exist and thus that the connotation of a word like 'horse' or 'yellow' which makes the word applicable to each of a number of things must be an abstract *idea*. The general word 'horse' has applications which are unquestionably correct, and there is a range of things to which its application is unquestionably incorrect. But in addition there is a range of things, actual or easily imagined, to which it is neither definitely and clearly correct nor definitely and clearly incorrect to apply the term. To illustrate, in a fairy tale a prince is changed by magic into a swan. Suppose the transformation from man to swan to be gradual and continuous. The word 'man' unquestionably applies to the prince before the onset of the change, and unquestionably fails to apply to the final result to which the word 'swan' unquestionably applies. But quite plainly there will be stages in the process of change with regard to which we should hesitate more and more to apply the word 'man', and stages with regard to which we should hesitate less and less to withhold applying the word 'swan'. This consideration would seem to show that the words 'man' and 'swan' do not have sharply defined boundaries, and this fact is taken to imply that the connotations of the words cannot be a common property which an examination of any object in its range of denotation will show it either to have or not to have.

Anything can be imagined gradually changing into some other thing, however different, a cow into a humming bird, and a drop of water into wax. And what can be imagined shows something about the use of common names: It shows that there are no sharp lines dividing things into two mutually exclusive and jointly exhaustive classes, those to which they apply and those to which they do not apply. Thus Locke wrote: 'For I demand, what are the alterations [which] may or may not be in a horse or lead, without making either of them to be of another species ... he will never be able to know when anything precisely ceases to be of the species of a horse or lead.' (1928, Bk. III, Ch. 3, Sec. 13). Locke's consideration also applies to words for colors, shapes, odors, etc. For exemplar colors given on color charts have vague boundaries: In a color continuum they imperceptibly shade into adjacent colors. The idea that emerges from this sort of consideration is that if there were properties which a number of things might share in and which were distinct from the things, there could be no undecidable cases. If φ is a property which could be thought of by itself apart from things it characterizes, it should always be possible to decide whether a given thing is an instance of it or not: There could be no things with regard to which it could not be definitely said that they have φ or fail to have it. If there were independent and common properties which existed as entities in their own right, the law

12

of excluded middle should apply without possible exceptions, and since it does not, the conclusion drawn is that there are no such things as common properties. What we call common properties are merely general ideas which the mind uses to classify things.

It cannot be doubted that the vagueness which inheres in our use of general words stands in need of explanation. But neither can it be doubted that general words are used to describe things, and that to describe things is to mention attributes which give them their character. It is also not subject to serious question that by means of general words we are able to describe things which no longer exist, or things which, like griffins, have never existed. The employment of language to describe what does not in fact exist, like the employment of language to describe things which do exist, also mentions attributes, in these cases attributes or sets of attributes which are not to be found in anything. The explanation of vagueness in our terminology will have to take this into account rather than explaining common properties out of existence. Wittgenstein gives us the therapeutic prescription to use the expression 'use of a word' in place of 'meaning of a word', undoubtedly because the first does not suggest an entity whereas the second does. In apparent agreement with this prescription some philosophers have observed that from the fact that a word has a meaning we tend to make the 'mistaken' inference that it means *something*. But although the injunction to substitute one form of words for another may help us avoid talk about universals, it does not enable us to dispense with them. The use of a general word to describe a thing, actual or imagined, involves mentioning an objective property, something which falls under the general designation 'meaning of a word': The property mentioned *is* the meaning of the word. Replacing 'meaning of a word' by 'use of a word' is a verbal way of avoiding the idea that meanings are abstract entities, but we may say it is an avoidance by a sort of failure of acknowledgement. For one cannot know the use of a general name without knowing its meaning, and as has been seen, the meaning of a general name is a common property which must guide our use of the word.

DOUBTS AND QUERIES

1. Russell has at times held that there are no universals and at other times that there are universals and that he has direct acquaintance with many of them. The question naturally arises, 'Why should someone think on

one occasion that there are such supersensible entities of which he has direct knowledge and at other times that there are none?' Is this a psychological question? Russell epitomizes within himself a historical disagreement among philosophers over the existence of universals, about which the same question arises. One thing that goes against this disagreement having a psychological explanation is that it has continued between so many philosophers over so many hundreds of years. It is unconvincing, as was Plato's rejoinder to Diogenes, to say that some people apprehend universals and others do not, that some people have a mental blind spot for them and others not. If we adopt this solution we should have to say that Russell had his blind spot on and off. When we ask for an explanation of the disagreement over the existence of universals, what sort of information is being requested, psychological, factual, or linguistic?

Does Church's claim that we apprehend abstract entities indirectly, through the intermediary of language, help explain the disagreement and its intractable persistence? Does his statement conflict with Russell's claim made on a number of occasions, to have direct acquaintance with them? How is this disagreement about the way in which universals are grasped to be explained?

To say that abstract entities are apprehended indirectly would seem to imply that we know the meanings of words indirectly. What does it mean to say the meanings of words are grasped indirectly? Is grasping the meaning indirectly comparable to seeing an object through a periscope? An object seen by this means could be seen with the naked eye. Could the meaning of a word which is grasped indirectly be grasped directly? What in addition to the way we grasp meanings in understanding words would be required to grasp the meanings directly?

Would understanding the sentence 'There is one and only one prime number between 32 and 40', without knowing what the prime number is, be a case of grasping the meaning of a phrase (here, 'prime and between 32 and 40') indirectly ? Does learning what the specific prime number is constitute acquiring direct knowledge of the meaning of the phrase? Obviously, if *all* meanings of expressions were known indirectly, the meaning of the name of the particular prime would also be grasped indirectly. Does Church's use of 'indirect' violate Wittgenstein's dictum that neither member of a pair of antithetical terms can function if the other loses its function? If all known meanings of terms are known indirectly, does 'indirectly' become a redundant term?

12*

According to Plato a general word is the common name of a number of things in virtue of the 'form' they have in common. When he charged Diogenes with not having the understanding with which to discern forms, did his observation imply that Diogenes was unable to use general words? If, as undoubtedly was the case, he knew how to use general words, why did Plato's charge not awaken his mind to the presence of universals? If the meaning of a word is a universal and Diogenes knew the meanings of words, how could he be unaware of universals?

In agreement with one Platonic theory Russell says that we apply a general word to each of a number of things 'because they all partake in a common nature or essence' (1943, p. 143) Does this imply that Russell could use general words when he was able to grasp universals and that he lost this ability when he developed blindness to universals? I.e., is Russell's on-and-off blindness paralleled by an on-and-off ability to use general words? If not, how is the continuous ability to use general words to be explained? Pragmatists have held that a theory in order to be genuine must make some practical difference, a difference which will eventually manifest itself in behavior, etc. Russell's philosophical views about universals seem to have had no discernible effect on his actual use of language. Does the rejection of the theory of universals on pragmatic grounds mean that the theory is false, or that it is literally senseless as some logical positivists have maintained?

2. It is important philosophically to bring conventionalism into connection with arguments which profess to show that universals can exist independently of language. Conventionalism is the doctrine according to which necessary statements record usage (see Ayer, 1951, Ch. 4). The statement 'Relations are not particulars, but universals', which Ayer takes to be necessary, he says is 'simply about words' (1951, p. 58). A circumspect way of expressing conventionalism is to say a sentence which expresses an *a priori* proposition, one about what is logically possible, logically impossible, or logically necessary, conveys only information about the use of expressions in the language in which the sentence occurs. For example, about the sentence expressing a logical necessity, 'Nothing can be colored in different ways at the same time with respect to the same part of itself', Ayer states: 'I am not saying anything about the properties of any actual thing ... I am expressing an analytic proposition, which records our determination to call a colour expanse which differs in quality from a neighbouring expanse a different part of a given thing,' (1951, p. 79). To sum up conventionalism without

attempting to be complete, statements about logical impossibility convey information to the effect that certain expressions lack use, statements about logical necessity convey information about relationships between the use of expressions, statements expressing logical possibilities convey information to the effect that certain expressions have a use in the language. It was argued that it is logically possible for there to be resembling things, from which the conclusion was drawn that the corresponding universal exists and is eternal. On the conventionalist view, to say that it is logically possible for there to be resembling things is only to convey the verbal information that the expression 'resembling things' has a use in the language. Supposing this is correct, is it possible to proceed to the inference that universals exist?

In attempting to answer this question the following consideration should be taken into account. The logical possibility of there being horses, for example, implies the existence of the property, or universal, *horse*, which could in principle be instantiated. But the existence of the property *horse* implies the logical possibility of there being horses. This is to say that the statement, 'It is logically possible for there to be horses', is equivalent to the statement, 'The attribute *horse* exists'. On the conventionalist view the first statement conveys the information that the term 'horse' has a use in the language. Since the second statement is equivalent to the first, it too conveys only verbal information. In the present case the statement, 'The attribute *horse* exists', conveys only the information that the word 'horse' has a use in the language. Does conventionalism imply that talk about universals is not talk about ontology, about 'what there is', but is instead talk about the use of terminology? How does conventionalism connect up with Wittgenstein's recommendation to employ 'use of a term' in preference to 'meaning of a term'?

3. The view that there are such supersensible entities as universals has been described as metaphysical. Ayer has said 'we may define a metaphysical sentence as a sentence which purports to express a genuine proposition, but does, in fact, express neither a tautology nor an empirical hypothesis. And as tautologies and empirical hypotheses form the entire class of significant propositions, we are justified in concluding that all metaphysical assertions are nonsensical' (1951, p. 41). According to this criterion the claim that there are universals is spurious, a piece of verbal nonsense parading as a claim about objects. How is the difference of opinion between Ayer and Russell to be construed? Russell identifies universals as meanings of general words. Does Ayer's criterion for literal

sense imply that it is senseless to say that general words have meanings?

4. If the disagreement between Ayer and Russell is not over whether general words have meanings, is it over whether meanings of general words are objects of some sort? Quine, for instance, has asked '...what sort of things are meanings? They are evidently intended to be ideas somehow – mental ideas for some semanticists, Platonic ideas for others. Obejcts of either sort are so elusive, not to say debatable, that there seems little hope of erecting a significant science about them' (1951, p. 91). If we look on the dispute as one about whether meanings are kinds of things, Russell, who has claimed direct knowledge of them, could be understood as holding that meanings are things, Quine that they are so elusive that their existence is debatable, and Ayer that it makes no literal sense to speak of meanings as being things. Is Quine's view that the claim that meanings are things debatable because the property of being a thing is, in the case of meanings, elusive? What sort of examination of meanings would be required to show definitely that meanings are things? What feature of meanings could Russell call attention to which would remove for Quine their elusiveness?

5. Ayer rejects the claim that there are universals, apparently on the ground that being supersensible their existence is not subject to verification in sense experience. On the construction of the theory of universals as stating that meanings of words are objects, does Ayer's rejection come to saying that it makes no literal sense to speak of meanings as being objects? Is Ayer's rejection of universals a rejection of the view that they are objects or of the view that they are supersensible objects? Consider this question in relation to the two resemblance views.

Could Ayer's application of the verifiability criterion have consisted in his entertaining the meaning of a general word and trying to determine whether it had the property of being an object? Could this have been Quine's procedure? What mode of verification would be appropriate to the three rival statements: The meanings of general words are supersensible objects, the meanings of general words may be objects, it is unintelligible to speak of them as being objects? What is the logical character of the statements?

6. In connection with Wittgenstein's *Gedankenexperiment* that we try to think of the meaning of a word without the word, a Berkeleian could claim success, because obviously it is possible to have the image of a horse, say, without having the general word 'horse' in mind, or to have a

specific color-image without having the name of the color in mind. How would a Berkeleian respond to the further *Gedankenexperiments:* 'Think of the meanings, without the words, of "not", "implies", "yesterday", "minute", "theory"? Russell stated that we cannot point to a time itself (1929, p. 125), for example, a minute, as opposed to an event occurring at that time. If a Berkeleian is not prepared to deny that there are such time intervals as minutes and years, and agrees with Russell's implication that they are not given to perception, how could he accommodate them within his general anti-Platonic position?

7. One of the reasons for the view that characteristics, or attributes, are particular and cannot belong to more than one thing is that to suppose that they could implies that a thing can be in local separation from itself, that is, can simultaneously be in several places. Some philosophers find no difficulty in supposing that abstract entities can be in a number of different places at the same time. And Frege stated that a universal could exist while being nowhere, as against a concrete thing which if it were nowhere would not exist. What feature distinguishing abstract from concrete things, apart from the one being abstract and the other concrete would lead a philosopher to say an abstract entity can be in local separation from itself or nowhere at all?

8. Many philosophers hold the particularity thesis, 'Everything which exists is individual and particular'. This thesis has led to a variety of views, one that there are no abstract entities or ideas and another that attributes themselves are individual and particular. Is the particularity thesis a generalization arrived at from the observation of things, or is it an analytic principle? That is, is it an inductive empirical thesis or is it *a priori?* If it is the first, the mode of verification relevant to it will be entirely different from what it would be if the thesis were *a priori.* How is one to decide which mode of verification is appropriate? Does the decision about this depend on an antecedent investigation of the logical character of the thesis, or is the logical character of the thesis to be determined by trying out different modes of verification? If the thesis is factual, that is, if the thesis states that as a matter of fact whatever exists is particular and individual, room is left open for the theoretical possibility of there being existents which are not particular and individual, just as the statement 'As a matter of fact elephants without exception are herbivorous' carries with it the *conceivability* of there being non-herbivorous elephants. Consider now the proposition that there could be abstract entities, which allows supposing that there are abstract entities. Is the proposition

'abstract entities exist' itself empirical, to be established or rejected on experiential grounds? If it is not, then its negation would not be empirical; i.e., 'There are no abstract entities' would not be empirical. What would this imply about the character of the particularity thesis from which it seems to follow?

Suppose the particularity thesis is *a priori*, to the effect that every conceivable existent is particular and individual. Understood in this way, does the statement violate the Wittgenstein principle that no term can function if its antithesis is deprived of its function? Does 'individual and particular existent' have a proper antithesis if 'being existent' entails 'being particular and individual'? Following Wittgenstein, it might be argued that if 'abstract entity' has no conceivable application to anything, no use to describe anything actual or theoretical, then 'particular and individual existent' would not serve to distinguish between possible existents. The meaning of this latter phrase would then vanish into the meaning of 'existent', with the result that the particularity thesis would state nothing more than the tautology, 'Whatever exists exists'.

REFERENCES

Recommended reading:
   H. H. Price (1953), *Thinking and experience*, Ch. 1.
Further readings:
   R. I. Aaron, *The theory of universals*, Ch. 12.
   George Berkeley (1871), *A treatise concerning the principles of human knowledge*, Introduction.
   Plato, *Parmanides*, sections 126 to 136,
   Bertrand Russell (1943), *The problems of philosophy*, Chs. 11, 12.

7. Rationalism and Empiricism

'To enquire into the original, certainty, and extent of human knowledge, together with the grounds and degrees of belief, opinion and assent'. This was Locke's program in his *Essay concerning human understanding*, and although earlier philosophers did not set out so explicit a program, the subject of inquiry had a long history before Locke, and the results of his inquiry had received both support and challenge long before him. Moreover, they continue to engage philosophers up to the present. Two great rival traditions in philosophy, rationalism and empiricism, have grown up around a fundamental divergence on answers to a cluster of related questions: 'What is the scope of human knowledge?', 'Of what kinds of entities, abstract or concrete, is knowledge possible?', 'Is reason, unaided by the senses, an adequate instrument for establishing not only truths of mathematics but also truths about the world of things?', 'Is there such a thing as sense knowledge?' Answers by proponents of extreme forms of both rationalism and empiricism have given rise to such paradoxical consequences as to prompt attempts to strike a compromise between them. This chapter will be given over to consideration of the questions which have divided the two schools.

Certain empiricists and certain rationalists alike have pointed out a distinction between kinds of truth of which knowledge might be claimed. Hume's distinction between relations of ideas and matters of fact is paralleled by Leibniz's distinction between truths of reason and truths of fact. It is customarily supposed, as was pointed out in Chapter 2, that two different modes of verification are relevant to propositions of these two kinds, and that an irreducible difference in logical character was associated with a difference in mode of verification. The use of the senses comes in play if truths of fact are to be established, and the use of reason unaided by the senses if relations between ideas are to be shown. To know facts which could be otherwise, empiricists like **Locke**, Berkeley, and Hume claimed that sense experience is required. But whether the senses are adequate to give us knowledge, or instead something which falls short of it, is one of the questions on which rationalists and empiricists have divided, although as we shall see, on this point some empiricist philosophers are as sceptical about the reach of the senses as are the rationalists. In general, the divergence between rationalism and empiricism can be said to center on the role of the senses in acquiring knowledge. In the end, as it turns out, neither position is consonant with common sense, and an attempt will be made here to see what can be said, against each, for the philosophical position G. E. Moore has developed in defense of common sense.

It should be pointed out first of all that the customary distinction between contingent propositions and *a priori* propositions, drawn explicitly by certain representatives of each school, has not gone unchallenged by others. However patent the difference may appear, that there is a difference has been denied by Mill, from the one side, and by Bradley from the other. The one has asserted that mathematical propositions, although usually cited as exemplars of the category *a priori*, are really inductions from experience, the other that despite appearances to the contrary, all true propositions are *a priori* necessities. How either position could hav suggested itself is a puzzle, since inspection of the propositions of natural science and of mathematics seems to disclose a clear distinction between the two. There seems to be all the difference between the empirical proposition arrived at by calculation from given empirical propositions, for example, that the length of a pool is x feet, given the magnitude of two sides and the contained angle, and the trigonometric identity, for example, $\tan 45° = 1$, which figures in the calculation. And even when a natural science is axiomatized, and deduction of theorems effected in the same way as from a body of mathematical axioms, a difference between the two sorts of axioms seems obvious, e.g., between 'Bodies in motion continue to move in the same direction with the same velocity unless acted upon by a new force' and 'Things equal to the same thing are equal to each other.'

Nevertheless we find Mill declaring that such propositions as the latter 'are experimental truths; generalizations from observation' (1856, p. 152). 'Whether the axiom [that two straight lines cannot enclose a space] *needs* confirmation or not, it *receives* confirmation in almost every instant of our lives. Experimental proof crowds in upon us in such endless profusion, and without one instance in which there can be even a suspicion of an exception to the rule, that we should soon have a stronger ground for believing the axiom, even as an experimental truth, than we have for almost any of the general truths which we confessedly learn from the evidence of our senses ... Where then is the necessity for assuming that the recognition of these truths has a different origin from the rest of our knowledge, when its existence is perfectly accounted for by supposing its origin to be the same?' (p. 153). Of arithemetic Mill admits that 'it is harder to believe of the doctrines of this science than of any other, ... that they are not truths *a priori*, but experimental truths ...' (p. 164). But he considers these likewise to be propositions about things and 'the Science of Number [to be] no exception to the conclusion we previously arrived at' (p. 167). – that its 'fundamental truths ... all rest upon the evidence of sense; they are proved by showing to our eyes and our fingers that any given number of objects, ten balls for example, may by separation and rearrangement exhibit to our senses all the different sets of numbers the sum of which is equal to ten' (p. 167). Mill is thus saying that the logical character of mathematical and scientific generalizations is the same because their mode of verification is the same.

Whether or not this reason is correct, the corresponding extreme rationalistic position cannot have the corresponding reason: that mathematical propositions and axioms of science are both in fact supported by *a priori* reasoning on concepts. Such a description of the procedure of natural scientists would flout the facts even more patently than does Mill's. Nevertheless, certain rationalists have maintained, either explicity or by implication, that all propositions, including those about the existence and nature of things, are *a priori*, and have argued that despite appearances to the contrary, no proposition is *established* inductively and that all truths *can* in principle be established by thought alone. The latter claim is sometimes bolstered by a metaphysical view about the nature of reality from which it follows; and sometimes the supposition that some truths might be otherwise is held to stem simply from ignorance, and a metaphysics is developed as an implied consequence. It is worthwhile canvassing a few of the reasons some rationalists have given for saying that the order of thought and the order of things are one and the same, and as Spinoza put it, 'In Nature there is nothing contingent ...' (*Ethics*, Prop. 29).

Bradley put forward this view explicitly in his doctrine that all relations are internal. According to him it is impossible for the terms of a relation to be what they are and not stand in precisely that relation. All relations, he held, are grounded in the nature of their terms, so that given all the qualities a term has, it will follow from this fact that it stands in the relation it does; and at the same time 'a relation must at both ends affect, and pass into, the being of its terms' (Bradley 1925, p. 364). The doctrine is thus to the effect that a thing's nature determines its relations, and its relations determine its nature. Bradley makes clear that by determination he means logical necessitation. For example, the property 6 has determine that it shall be 1 greater than 5, and any number which is 1 greater than 5 necessarily must be 6. That other relations, say spatial nextness or similarity, seem to 'the eye of common sense' (p. 394) not to be of this sort is due to ignorance and a sort of philistine dogmatism. What happens in the case of a given element for which 'we do not perceive in its content the internal relations to what is beyond it [is that] upon the ground of this failure, we go on to a denial, and we insist that no such internal relations are present' (p.392). 'As to that apparent externality there can be no doubt. Why this thing is here and not there ... remains unknown ... [But] somewhere there must be a reason why this and that appear together' (p. 577). To suppose a relation is merely external, that is, such that its terms could exist and be what they are and yet the relation not hold, is to suppose the terms are related for no reason at all. What constitutes a reason is the nature of the terms. A necessity, to use Descartes' phrase, 'lies in the things themselves' (*Meditation* V). The failure to grasp this, e.g., to see that one man is similar to another necessarily, is because we do 'not know the ground, the how and why, of his relation to the other man', so that it 'remains for [us] relatively external, contingent, and fortuitous. But there is really no mere externality except in [our] ignorance' (Bradley, 1925, p. 581).

We find the same thesis in Leibniz, who begins with an explicit distinction between truths of fact and truths of reason, i.e., between contingent statements and *a priori* ones, and proceeds to abolish it by maintaining that 'one who perfectly understood the notion of the subject would judge also that the predicate belongs to it' (1900, p. 214). God, who could make the infinite analysis required to apprehend the 'foundation and reason of all the predicates' of an individual substance, that is, the necessary connection between the subject and predicates, would find no distinction between propositions: All would be analytic. The distinction we make between necessary and contingent connections has no counterpart in reality, and we make it because of our limitations. Were we able to embrace the infinite complexity of a subject 'in one intuition', we could, for example, know '*a priori* (and not by experience) whether [Alexander] died a natural death or by poison' (*Ibid.*); we should see that all connections are necessary, that is, that all propositions are *a priori*.

We find a similar view about the specific relation of causation in a contemporary idealist, Dr. A. C. Ewing. He writes: 'I can attach no meaning to a causation in which the effect is not necessarily determined, and I can attach no meaning to a necessary determination which would leave it perfectly possible for the necessarily determined event to be different without contradicting either its own nature or the nature of that which determines it' (1935, p. 77). He admits that 'the scientist does not see the [entailment] connexion', but holds that 'his inductive arguments logically presuppose its presence. For he certainly argues from cause to effect, and how can he possibly be justified in doing that if they are not connected by any relation of entailment? '(p. 78).' If we are to argue from C to E, it would seem that C must entail E. But we do not see that it does entail E, so how can we use causal arguments at all in regard to the physical world? The answer is that, while it is necessary, if we are to argue from C to E, that we should have grounds for supposing that C entails E, it is not necessary that we should ourselves see the entailment to hold' (p. 79). Therefore only when an entailment is seen to hold do we have knowledge. Otherwise we fall short of it.

It is important to note that this form of rationalism, as distinct from other forms to be discussed, and against all forms of empiricism, takes reason to be capable, at least in principle, of supplying us with knowledge of the world. As Descartes said in *De Mundo*, 'Whoever examines carefully the rules I have laid down and the truths thereby reached, will be able to proceed to demonstrations *a priori* of everything that occurs in the world' (1929, Ch. 7). Leibniz expressed the same confidence in reason, once an art of *a priori* calculation (1900, p. 140) were developed, in the following quaint words: '...if controversies were to arise, there would be no more need of disputation between two philosophers than between two accountants. For it would suffice to take pencils in their hands, to sit down to their slates, and to say to each other (with a friend as a witness if they liked): Let us calculate' (1900, p. 170). Whether or not the ideal of attaining knowledge by inspecting and calculating with concepts can be realized, it is clear that the possibility in principle of doing so implies something about the nature of the world: that it is a system of necessary connections, or equivalently, that it can be described by a set of *a priori* truths. Knowledge of the world is knowledge of the relations of concepts, and it is possible because the order of things is an *a priori* order. Parmenides asserted the connection between knowledge of reality and the nature of reality in the words, 'What is and what can be thought are the same'.

It is clear that this form of rationalism implies the impossibility of anything in the world being other than it is, of undergoing change. For *a priori* true propositions cannot become false, and if they describe the world, then the eternality of truths has as its consequence the eternality of what they describe, and thus the unchangeability of what there is. Change cannot occur and contingency cannot be. And this denies the appearances. For things seem to come into existence, change, and pass away. At least so our senses indicate. Rationalism must therefore either justify the claim that all truths about reality are *a priori*, or admit that there can be truths about the changing appearances which are at the same time truths about what is real, i.e., propositions whose truth-values depend on, change with, the changing states of affairs. To decide between these alternatives comes to adjudicating between the philosophical position that knowledge of things can be obtained by thought alone and the position that such knowledge can be obtained only through the senses.

The most extreme form of rationalism, propounded by Parmenides and by Bradley, his twentieth century counterpart, makes no compromise with the appearances and dismisses them as unreal. If the senses attest to anything in conflict with what reason affirms, then the rule of rationalism enjoins us to heed the voice of reason. When Parmenides condemned the eye as blind, and urged philosophers to 'bring the test of reason' to the investigation of reality, the implication was that reality is reached only in thought, that it is hidden from sight, and in fact that the sensible manifold we take to be our world is a cosmic mirage. As was seen in Chapter 4, sense appearances were dismissed on strictly *a priori* grounds. By professing to demonstrate a contradiction in the notions of relations, qualities, and things Bradley ruled out, as insubstantial appearance, the world of discrete things standing in diverse relations to each other. Granting that the only possible evidence for the existence of chairs, tables, human bodies, etc. is sense-evidence, then the only possible evidence has to be rejected as systematic delusion if it is self-contradictory that such things should exist. What is real *must* conform to the criterion of consistency. Parmenides relied on reason to assure him that something exists and what its properties are. That something turned out to be a reality transcending sense-experience.

The focal point of dispute between empiricists and rationalists has been the adequacy of the senses for yielding knowledge. But although rationalists are agreed that thought is the only source of knowledge, not all are agreed that the senses deliver only illusion. Other forms of rationalism make some attempt, as Parmenides and Bradley did not, to 'save the appearances', and concede to the senses the possibility of providing grounds, however inadequate, for believing that a world of sensory objects exists. And this implies the possibility of there being such objects and of there being facts about them which determine the truth-values of assertions we make about them. That is, it requires maintaining the distinction between *a priori* and contingent propositions, a distinction made by representatives of both of the rival schools, for example, by Locke and Hume on the one hand, and by Leibniz on the other. Now the denial of this distinction has a consequence which, once seen, puts one who denies it in an untenable position. It is worthwhile elaborating this consequence.

Consider first the extreme rationalist position that all propositions are *a priori*, either *a priori* true or *a priori* false. Truths which are taken to be truths of fact are held ultimately to be truths of reason. This means that in principle there can be no proposition which is a contingent truth (or falsity), and that all conceivable propositions fall into the class of *a priori* propositions. So the phrase '*a priori* proposition' will not serve to set off one class of propositions from another *possible* class, which is to say that its antithesis, 'contingent proposition', has lost its use. And this makes the characterization '*a priori*' empty; its function of distinguishing amongst propositions is destroyed once its antithesis has no conceivable application. To use Wittgenstein's metaphor, once the tiller is detached from the rudder, the function of both is destroyed. 'All propositions are *a priori* propositions' reduces to the uninformative tautology 'All propositions are propositions'. And exactly the same consideration applies to Mill's claim that all propositions, mathematical as well as scientific ones, are really empirical. 'Empirical' is thereby made to lose its function to distinguish among possible propositions those which are empirical from those which are *a priori*, so that Mill's claim likewise reduces to a contentless tautology.

With an intact distinction between empirical and *a priori* propositions, a less extreme form of rationalism, of which Plato was a representative, attempts a compromise between the claims of reason and those of the senses. The primacy of reason as a means to knowledge is maintained, but its sphere is no longer 'all time and all existence' but a world of timeless being, inhabited by abstract entities, 'the invisible, intangible essences'. To these entities (universals) Plato attributed properties which in the Parmenidean view characterized Being. Uncreated and indestructible, without change, motion, or any sensible qualities, they are intelligible objects which transcend the grasp of the senses. Of these true knowledge is possible. The mind 'by a power of her own' apprehends the truths of reason. But as for the Heraclitean world which changes and perishes, only opinion is possible; truths about it cannot be known. The senses are poor witnesses, not because they of necessity disclose only illusion, as Parmenides and Bradley held, but because they are inadequate to establish any truths of fact. Use of the senses can at best make it likely that sense-objects exist, and what their nature is, but never certain. This is the Platonic compromise with Parmenides and Heraclitus. Its metaphysics makes room both for a world of changeless being and a shadow world of things in perpetual becoming. Of the first there is knowledge – mathematical knowledge is of this sort; of the second there is only opinion. The opinions could be true, something impossible according to the extreme rationalistic claim that appearances are all self-contradictory; but the limitations of the senses preclude, in principle, the attainment of anything better than opinion.

Opinions are, of course, capable of being either true or false, so this form of rationalism clearly implies a distinction between propositions known by reasoning on their constituent concepts and propositions whose truth-value is contingent upon something external to the propositions themselves. The modes of verification relevant to propositions of the two sorts will thus be different. The rationalistic thesis is that although sense-verification is the only relevant mode of verification of propositions about the existence and nature of concrete objects, nevertheless no amount of sense-evidence justifies a claim to knowledge. And as a corollary, disclosures of the senses have no bearing on the truth of *a priori* propositions, whence it would appear that *a priori* propositions can state no truths about the world of things. The latter, as we have seen, was denied by Leibniz. *A priori* truths, he held, were truths about all possible worlds and therefore about this one. Further, such truths are all analytic: To see that they are 'requires an infinite analysis, which God alone can accomplish' (1900, pp.221–222), but such is nevertheless their character.

In opposition, Kant denied that any proposition of the form *ab* is *a* is in any way informative about things. But he did not assert that all *a priori* truths are uninformative; and against empiricists he maintained that although all our knowledge of things begins with experience, knowledge of things does not all come from experience. Certain very general laws of nature, such as that every event has a cause, although suggested by experience, can be known to be true; and since experience could not establish such a general truth, and in particular, one which asserts what necessarily is, such knowledge is *a priori*. That every event has a cause is very different from the proposition that every effect has a cause, which analyzes as 'Every caused event has a cause'. Being of the form *ab* is *a*, the latter is analytic, whereas the former Kant held to be 'ampliative' – to add, in its predicate, something not contained in the subject. As was pointed out in Chapter 1, this category of statement was held by Kant to have the features of both synthetic and *a priori* propositions: They give factual information, as does any empirical proposition, and at the same time have the 'inward necessity' of analytic propositions. Experience first informs us of the connection between subject and predicate, but reason informs us they are linked by necessity. Lacking necessity, the proposition 'Every event has a cause' could not according to Kant serve as a foundation from which science could proceed to establish particular invariances in nature.

Although Kant assigns to reason a scope which would not be conceded to it by strict empiricists, he at the same time assigns it limits which would be denied by many rationalists. According to him reason cannot profitably proceed beyond the bounds of sense to propositions involving 'concepts to which experience can never supply any corresponding objects' (1929a, p. 45) – such concepts as God, the soul as a simple subject of mental activities, things as they are in themselves apart from their phenomenal attributes. In fact knowledge which transcends the bounds of all sense-experience is claimed to be impossible. Nature conceived of as 'the existence of things in themselves (1929b, Sec. 14) can be known neither *a priori* nor *a posteriori*'. 'Since the oldest days of philosophy', Kant writes, 'inquirers into pure reason have conceived, besides the things of sense, or appearances (phenomena), which make up the sensible world, certain creations of the understanding ..., called noumena, which should constitute an intelligible world ... Our critical deduction by no means excludes things of that sort ..., but rather limits the principles of the Aesthetic (the science of sensibility) to this, that they shall not extend

13

to all things ... but that they shall only hold good of objects of possible experience ... [It is a] rule which admits of **no** exception "that we neither know nor can know anything at all definite of these pure objects of the understanding ... as soon as we leave this sphere [of objects of possible experience] these concepts retain no meaning whatever"'(*Ibid.*, Sec. 32). Beyond experience 'no concepts have any significance, as there is no intuition that might offer them a foundation' (Sec. 34).

Except for the proviso that the existence of things transcending sense-experience 'is not excluded', these words might well have been written by present-day logical empiricists. The principle of verifiability in sense-experience would of course exclude as meaningless any claim to the existence of noumena. It would also eliminate, on the same ground, the claim that there exist ideas which derive from some other source than sense-experience. The existence of innate ideas has been historically a focus of controversy between rationalists and empiricists. As we saw in Chapter 5, according to Descartes we could not have framed the idea of God by ourselves; the idea of an infinite being has to be implanted in our minds by an Infinite Author. Leibniz' metaphysics implies that *all* ideas are innate, since the monad receives no ideas from outside itself. And all abstract ideas according to Plato were present to the mind at times preceding the existence of bodily senses. Against the rationalists Locke maintained that the mind is a blank tablet on which experience writes – that there is nothing in the intellect which was not first in experience. All our ideas are acquired either by sensation or by reflection upon what goes on within us. And we begin to think only when experience furnishes us with the materials. Bishop Berkeley goes further: the general ideas with which thought is engaged are merely particular ideas, any one of which a given general word 'indifferently suggests to the mind' (1871, Intr., Sec. 11). 'An idea, which considered in itself is particular, becomes general, by being made to represent or stand for all other particular ideas of the same sort' (*Ibid.*, Sec. 12). So general ideas on this account not only derive from experience but are not different in kind from the data of sense. Far from being supersensible objects, they are sensible objects, and consequently only exist at the time of apprehension.

Various rationalistic theses about the existence and nature of either universals or innate ideas, and the empiricist counterclaims, are, however, not integral to the central question at issue between the two schools: whether knowledge of things can be had solely by means of sense-experience, or even by sense-experience at all. We return then to this issue, and shall confine discussion of it to those forms of the rival schools which admit both the existence of propositions whose truth-values are contingent upon states of affairs which could be otherwise and the existence of truths of reason. We have seen that although Kant supposes reason to be incapable of proceeding to knowledge of objects beyond the limits of possible experience, he nevertheless supposes that about nature conceived of as 'the complex of all the objects of experience' (*Ibid.*, Sec. 16) *a priori* knowledge can be had. Between Kant and all empiricists this is a central point of disagreement. Quite apart from the question whether some of the propositions which Kant singled out as synthetic *a priori* (e.g., that every event has a cause) are indeed so, there is, as has already been seen, a serious question whether any *a priori* proposition, synthetic or analytic, makes any assertion about matter of fact. Against Leibniz's view that truths of reason hold for all possible worlds, it can be argued that what is compatible with every state of affairs says nothing about any of them. And it is a puzzle what sort of procedure is relevant to deciding between claim and counterclaim.

Suppose the empiricist view on this point is correct: that the logical connections between concepts, which reason can discover, are not at the same time factual connections between things falling under the concepts. Rationalism seems then to be left with nothing but its initial distrust of the senses, though this distrust need not take the extreme form that the senses can only delude us. Some rationalists, however, have not been content to make a blanket dismissal of the use of the senses in investigating reality and have attempted to justify it by an *a priori* argument. Descartes, for example, brought such charges against the senses that it appeared to him impossible that any justification for their use was ever to be found in sense-experience itself. The usual procedure of both scientist and ordinary man in establishing the existence of things is, in any case of doubt, to take extra precautions by re-checking or by bringing in the other senses. But this gives no warrant according to Descartes for supposing that either before or after checking one's perceptions one has acquainted oneself with what really exists as against what merely appears to exist. The fact that sensory experiences present themselves independently of the will is no good reason against supposing that one might have been 'so constituted by nature [as to] be deceived even in matters which seemed to ... be most certain' (*Meditation* I). If it were a reason it would constitute a refutation of Leibniz's doctrine that the monad's sense-contents have no outer sources, which it is not. The thesis that no justification for the use of

13*

the senses is to be found in sense-experience itself Descartes supported with a further reason, extant from antiquity, namely, that '. . . there are no certain indications by which we may clearly distinguish wakefulness from sleep . . .' (*Meditation* VI). 'I have never believed myself to feel anything in waking moments which I cannot also sometimes believe myself to feel when I sleep, and as I do not think that these things which I seem to find in sleep, proceed from objects outside me, I do not see any reason why I should have this belief regarding objects which I seem to perceive while awake' (*Meditation* I). And as Berkeley pointed out later, '. . . what happens in dreams, frensies, and the like, puts it beyond dispute that it is possible we might be affected with all the ideas we have now, though no bodies existed without resembling them. Hence it is evident the supposition of external bodies is not necessary for the producing our ideas; since it is granted they are produced sometimes, and might possibly be produced always, . . . without their concurrence' (1871, Pt. I, Sec. 18).

Without some warrant that this is not the case, that we are not systematically deluded, Descartes thought that neither the scientist nor the ordinary man could continue to take for granted that the senses are generally reliable, and when deceptive, that their deliverances are correctible by further use of them. Accordingly he attempted an *a priori* demonstration that external causes of our sense-contents exist and that we are not perpetually in the condition of merely seeming to perceive an existent rather than actually doing so. Obviously if the senses are on trial, the only justification for the common belief that their testimony can be relied on must be nonexperiential. Additional sense testimony can never bolster the sense testimony at hand if the trustworthiness of every sense-experience is in question. Descartes' justification was theological: The existence of corporeal causes was deduced from the nature of God. '. . . I recognise it to be impossible that He should ever deceive me; for in all fraud and deception some imperfection is to be found . . . and accordingly cannot be found in God' (*Meditation* IV). The part God plays in the production of our ideas is then described as follows: '. . . since God is no deceiver, it is very manifest that He does not communicate to me these ideas immediately and by Himself . . . For since He has given me . . . a very great inclination to believe that they are conveyed to me by corporeal objects, I do not see how He could be defended from the accusation of deceit if these ideas were produced by causes other than corporeal objects. Hence we must allow that corporeal things exist' (*Meditation* VI). God, then, entitles us to the assurance that there is a world external to us, and the *a priori* demonstration thus implies that sense testimony need not always be dismissed as delusive.

One difficulty with this assurance is that it in no way excludes the possibility of specific errors of perception. God's goodness and power may preclude systematic deception, but they do not preclude deception in specific cases. Descartes admitted that 'experience shows me that I am subject to an infinitude of errors', and that this gives rise to a new problem inasmuch as 'God could have created me so that I could never have been subject to error' (*Meditation* IV). The admission brings us back to the original question about the senses, whether one is ever in a position to discriminate among sense deliverances those which are veridical and those which are not. In the case of any specific sense-experience, can the use of the senses ever justify one's 'inclination to believe' that it is in fact a case in which a physical object, of the indicated nature, is present to the senses? The question put by Socrates to Theaetetus remains to trouble one's natural confidence: 'How can you determine whether at this moment we are sleeping, and all our thoughts are a dream; or whether we are awake, and talking to one another in the waking state?' Descartes' demonstration *a priori*, from the nature of God, that corporeal objects do indeed exist does nothing to allay this doubt. Neither does Leibniz's account of the truth of (apparently) contingent propositions as due to a synchronization, arranged by God, between the inner states of the monad and the outer world of other monads external to it.

It would appear that whatever the variations in the form rationalism takes concerning the kind of objects of which reason is capable of attaining knowledge, there remains a point of general agreement, namely, that the senses are inadequate, for one reason or another, to give knowledge of the sense world around us. This has been a constant theme from Parmenides through Plato onwards. And what started with Empedocles as a counteroffensive, in defense of the senses as avenues to knowledge, is an equally invariant theme with empiricism. 'Go to now', said Empedocles, 'examine by every means each thing how it is clear, neither putting greater faith in anything seen than in what is heard, nor in a thundering sound than in the clear assertion of the tongue, nor keep from trusting any of the other members in which there lies a means to knowledge, but know each thing in the way it is clear' (in: Nahm, 1947, p. 129). There is no hint in these words that some sort of justification of the use of the senses is required which is not found in sense-experience, that the senses by themselves are inadequate. Locke said, 'I think nobody can in earnest be so sceptical as to be uncertain of the existence of those things which he sees and feels'. 'The notice we have by our senses of the existence of things without us, though it be not altogether so certain as our intuitive knowledge, or the deductions of our reason employed about the clear abstract ideas of our minds; yet it is an assurance that deserves the name of knowledge' (1928, Bk. IV, Ch. 11, Sec. 3).

Contemporary empiricists have coupled with this affirmation of faith in the senses an explicit claim about the limitations of thought in revealing any matter of fact. Thought can determine 'the relations of ideas', but it cannot proceed beyond them to establish truths of fact. Kant's position was a half-way house: that reason could only be employed about the objects of possible sense-experience. But about these Kant thought *a priori* knowledge to be possible. Ayer holds that reason can calculate the truth-values of *a priori* propositions only, that, so to speak, the sphere within which reason operates is the *a priori;* but he maintains that all *a priori* truths are analytic and therefore empty of factual content. That is, reason is incapable of establishing any truths about things. For these the use of the senses is required.

At first sight the empiricist position appears to be the position adopted by common sense and the natural sciences. But the consequences of tenets integral to empiricism show that this impression is entirely mistaken. Far from being consonant with common sense, it eventuates in a pervasive scepticism which easily matches the scepticism premised by Cartesian rationalism. This surprising consequence of empiricism is a consequence of a tenet it has in common with certain forms of rationalism. G. E. Moore gives a philosophical defense of common sense centering about a set of statements which 'men have believed ... almost as long as they have believed anything' (1953, p. 3), of which he claims, for common sense and against sceptical denials, we all have knowledge. Of certain of these statements, those about sense-objects, Plato denied that we have anything more than mere opinion. We find Locke saying, less bluntly but in words hardly less damaging to the assurance of common sense, that 'There is, indeed, another perception of the mind, employed about the particular existence of finite beings without us; which going beyond bare probability, and yet not reaching perfectly to ... the degrees of certainty [possessed by intuition and demonstration], passes under the name of knowledge' (1928, Bk. IV, Ch. 2, Sec. 14). The same thing could be said, and has been said, about the nature as well as the existence of 'finite beings', whether physical objects or other persons and their inner states, and about events belonging to both the future and the past. In what follows it will be shown how it is that empiricism, which begins in common sense, ends by making common cause with rationalism against it, and how its consequences may be challenged in defense of Moore's commonsense position.

We find in Locke's account of knowledge the source of the paradox: 'Since the mind, in all its thoughts and reasonings, hath no other immediate object but its own ideas, ... it is evident, that our knowledge is only conversant about them. Knowledge then seems to me nothing but the perception of the connexion and agreement, or disagreement and repugnancy, of any of our ideas. In this alone it consists (Bk. IV, Ch. 1, Sec. 1–2). He then notes that it follows from this that 'we can have knowledge no farther than we have ideas' and that 'we have knowledge no farther than we have perception of their agreement or disagreement. Which perception being, 1. Either by intuition, or the immediate comparing any two ideas; or, 2. By reason, examining the agreement or disagreement of two ideas, by the intervention of some others'; and to these he adds a third: 'By sensation, perceiving the existence of particular things' (Bk. IV, Ch. 3, Sec. 1, 2). It is reasonably clear that if our knowledge is confined to our ideas, then there is no explaining a claim to knowledge of 'actual and real existence agreeing to any idea' (Bk. IV, Ch. 1, Sec. 7). Locke gave several reasons in justification of his claim that our perceptions must be produced by exterior causes: because people without sense organs lack them, because most data of sense, in contrast to those called up by memory, come to us without our consent, and are sometimes accompanied by pain, and finally, because our senses mutually support each other. But it is clear that any sceptic would deny that these grounds would justify anything beyond mere belief. Gorgias in ancient times stated unequivocally that if anything did exist it could never be known. How he supported his claim is conjectural, but his reasoning may well have borne on the last of Locke's considerations, that our senses bear witness to each other. Consider what we do in checking our perceptions. We are never, conceivably, in a position to compare a perception with its exterior cause, with the thing as it actually is, simply because the cause *is exterior to* the idea. A curtain of ideas stands between us and reality outside; the best we can do is to compare one perception with another perception. This is 'the ego-centric predicament'. Knowledge is confined to the contents of one's own sense-experience.

Locke abandoned this position concerning the scope of knowledge, no doubt at the prompting of common sense, for the position that by sensation we have 'an assurance that deserves the name of knowledge' (Bk. IV, Ch. 11, Sec. 3). He explained, however, that 'The mind knows not things immediately, but only by the intervention of the ideas it has of them' (Bk. IV, Ch. 4, Sec. 3). This is to say that knowledge of things is based on inferences from our ideas. Inasmuch as such inferences are nondemonstrative, they are on Locke's admission not 'so certain as . . . the deductions of our reason employed about the clear abstract ideas of our minds'. (Bk. IV, Ch. 11, Sec. 3). He nevertheless claims that they 'go beyond mere probability', as is not the case with inferences to things not actually present to our senses. It is of interest that a present-day empiricist such as Hans Reichenbach in effect says the same thing: Sense-perception can never attain to certainty but cannot on that ground be denied to give us 'genuine knowledge '(1948, p. 335). One cannot help feeling that an honorific name has been given to what Plato called opinion, and that what is not certain should rightly be called 'merely probable'. And in fact we find Ayer asserting that statements about physical objects and physical occurrences are and must remain hypotheses. 'No proposition, other than a tautology', he says, 'can possibly be anything more than a probable hypothesis' (1951, p. 38). 'There are no absolutely certain empirical propositions. It is only tautologies that are certain. Empirical propositions are one and all hypotheses, which may be confirmed or discredited in sense-experience. And the propositions in which we record the observations that verify these hypotheses are themselves hypotheses which are subject to the test of further sense-experience. Thus there are no final propositions' (pp. 93–94). It would appear then that empiricism has come round to agreement with the less extreme form of rationalism on the scope of the senses: They can render more and more probable any statement about sensory objects, to any degree we please, *short of certainty*.

The usual corollary is that, among empirical propositions, we can be certain only of those about our own sensations. 'The only existence of which we are certain', says Hume, 'are perceptions . . . as no beings are ever present to the mind but perceptions. . .' (1888, Bk. I, Pt. IV, Sec. 2). Solipsism is the immediate consequence: If one can be certain only of one's experiences, there is no possibility of knowing that anyone else is having an experience, nor what his experiences are like. This point is nicely brought out in the quaint tale of two Chinese philosophers standing on a bridge, who engaged in conversation as follows: 'See the little fishes dart and play; therein consists their pleasure', to which the reply was, 'How can you, not being a fish, know wherein consists their pleasure?' And to this came the counter-reply: 'And how can you, not being me, know that I cannot know wherein consists their pleasure?' Of course the sceptic would maintain, against these challenges, that *if* what anyone can be certain of are the contents of his own mind, then one can know that he could not know the contents of any other mind. Gorgias' third sceptical thesis, that if one did know of the existence of anything, this could not be communicated, follows directly out of solipsism. Communication implies making someone else aware of one's own thoughts, conveying to him by means of written or spoken words the meaning associated with those words. Suppose the meanings are taken to be thoughts, and viewed as 'subjective entities' (Bochenski, 1956). The sceptic maintains that even though another person could be made aware of the words, as physical occurrences, he could not be made aware of the thoughts associated with the words. Thoughts belong to each person's private history and cannot be exhibited in the way in which words are exhibited. On this view words and their meanings are given by psychological contiguity, words to sight or hearing (or to touch, as in the case of Braille), and meanings to the understanding. And although one type of object may be objective and public, the other is subjective and private. Thoughts are accessible only to him who has them. So one's words might reach a hearer or reader but not the thoughts attached to them.

The same conclusion obtains even though it be held that two minds can entertain one and the same meaning, that a meaning is an 'objective entity' which is the content of an act of thought. It might be supposed that distinguishing between the act of thinking and the content of the mental act, the one being private to the thinker and the other objective, would enable us to maintain the possibility of communication: If one and the same content can be the object of thought for any number of different thinkers, then it can no longer be argued that communication implies sharing what is private. It can, however, be argued that although, as Plato held, meanings of general words and sentences are objective, communication is nevertheless impossible. For communication implies at least the possibility, on the part of both parties, of verifying that certain specific meanings have been imparted. Consider now the word 'blue', and the meaning, or universal, named by it. It can be argued that no one could be certain that anyone else used it to name the same universal without being certain that he applies it to instances of the universal.

And there is no way of knowing that a person applies a word to instances of a certain universal without being aware of those instances. For me to know that you mean by the word 'blue' what I mean by it, I should have to know that you apply the word to color instances like those that I apply it to, that is, to color instances to which I would apply it. Only in this way could I be sure that you use the word for the same objective property I use it to stand for. But to do this I should have to enter into your mind and see your seeing of the instances. And this would be possible only by my being you. I can see your seeing a color or shape, or smell your smelling an odor, or have your taste sensation, only by being you. But if *I* am the person who has, for example, a perception of a color quality, and applies a certain word to it, this would not be a case of my knowing that someone else, someone *other* than myself, uses the word for the same color that I use it to stand for. If you were I, then you as a distinct individual would no more exist than Alice would exist if she were only a thing in the Red Knight's dream. Thus, although meanings are objective, I nevertheless could not know that anyone else's words have the meanings I apprehend when I understand the words. And hence what is implied by communication, namely, the possibility, in principle, of knowing that what one meant had been imparted, is cut away. Quite apart from considerations about the status of what is imparted, knowing that something has been imparted to another mind requires knowing that there is another mind. And if all one can be certain of are the contents of one's own mind then this would require that another mind be one of one's own mental contents, which is absurd.

How the view that knowledge is limited to the contents of one's own mind bears on one's natural confidence in inductive inferences from past to future is now clear. The sceptic maintains that any connections between one's perceptions beyond what introspection discloses at the time they occur can never be known. Even granting that our memory can be trusted and that connections between certain sorts of percepts have in the past had a coherence and constancy which makes their association seem natural to us, this provides no ground for supposing the associations will be preserved in the future. 'When the mind looks farther than what immediately appears to it, its conclusions can never be put to the account of the senses; and it certainly looks farther, when ... [it] supposes the relations of resemblance and causation betwixt them... (Hume, 1888, Bk. II, Pt. IV, Sec. 2). That future associations will be like past ones can of course never be justified by our senses; it would be contradictory to hold that the senses could inform us of what does not appear to the senses. Neither can it be justified by reason, since it is perfectly clear to reason that 'there can be no demonstrative arguments to prove, that those instances, of which we have had no experience, resemble those, of which we have had experience' (*Ibid*, Bk. I, Pt. III, Sec. 6). For 'wherever a demonstration takes place, the contrary is impossible, and implies a contradiction. There is no demonstration, therefore, for any conjunction of cause and effect' (Hume, 1938, p. 14). These remarks apply to the items of our sense-experience and *a fortiori* to causal connections between objects assumed to correspond to these items. As Hume says, 'Any degree of regularity in our perceptions, can never be a foundation for us to infer a greater degree of regularity in some objects, which are not perceived' (1888, Bk. I, Pt. IV, Sec. 2). Nor, of course, can it be a foundation for inferring any regularity at all. Hume writes: 'Were a man, such as *Adam*, created in the full vigour of understanding, without experience, he would never be able to infer motion in [one billiard ball] from the motion and impulse of [another]. It is not anything that reason sees in the cause, which makes us *infer* the effect. Such an inference, were it possible, would amount to a demonstration, as being founded merely on the comparison of ideas. But no inference from cause to effect amounts to a demonstration. Of which there is this evident proof. The mind can always *conceive* any effect to follow from any cause, and indeed any event to follow upon another. Whatever we *conceive* is possible...' (1938, pp. 13–15). Neither reason nor past experience can justify the supposition that 'like causes, in like circumstances, will always produce like effects ...' 'Tis evident, that *Adam*, with all his science, would never have been able to *demonstrate*, that the course of nature must continue uniformly the same, and that the future must be conformable to the past ... 'tis possible the course of nature may change, since we can conceive of such a change' (*Ibid.*, p. 15). Nor can those cases in which inferences from the past to the future have been borne out be used to justify the *generality* that the future is always conformable to the past. That is, it cannot be justified *inductively* either. For those specific inductions from past experience themselves rest on the supposition that this conformity exists, so that such an attempt at justification would be circular.

This, then, is Hume's answer to the question whether induction can be justified: It cannot. He defends his conclusion by reference to a guiding empiricist principle, namely, to confine himself to what experience reports. Inspection of his perceptions never reveals any bond between them, such that the occurrence of one compels the other. 'All events seem entirely loose and separate', he says. 'One event follows another; but we never can observe any tie between them. They seem *conjoined*, but never *connected*' (1902, Pt. II, Sec. 7). And of course even though there were a 'discoverable connexion' in a given case of conjunction, this would augur nothing for the future conjunctions, nor that there would be future conjunctions. The senses, he says, 'convey to us nothing but a single perception and never give us the least intimation of anything beyond' (1888, Bk. I, Pt. IV, Sec. 2). The senses not only give us no knowledge of future concomitances; they do not even *make it probable* that if A and B have without exception been associated in the past, A will be associated with B on its next occurrence. For such an inference, Hume says, would rest on its being probable, in general, that future associations would resemble past ones. In his words: 'Nay, I will go farther, and assert, that [one] could not so much as prove by any *probable* arguments, that the future must be conformable to the past'; for specific probable arguments, from which this might be inferred inductively, 'are built on the supposition, that there is this conformity betwixt the future and the past' (1938, p. 15). If one accepts, as Hume does, Locke's first position that knowledge is only conversant about the mind's own ideas and extends no further than these, the consequence is that we have no knowledge of an external world, of other minds, or of either the future or the past. This is the end of the road on which the empiricist set out to defend sense observation as a means to knowledge. And it is the junction at which the empiricist and rationalist meet on common ground.

The trouble with this consequence according to Reichenbach is to be found in the invidious comparison, explicit in Locke, between 'the notice we have by our senses' and intuitive and demonstrative knowledge, which are superior to it in giving us certainty. Reichenbach asserts that 'the empiricist unconsciously accepted the fundamental thesis of rationalism, according to which genuine knowledge has to be as reliable as mathematical knowledge' (1948, p. 335), mathematics being 'the prototype of all knowledge' (p. 338). He goes on to say that 'the empiricist skeptic is the philosopher who . . . regards empiricism as a failure because it cannot attain the very aim which was set up by rationalism, the aim of an absolutely reliable knowledge' (p. 335). The suggestion of these words is that sense knowledge is not absolutely reliable knowledge, and in fact he is explicit that sense testimony can make a proposition more and more probable but can never make it certain. As for predictions we make about future concomitances, these rest on a 'blind posit', that is, a presupposition that is nothing more than an article of faith. The posit is to the effect that 'the frequency found in a finite number of observations will remain approximately constant however much the number of observations may be increased' (Russell, 1948, p. 413). It is obvious that whatever objections are raised against the inductive principle, stated roughly as 'the future will resemble the past', can be raised against the blind posit.

What the status of this principle is has been the source of much puzzlement. Hume takes it to be an empirical principle for which no proof is possible, since it would itself be presupposed in any attempt to establish it. And for the same reason it is not even probable. Surprisingly, it is sometimes taken to be a logical principle, although as Hume says, it is conceivable that the course of nature might change. Here then is a principle whose logical character is in dispute, and for which there appears to be no means of settling what it is. Whatever its status, Bertrand Russell takes it that it must be assumed as a premise of any inductive argument. It 'alone can justify any inference from what has been examined to what has not yet been examined' (1943, p. 106); the observational evidence itself is insufficient. He formulates the required premise in the following way: '(a) The greater the number of cases in which a thing of the sort A has been found associated with a thing of the sort B, the more probable it is (if no cases of failure of association are known) that A is always associated with B; (b) Under the same circumstances a sufficient number of cases of the association of A with B will make it nearly certain that A is always associated with B' (p. 104). Without this principle, past experience of the sun rising every day gives us no ground for expecting it to do so tomorrow, 'or for expecting the bread we shall eat at our next meal not to poison us.' Russell makes it clear that he is not seeking a proof that these expectations '*must* be fulfilled, but only for some reason in favour of the view that they are *likely* to be fulfilled' (p. 96).

It is reasonably clear that if empiricists are willing to conclude that anything more than merely probable knowledge is impossible, their position certainly provides no counter to the rationalist attack on the senses. And in fact if what we claim to know must be such, as Ayer says, that we are both sure of it and have a right to be sure of it, then it is not at all clear how the empiricist can extricate himself from solipsism of the present moment. Any experience beyond the present one, whether future or past, must be inferred, and the inference is admittedly not deductive. Conceivably any prediction of a future experience which will check on a supposedly past experience, or bear out what the commonsense man naturally expects as a sequel to present experience, may be false. And if the inference is inductive but must be justified by a general principle whose logical status is in dispute and may be as subject to Hume's challenge as the inference itself, then the empiricist who begins with sense-experience seems unable to make a rational inference to any experience beyond it. What one has a right to be sure of is the existence and character of the experience of the moment. Locke's dictum could be amended to read, 'Knowledge is only conversant about the ideas present to us'.

If the empiricist is reduced to claiming only probable knowledge of a predicted future experience or an inferred past experience, his situation is even more precarious with respect to objects scientists infer and to those objects which figure in what Moore singled out as 'beliefs of common sense'. Scientists infer the existence of electrons and protons from their alleged effects; and on a view such as Locke's, our access to physical objects, events of the past (as against memory experiences), and other minds is equally indirect. Sense-experiences are but signs from which the existence of physical objects is inferred; from the existence of those physical objects we take to be human bodies we infer the existence of other minds; and from inferred physical records or from items in memory experience belonging to our present we infer the existence of past events. And these objects and events are on Locke's view incapable, in principle, of being experienced. There is no such thing as checking an inference by comparing the inferred object with experience: There is no way of checking an induction from premises about present data of sense to a conclusion about things which can never be data of sense – physical objects, other minds. Even supposing that on the basis of sense-experience we are justified in predicting the occurrence of other sense-experiences, 'the position', as Ayer says, 'is quite different when the things whose existence we are claiming to infer not merely are not given to us in experience but never could be ... Some philosophers even consider it to be nonsensical to assert the existence of an object which could not, at least in principle, be observed; and clearly no amount of inductive evidence can warrant a meaningless conclusion' (1947, p. 77). Even supposing the inductive conclusion is not conceded to be meaningless, the consequence of Lockeian empiricism is that we have no right to be sure of the existence of physical objects or past events, nor *a fortiori* of objects inferred from them, viz., other minds and objects of science. These are unknowables.

Another consequence, and this is asserted explicitly both by empiricists such as Mill and Russell and by Cartesian rationalists (see *Meditation* II), is that inferred objects are not really perceived – physical objects no more than minds or the events of the past. 'I affirm', said Mill, 'that I hear a man's voice. Thir would pass, in common language, for a direct perception. All, however, which is really perception, is that I hear a sound. That the sound is a voice, and that voice the voice of a man, are not perceptions but inferences. I affirm, again, that I saw my brother ... If any proposition concerning a matter of fact would commonly be said to be known by the direct testimony of the senses, this surely would be so. The truth, however, is far otherwise. I only saw a certain colored surface; or rather I had the kind of visual sensations which are usually produced by a colored surface; ... observation extends only to the sensations by which we recognize objects ... The logic of observation, then, consists solely in a correct discrimination between that, in a result of observation, which has really been perceived, and that which is an inference from the perception' (1956, Bk. IV, Ch. 1, Sec. 2). In similar vein Russell writes: 'The table as a physical object lies outside my experience. I do not "see" the furniture in my room except in a Pickwickian sense ... We do not actually see physical objects any more than we hear electromagnetic waves when we listen to the wireless' (1948, p. 311). 'It is a fallacy to suppose that a man can see matter. Not even the ablest physiologist can perform this feat. His percept when he looks at a brain is an event in his own mind' (p. 229).

Once the distinction is made between what is perceived and what is inferred. (See also **Berkeley,** (1925), *First dialogue:* '... the senses perceive nothing which they do not perceive *immediately:* for they make no inferences'), the consequences which are so paradoxical to common sense, namely, that bodies are not 'really seen' and that we have no right to claim knowledge of them, are equally unavoidable for phenomenalism. The phenomenalist position, according to which a thing is a class of actual and possible sensations and nothing more, escapes the difficulty Locke's view presented of verifying the existence and character of an unknowable cause of knowable effects. Each of the sensibilia constituting a physical object is theoretically knowable, for any inference to a future sensibile is capable of being checked directly. That is, each is 'strongly' (Ayer, 1951, p. 9), i.e., conclusively, verifiable. But this is not to say that the totality is. Since there are as many senibilia constituting a thing as there are possible points of view, a thing will be an infinite system of sensibilia. Hence any knowledge of a thing would be knowledge of more than could be given in any perception and would therefore be inferential. And since no finite set of statements about sense data is sufficient for deducing the existence of a physical object, such knowledge would be probable merely.

Ayer puts the position as follows: 'However far they may be extended, our sense-experiences can never put beyond question the truth of any statement implying the existence of a physical object; it remains consistent with them that the statement is false' (1956, p. 125). That is, such a statement 'cannot be strongly verified by any finite number of experiences: it is possible that there should not, in fact, be a clock on the mantelpiece now even though there appears to be one whenever I (or indeed other people) look' (Braithwaite, 1938, p. 276). Thus a statement about a physical object is at best 'weakly verifiable', that is, such that experience can render it probable (Ayer, 1951, p. 9). In order for it to be strongly verifiable an infinite series of sense-tests would have to be made. And in order to perceive a *physical object* an infinite number of sensibilia would have to be encompassed, to use a phrase from Leibniz, 'embraced in one intuition'. The conclusion that empirical statements are one and all hypotheses thus derives from the logical impossibility of making an infinite number of observations, or, if indeed it makes sense to speak of making an infinite number of observations, from the logical impossibility of knowing that they are not all hallucinatory. Similarly, the hypothesis that an unknowable cause gives rise to our sense-experiences is no more than probable because of the logical impossibility of conclusively establishing it. The question arises whether what is not strongly verifiable 'deserves the name of knowledge'. Both Reichenbach and Russell call it 'probable knowledge'. Locke calls it sensitive knowledge. These terms are no cover for the fact that what is called knowledge is not certain. Plato and other rationalists called it opinion.

Must we then arrive at the same dead end from both directions? Must we accept the consequences to which argument has driven the empiricist despite his attempts at escape? If we must, then we are committed to holding that we do not know, with certainty, any external fact, that no past conjunctions of experiences give any ground for inferring even the probability of a future similar conjunction, let alone of a conjunction of their external causes, and that no one ever perceives those external causal objects. Moore's counter to these views is simply that he, and furthermore, the philosophers who hold them, knows them to be false. 'It is absurd', he says, 'to suggest that I do not know any external facts whatever; that I do not know, for instance, even that there are any men beside myself' (1922, p. 157). As for other philosophers, he brings into the open an extraordinary paradox which has through the centuries lain in comfortable concealment: 'that [they] should have been able to hold sincerely, as part of their philosophical creed, propositions inconsistent with what they themselves *knew* to be true' (1959, p. 41). And to believe propositions directly inconsistent with what one knows to be true is to believe what one knows to be false. Moore grants that such propositions are believed but they are not the ordinary, everyday variety of beliefs, which find their expression in the affairs of daily life. Rather, they are beliefs which can only be held in 'a philosophic moment', that is, when philosophizing. In Wittgenstein's view, what makes it possible for such propositions to be put forward is a kind of bewitchment induced by language. Regardless of what their source may be, Moore's position on the arguments cited in their support, a position he asserts forthrightly, is that 'it would be at least as easy to deny the arguments as to deny that we know any external fact' (1922, p. 163). In fact it is immeasurably easier; and not only this, it is immeasurably more rational than to hold views one knows to be false, views which in any case do not survive the philosophic moment.

Moore sets out a group of commonsense beliefs which he lays down as truisms – such beliefs as that there are other things to which one's own body stands in various relations, and other human beings who have had experiences like one's own. Regarding these we can construe his position as being to the effect that it would be irrational to accept as valid any argument which goes against them – even though no fallacy in the argument has been brought to light. The truth of these commonsense propositions does not hang on refuting such an argument. Moore may be described as the philosophical Alexander, who cuts the Gordian knot instead of untying it. A sceptical argument is a puzzle which one may not be able to untangle; but this fact in no way shows the argument to be valid. It would be the height of irrationality not to reject it as fallacious. It may be observed, as an aside, that no philosopher is so irrational as to behave as though his arguments are correct. His behavior shows that regardless of his philosophical talk, he thinks with the nonphilosopher.

As for positive proof of what Moore calls 'the commonsense view of the world', Moore implies that it is idle to ask for one: 'The only proof that we do know external facts lies in the fact that we do know them' (1922, p. 160). Moore in effect is saying that there is no proof, that is, no

14

demonstration. But he denies that this requires us to grant that we do not know these commonsense propositions to be true, that we merely believe them or know them to be highly probable. We can know things, he says, which we cannot prove, i.e., which do not follow from anything we know. For example, about our inductive knowledge of causal connections he says, 'We must, I think, grant the premiss that, from the fact that two things have been conjoined, no matter how often, it does not strictly *follow* that they *always* are conjoined. But it by no means follows from this that we may not *know* that, as a matter of fact, when two things are conjoined sufficiently often, they are also *always* conjoined. We may quite well know things which do not logically follow from anything else which we know' (1922, p. 161).

In his paper, 'Proof of an external world', Moore purported to prove the existence of two material objects in the world by deducing this from what he expressed by certain gestures and the words 'Here is one hand' and 'Here is another'. But as for proving there are two hands, he admits he has not given a general statement as to how a proposition of this sort may be proved (1959, p. 149), and he believes it cannot be given, since in order to do this he would need to be able to prove that he is not dreaming. But this fact does not make it incumbent on him to admit that he accepts the existence of his hands 'merely on faith'. 'I can know things' he says, 'which I cannot prove; and among things which I certainly did know, even if (as I think) I could not prove them, were the [two] premises, ['Here is a hand' and 'Here is another'] (p. 150). 'How absurd it would be', he writes, 'to suggest that I did not know it, but only believed it, and that perhaps it was not the case! You might as well suggest that I do not know that I am now standing up and talking – that perhaps after all I'm not and that it's not quite certain that I am!' (pp. 146–147). (It is surprising, in the light of what Ayer has said about our knowledge of empirical propositions, that we find him making a similar sort of comment [*The problem of knowledge*, 1956]. Citing the fact that statements about the existence of material objects cannot be deduced from any finite set of statements about sense data, he objects to this fact being 'expressed in the form that no statement about a physical object can be conclusively verified' (p. 125), that 'however far they may be extended, our sense-experiences can never put beyond question the truth of any statement implying the existence of a physical object'. He then raises Moore's sort of question, 'But is this really so? Can there be any doubt at all of the present existence of the table at which I am seated, the pen with which I am writing, the hand which is holding the pen? Surely I know for certain that these physical objects exist?' He concludes with the assertion that present and past experiences taken together 'entitle [him] to regard the existence of these and many other physical objects which [he] can now perceive as conclusively established'.)

The sceptic's reply is obvious: that the existence of external facts has merely been asserted, not demonstrated, and that knowledge of these alleged facts has been claimed without the least justification. For Moore to claim that he knows that there are two physical objects in the world on the ground that he knows the premises from which this follows, namely, 'Here is one hand' and 'Here is another', the sceptic would say begs the question. If there is any question about whether there are physical objects there will be the same sort of question about whether there are hands. And indeed Moore's proof, construed as supporting a common-sense truism, viz., that we know that physical objects exist, does seem to fall before this charge. His defense of the truth of commonsense beliefs, in default of showing a fallacy in sceptical arguments, appears to be merely a dogmatic affirmation, an emphatic restatement of the beliefs themselves. And as Wittgenstein remarked, one cannot defend common sense by restating its views. The dispute between the common-sense philosopher and the sceptic looks like a stalemate, the assertion of view and counterview, with the sceptic supporting his view by arguments whose validity is dismissed on the ground that it would be irrational to accept them in the face of what we all know to be true.

We have, however, a different perspective on the dispute if we look at it through an interpretation of both sceptical and commonsense claims which has been given them by so-called ordinary language philosophers such as Norman Malcolm. On this interpretation certain unpalatable consequences of the sceptical position show up which must be faced before embracing sceptical conclusions because no fallacy has been dis-covered in their supporting arguments. It is these consequences which throw one back upon the commonsense position. Moore's work was explicitly directed to defending the *truth* of commonsense beliefs, and the sceptic's arguments are correspondingly construed as necessitating the denial of their truth. An ordinary language philosopher takes both po-sitions to bear, not on the truth of what is asserted, but on the language in which the assertions are made. Instead of construing Moore's assertions as iterating the truth of commonsese beliefs, they are construed as defending the language the common man uses. And when the sceptic

14*

says physical objects are not really perceived, and that we can only know it to be probably true that there are things, other minds, and causal connections, ordinary language philosophers take these assertions to constitute, by implication, an attack on common language rather than on common beliefs.

There is some justification for this interpretation. For if we look at sceptical arguments carefully, despite their appearance of making factual denials, we see that they are intended to establish the logical impossibility of many ordinary statements being true. And between the logical impossibility of a proposition and a linguistic fact about the expression which denotes it there is a close connection. A simple example will show this. Consider the proposition that two straight lines cannot enclose a space, and the sentence 'It is logically impossible for *two straight lines to enclose a space*'. In this sentence the italicized expression, what one might call its descriptive part, denotes nothing conceivable, and therefore has no use in the language to describe any state of affairs. Nor has it any use in expressions of questions, orders, requests, etc. If it is logically impossible that two straight lines should enclose a space, then the expression 'two straight lines enclose a space' has no more descriptive use than a nonsense combination of syllables, a mere jingle. Thus a sentence which asserts that something is logically impossible does not assert that something is not in fact the case. For what is not in fact the case could be the case. Inasmuch as the descriptive part of the sentence does not stand for something conceivable, seeing that a sentence of the form 'It is logically impossible that --' is correct has the effect of precluding the intelligible use of an expression.

The bearing of this on the sceptic's arguments is clear. If correct, they do not have the effect of upsetting a matter of fact; instead, they carry with them the consequence that parts of everyday discourse are devoid of intelligibility. How acceptable this consequence is can be determined by examining the sceptical views which have been under consideration. Take the view that no one really perceives physical objects. It is clear that it is intended to assert the logical impossibility of anyone's perceiving them. What the senses disclose *can never be* either the cause of one's data or the class of which one's data are members, inasmuch as it is inconceivable that in perception we should go beyond what is given in any one sense disclosure. On either the Lockeian or the phenomenalistic view our senses can give no conclusive reason for holding that a physical object exists as against merely appearing to exist. We can neither check our data with their cause nor with the infinite class of which they are members. And if it is logically impossible to determine that we are seeing a thing as against seeming to see it, this means that the concept *seeing a thing* is impossible, in principle, to apply. The corollary for language is that the words 'seeing a thing' have no use to describe an activity, actual or possible.

Of course it is undeniable, and Moore points this out, that 'we do, in ordinary life constantly talk of *seeing* such things as doors and fingers', and he goes on to say that 'when we do so, we are not using language incorrectly...' (1922, p. 226). The burden of the sceptical argument is that we are. But if we are, then a consequence obtains which undermines the sceptic's conclusion, namely, that his argument destroys the distinction which the expression of his position requires. Both the sceptic and the ordinary man distinguish between seeing a thing and seeming to see a thing. The difference between the ordinary man's distinction and the philosopher's is that the ordinary man takes it for granted he can subject to check, by further use of the senses, any case in which he questions whether he is really seeing a thing when he seems to see one. If there is any doubt whether he is seeing a thing rather than merely seeming to see it, for example, if he is unsure he is seeing a lake in the desert, he makes further sense tests to determine whether he seems to see a thing and really sees it, or seems to see it but does not see it. Both expressions, 'seems to see it and really does' and 'seems to see it but does not see it', properly describe possible situations, as language now is. That is, the expression 'see a thing', which functions within the expression 'seems to see a thing', in ordinary language leads an independent life, serving sometimes truly to describe what we do and sometimes not, just as 'tiger' sometimes truly applies to something we see and sometimes not. It is reasonably clear that if as a consequence of sceptical arguments 'seeing a thing' is unintelligible, so is 'seeming to see a thing'. 'Seeming to see a thing' has no more use than 'seeming to runcillate'. But the view that we never really perceive things requires the possibility of retreating to a weaker position: that we merely seem to see them. Without the contrast between perceiving and seeming to perceive, the philosopher who says we always merely seem to perceive things lacks the means of saying what it is we seem to do and hence lacks the means of denying that we ever perceive things when we seem to perceive them.

It is similarly the case that the sceptic's insistence on the *necessary* limitations of the senses has the effect of eliminating the current distinction between the words 'probable' and 'certain'. In defense of empiricism

Reichenbach labels it a prejudice that 'mathematics is the prototype of all knowledge' (1948, p. 338). Yet the invidious comparison between what the senses can provide and what reason can provide is admitted if the senses are held incapable of establishing the truth of an empirical proposition referring to something more than an immediate experience. The senses, in attaining only to probability, are admitted to fall short of a goal, viz., the indubitable knowledge got by reasoning on concepts. But is this a conceivable goal? *What* such propositions fall short of they could not conceivably attain: the logical certainty of *a priori* propositions. This they could attain only by being *a priori*. Reichenbach correctly pointed out that realizing the ideal of logical certainty cannot be achieved by propositions about material things. But one cannot proceed from this to hold that observation can make the probability of such statements amount 'almost to a certainty'. For if they could be made *almost* certain, they could *be* certain, that is, they could be what is impossible, *logically* certain. There is no approaching a goal where there is no goal, and a goal which cannot, in theory, be reached is not a goal. The linguistic consequence of the sceptic's view is that the word 'certain' has no function to distinguish one proposition about things from another such proposition. The terms 'probable' and 'certain' are no longer antitheses which divide the class of these propositions into those which are problematic and those which are certainly true or certainly false. And this is to say that *both* terms, 'certain' and 'probable' (i.e., '*less than* certain'), have lost their use to characterize empirical propositions about things. Instead, like the terms 'empirical' and '*a priori*', they make a distinction concerning the logical character of two sorts of propositions, and the characterizations are like 'even' and 'odd' as attributes of numbers: Both cannot characterize the same thing.

The sceptic seems to have one way of meeting this criticism, namely, by maintaining that the attributes *probable* and *certain* do, with qualifications, both apply to empirical propositions, so that there is no need of his being committed to the absurdity that any empirical proposition must be *a priori* in order to be certain. He could hold that sense observation can render an empirical proposition about things probable and a proposition about one's immediate experience certain, and thus that both antithetical terms, 'certain' and 'probable', apply to the class of empirical propositions. He asserts the attribute *certain* of basic propositions (e.g., 'I am feeling pain'), and denies this attribute to statements about external fact. In the one case sense observation is said to constitute conclusive verification, in the other not. Braithwaite says of the former: 'Any proposition about a present experience of mine is verified by my having the experience or falsified by my not having the experience ... the proposition that I am now seeing blackish patches is "conclusively established" in my experience the proposition that I am now in pain is conclusively disestablished in my experience' (1938, p. 271). It follows then that these can be known to be true. As has been seen, the remaining class of empirical propositions can only be known to be probable. The two tenets taken together imply solipsism.

It is important to see that this denouement of empiricism is a consequence of a use of 'certain', 'known', 'conclusively established' which does not exist in ordinary language. These descriptions of propositions about immediate experience appear to designate a standard which these propositions come up to while other empirical propositions do not. Sceptical claims have the air of using these words to ascribe to some empirical propositions one and the same attribute which they deny to others. But it will be noted that 'conclusive establishment' cannot mean, in connection with such propositions as 'I am feeling pain', establishment by relevant observations – as though one could *get to know* one was feeling a pain, after first being ignorant of having it. The claim that one conclusively establishes the proposition that one has a pain by having it uses 'conclusively establishes' to mean merely 'makes true'. It would be an impropriety of language to ask, 'Have you made sure you have a pain?', 'Have you checked it?' If it were not, then at some point in the verification process one could intelligibly say of one's own immediate experiences that it was probable that one was having them. The sceptic is aware that it would not make sense to say this; at the same time his view precludes its being intelligible to say of any physical object that its existence is certain. So it is clear that the class of empirical propositions is on the sceptical view split into two sub-classes, basic propositions and hypotheses, and that to members of these two classes one of the terms, 'certain', 'probable', applies, but not both. That is, in each range of application there is no function for one of the two antithetical terms. One cannot say intelligibly either that it is probable that there seems to be a pen in my hand or that it is certain, or known, that there is a pen in my hand.

How is it now in common discourse? Wittgenstein points out what their use is as follows: 'One says "I know" where one can also say "I believe" or "I suspect"; where one can find out' (1953, p. 221). "I know..." may mean "I do not doubt..." but does not mean that the words "I doubt..." are *senseless*, that doubt is logically precluded'

(*Ibid.*). These remarks bear on the two connected claims, that one can know one's immediate experiences and that one can merely believe statements about physical objects, other minds, future and past events. What he is saying indicates that the sceptical position constituted by these two claims involves a reversal of the ordinary linguistic proprieties – that it is instead incorrect, for example, to say 'I know I am in pain', and correct to say 'I know he is in pain'. Leaving aside any question about the propriety of describing basic propositions as known, or certain, there is no question about the propriety of describing propositions referring to external facts either as probable or as certain, as doubtful or as known. It is proper English to say either that such statements are conclusively established or that they are rendered probable, the same mode of veri-fication serving to do either. By looking, feeling, etc. we make it probable that an assertion about something beyond the content of an immediate experience is true, and by the same means we make certain, or get to know this. As G. A. Paul wrote: 'The way to find out whether one has seen a thing right, if one is in doubt, is to get nearer and try to touch it, pick it up, use it ... I. e., by further activity I tell whether I was right or wrong in taking there to be a pen there or the apples to be real ones' (1937, p. 72). Probability ranges from 0 to 1 – from certainly false to certainly true – and it is proper English to say that empirical investigation can confer on a proposition not only some value between these extremes but the extreme values as well. That is, the antithetical pairs, 'certain', 'probable', and 'known', 'believed', correctly apply to one and the same statement. They are not used to mark out a distinction in logical character between two sorts of empirical propositions, basic propositions and propositions about external facts. Were it logically impossible for a statement about things or other persons to be known or made certain, then it would never be a proper and correct description of someone, as it now is, to say that he at one time had insufficient evidence for anything more than belief but now he knows what he once believed. The sceptic might retort that ordinary language is in need of reform. But if in accordance with the reforms in-troduced it would be logically impossible for any of a whole class of propositions to be certain, then not only would it make no sense to speak of their being certain; it would also make no sense to speak of their being *less than certain*. To be less than certain, propositions about external fact would have to fall short of being propositions solely about one's present experience. And this absurdity shows that where there can be no certain knowledge there can be no probable knowledge.

Analogous critical observations apply to Gorgias' third sceptical thesis, which follows out of solipsism, that if one did know of the existence of anything it could not be communicated. It will be recalled that one reason backing this view is that one could never know that someone else was attaching to words the same meaning he himself attached. The false picture linked with this claim is, in Wittgenstein's words, that 'A man's thinking goes on within his consciousness in a seclusion in comparison with which any physical seclusion is an exhibition to public view' (1953, p. 222). There is no comparing physical seclusion, from which one can, conceivably, break out, and logical seclusion, from which one cannot. When Gorgias implies that one can never know what someone is asserting or that what one is asserting is understood, it is a logical impossibility which stands in one's way. The *belief* that a speaker's words mean what we mean by them, a belief which can never become knowledge, is like the probability which always falls short of certainty. Where there is, in principle, no knowing, believing cannot be contrasted with it.

It remains now to examine the sceptical claim that past conjunctions of events confer on future conjunctions not even so much as a probability that one type of event is the cause of the other. Observational evidence by itself is held to be insufficient to make anything probable. Hence the search for a general premise which when adjoined to the evidence will justify the probable conclusions we all draw. Some philosophers have taken the position that such a premise is not required for justifying induction, and it is worth considering this position and the difficulty the sceptic would find in it. The position is that given the English usage of the word 'probable' it is a necessary truth that *some number* of cases of association of A and B makes it probable that they are always associated (Lewy, 1938, pp. 89–90). That is, the proposition 'for some values of x (of which there is a lower limit) x cases of association ... make p probable' is treated as strictly analogous to 'for some values of x, x is divisible by 2'. 'x cases ... make p probable' and 'x is divisible by 2' each has a series of necessarily true values (and of course others which are not). To assert an observational premise reporting a number of cases of association equal to or greater than a certain minimum and to deny that the conclusion is probable will be a self-inconsistency. The difficulty of course is to know at what point an entailment relation holds between evidence and conclusion, granting that some number of observed concomitances does guarantee this. As the number of cases

of association is diminished we find ourselves unable to decide the precise point where '*p* is probable' cannot be said to follow from the observational evidence. If a hundred cases of association of *A* and *B*
warrant inferring that it is probable *A* is always associated with *B*,
will fifty, or forty-nine? It is an impressive fact that on substituting
consecutive values in the expression '*x* cases ... make *p* probable'
we derive a numerically ordered sequence of propositions with regard to
which there is no reason for saying one is necessary and its immediate
predecessor not. Apparently C. D. Broad was so impressed by this fact
that he was willing to deny that any of them is necessary, which is to
deny that any number of cases makes *p* probable.

No doubt part of the philosophical dissatisfaction with inductive
inference is that there are no rules, as there are in deductive inferences,
for determining when '*p* is probable' follows from the evidence. That is,
there are no rules for deciding that the number of observed cases is
sufficient. One knows by inspection which values of *x* in '*x* is is divisible
by 2' result in a necessary proposition. But one does not similarly know
which values of *x* do this for '*x* cases make *p* probable'. 'Some number of
cases makes *p* probable' may give the appropriate context for probability
statements, but it does not tell us specifically with what number of cases
'it is probable that *p*' follows. In deductive inferences, at least in simple
cases, we have criteria which enable us to decide whether a conclusion
can be validly inferred. To have such criteria for inductive inferences
would be to have criteria *fixed by the number of cases*, such that from a
definite number of cases it could be known that '*p* is probable' follows.
To draw a sharp line between correct and incorrect inductions, scores
of criteria would need to be formulated, and all would appear to be quite
arbitrary. For example, why should fifty cases be ruled sufficient for an
inductive conclusion, and not forty-nine?

It would appear that philosophical dissatisfaction with the fact that
we do not in a given case know whether the evidence is sufficient nor
how to test whether the evidence is sufficient is merely another example
of the dissatisfaction with the fact that inductive inference is not deductive. Hume made much of the point that there are no demonstrative
arguments to prove that the future must be conformable to the past. The
search for a premise which when adjoined to the observational evidence
would warrant an inductive conclusion appears to be of a piece with this
general dissatisfaction. But if this is a correct appraisal of the sceptic's
dissatisfaction, then it must be noted that to be discontented with the

fact that inductive inference is not deductive is to wish for what is logically impossible.

To return to the sceptic's view, it will always be unintelligible, not false, to say that any number of cases makes a statement probable, for example, that thousands of cases of water freezing, without fail, at 32° F makes it probable (let alone certain) that it will always, or in the next case, freeze at that temperature. Furthermore, on Hume's account one does not even know what it is like for a temperature of 32° F to *cause* water to freeze – as against preceding its freezing constantly. Against the background of ordinary language in which the distinction between caused and accidental occurrences exists, Hume's language seems merely to express a fact of nature – that no events are in fact caused. But his reasoning makes it clear that something much stronger is being asserted: that it is inconceivable that there be any productive agency between events. And this means that the distinction between caused and accidental events is eliminated. 'Caused occurrence' will have no use to describe any occurrence, whence neither will 'uncaused occurrence'.

Critical considerations which have been addressed here to the tenets that things are not perceived, that we can only know it to be probably true that there are things and other minds, that it is not even probable that there are causal sequences, nor possible, on Hume's view, that there be such sequences, and finally, that communication is impossible, are intended to show the consequences of these tenets for ordinary discourse. They constitute a defense of common language. They are not directed to defending what Moore explicitly stated he wished to defend: the truth of commonsense beliefs. By translating sceptical views into the concrete Moore intended to bring out the paradoxes they entail: that all such statements as 'I saw a house', 'I knew there were ore deposits', 'I understood what Smith said and know that he exists', ' I looked for and found the cause of the symptom' are under every circumstance false. The reinterpretation of sceptical views as constituting an attack on the language of common sense is intended to bring out consequences much more drastic than that it is not *true* to say such things. On this interpretation it will always be an improper use of language to say such things. It is clear that an analogous interpretation of Moore's defense of common sense will turn it into a defense of the linguistic *status quo*. Moore could direct against the linguistic sceptic a consideration parallelling his earlier rejection of arguments against holding commonsense beliefs: that it is more rational to suppose ordinary language is all right than to suppose that arguments which in effect strip parts of language of its sense contain no hidden mistakes. And the linguistic sceptic shows by his behavior that he agrees with Moore. It needs hardly be remarked that he does not give up the forms of expression which, if his arguments were correct, would be nonsensical. He uses them along with Everyman, and only in a philosophic moment apparently forgets that he votes against his own scepticism by his everyday behavior and talk.

DOUBTS AND QUERIES

1. What does Ewing's supposition come to, that a causal connection is an entailment relation which we do not see (but of a kind which throughout nature must be assumed to hold within repeated conjunctions if these are not to count as 'monstrously improbable coincidences')? Does not seeing an entailment connection mean that we mistake the logical character of a causal proposition, i.e., fail to see that it is *a priori* true or *a priori* false? What component in a case of causation, if perceived, would show that a causal proposition is necessary? Consider cases in mathematics in which people have failed to recognize that a proposition is self-contradictory, e.g., the proposition that it is possible to trisect an angle with straight edge and compass, or that there is a rational number equal to $\sqrt{2}$. How is discovery that they are self-contradictory made? Suppose we hold that when we discover A is not the cause of B, say, by finding a case in which A occurs but B does not, we establish the self-contradictoriness of 'A causes B', and that this is exactly analogous to establishing the self-contradictoriness of 'there is no prime between 27 and 30' by finding a number in this range which is prime. Philosophers who deny that the two propositions are analogous would say that finding a countercase to a causal statement by observation precludes the statement's being *a priori*, to which a rationalist might reply that the same sort of reason, finding a countercase to 'there is no prime between 27 and 30', would show that proposition not to be *a priori*.

Can one hold that sense observation is merely a less sure means of establishing *a priori* truth or falsity than calculation or demonstrative inference?

2. The general question arises whether necessary propositions and contingent propositions differ only in appearance – whether certain truths of reason only appear to be truths of fact. This seemed to be Leibniz'

view about propositions which we do not recognize as identical truths. A mind capable of making an infinite analysis would see that they are analytic. His view seems to rule out the possibility of a statement's being other than an identical truth. But there is a crucial question here: If it is logically impossible for there to be non-identical truths, *could* a proposition appear to be a non-identical truth? The appearance of there being non-identical truths implies the theoretical possibility of there being such truths. Can there be such an appearance if it is *in principle* impossible, as Leibniz holds, to provide a single instance? Is not being able to provide an instance in these cases comparable to not being able to provide an instance of a unicorn?

3. What is implied by the position that all false propositions are logically impossible? It is customary to distinguish between the impossible, the possible, and the necessary. But if what is false *could* not be otherwise, i.e., is self-contradictory, it can be argued that the necessary and the possible coincide – that if it is possible for something to be the case, then necessarily it is the case. Will possibility, as a distinct category, drop out? Given an identity between the false and the impossible, what is possible will coincide with what is true. Then can what is possible be false?

4. It is usually allowed that the objects and occurrences constituting nature could fail to exist, that there was a time when they did not exist and that there will be a time when they cease to exist. Also, it is allowed that their changing in various ways is possible – that creatures age, mountains become smoother, lakes dry up. But this implies that there are propositions whose truth-values are determined by whatever state of affairs happens to exist. That lions exist, for example, is true but could be false. But if all propositions are *a priori*, could what exists fail to exist eternally? Could what exists go out of existence, or could what does not exist come into existence? And if the existence of change implies the existence of propositions whose truth could conceivably be upset, would the rationalist position that there are no truths of fact preclude change? If there can be no propositions whose truth-values are contingent, will it follow that the facts which entail their existence also cannot exist? In other words, does the view that all true propositions are eternal truths imply that the world of ordinary things cannot exist?

5. Bradley held that moving planets, living creatures, phenomena of change were unreal because the concepts of such things are self-contradictory. Nevertheless he held that there are the self-contradictory appear-

ances of such things: Although reality cannot be self-contradictory, appearances can be. Consider the following claim, if not made in a philosophic moment: I cannot be wearing a blue jacket which is uniformly brown, but I could sensibly appear to be wearing a blue jacket which is also brown. Could what is logically impossible be pictured? If a consequence of any position which denies that there are contingent propositions is that contingent things cannot exist, can there be sensible appearances of such things? Does the existence of a sensible appearance imply that there is at least one contingent proposition?

6. Bradley gave an analytical argument, from concepts, against the reality of time, space, material objects, etc. Moore refuses to accept the concrete consequences of this position, and cites temporal facts, the existence of hands, etc. as a refutation of it. This kind of refutation has been characterized as begging the question. Could a defense of Moore's procedure be given, by reference to the mode of verification relevant to establishing that there are such things as temporal facts and spatial objects?

Consider, however, the propositions Moore attempted to refute by citing such things: propositions to the effect that the existence of temporal facts and spatial objects is self-contradictory. Can a matter of fact be relevantly brought against a claim that a certain proposition is self-contradictory? If the proposition is contradictory, there can be no refuting instances, i.e., instances showing it to be true, and if there is a refuting instance, actual or describable, then the proposition it is brought against cannot be self-contradictory. Can a matter of fact show that a proposition which a philosopher represents as being contradictory is not contradictory?

7. Consider Mill's view that all propositions are contingent, and that the only reason we take some of them to be true *a priori* is that no counter-cases have been found. In the case of unrestricted universal generalizations we could find a counterexample by examining an infinity of instances. Such an examination is impossible, and on Mill's view, factually impossible. Can one establish this impossibility by trying to surmount it and failing? Is it an answer to say that we cannot count cases fast enough, or live long enough, to encompass an infinity? that we cannot do what an all-powerful being could do, namely, tabulate the cases faster and faster, say, in successively shorter intervals, $1, \frac{1}{2}, \frac{1}{4}, \frac{1}{8}, \ldots$? Could we say the he would have tabulated them all at 2, the sum of this sequence of intervals? See 'The limits of empiricism', by Bertrand Russell (1936),

who said it is 'medically impossible' to run through an infinite sequence. Is the difference between us and an infinitely powerful being a medical difference?

8. Consider the view that we can never know with certainty that we are perceiving things, that we can only believe this. In examining this position it was pointed out that the concepts *believe* and *know* are so linked with each other that what is believed could in principle be known, and conversely. If what can be believed can be known, then what cannot be known cannot be believed either. Now, if it is *logically* impossible to know that our perceptions are not delusive, will it follow that it is logically impossible to believe this? To see that it does follow it is important to distinguish between incredibility and logical impossibility. In general, the logical impossibility of believing *p* implies that *p* itself is inconceivable. If *p* is conceivable we can at least imagine a circumstance in which it would be believed. The only ground for its being logically impossible to believe a statement would be that statement's logical impossibility. So if it is logically impossible to know that any of our perceptions are veridical, hence logically impossible to believe this, it will follow that it is logically impossible for our perceptions to be veridical. In other words, it would seem to follow that the existence of objects corresponding to our perceptions, objects which are actually perceived, is logically impossible.

This is a consequence of the tenet which both empiricism and the less extreme form of rationalism have in common, namely, that nothing more than probable knowledge can be had of the world of common objects. Can the above consideration be used to reduce the less extreme form of rationalism to the extreme form, according to which the world of sense-experience is self-contradictory?

9. Suppose that all of life is a dream, that is, that all so-called waking-life experiences are merely more coherent experiences but no less delusive than those we customarily call dreams. Could the sceptic free himself from the objection that if *he* were to demonstrate that all of life is a dream he at least must stand outside the dream – that he himself is not in the egocentric predicament his view represents everyone as being in?

10. One of the main arguments for the view that I can know only propositions about my own sense contents is that I could have information about an existent other than a sense content of my own only if I could compare it with my sense content. But in attempting to make a comparison I only succeed in comparing a present sense content with another sense content, or rather, with what is remembered of another sense con-

tent. There seems no escape from the egocentric predicament. The case seems to be made for saying that the concept *knows things which are not merely one's own sense contents* has no possible instances. Of course the concept *knows only one's own sense contents* has, or could have, instances. Can an antinomy be developed from this solipsistic view? Consider the concept *knows only one's own sense contents*. What is implied? Can the concept *knows only x* function in isolation from the concept *knows something besides x?* That is, does it imply the *possibility* of knowing things other than one's sense contents? If the force of *only* is not to distinguish among things that might possibly be known, things that are one's own sense contents and things that are not, then will the concept *knows only one's own sense contents* reduce to, become identical with, *knows one's own sense contents?* If it does, its use to make a contrast is lost. Does the philosopher who concludes that one's knowledge is solipsistically bounded need this contrast to set out his position against a counter view? Consider now the *argument* for solipsism. It is directed to showing that the concept *knows things other than one's own sense contents* could not possibly have instances.

11. It is instructive to compare 'He alone can know what he intends' and 'He alone can know what he will do' (See Wittgenstein, 1953, pp. 223–224). The sceptic maintains that one's own intentions, and the like, one can oneself know, but that no one else can. And against the criticism of this claim, that the word 'know' (equally with its antithesis 'believe') has no use in nonphilosophical contexts, he could cite exclamations in ordinary language such as, 'But I must know what I intend', 'Surely I must know better than you that I am in pain'. To assess such retorts one needs to inquire about their purpose (1953, p. 221.) Do they imply a fact about our knowledge? Does 'I know I am in pain' assert something about one's knowledge and also something about one's condition? If one is making a factual report, could one succeed as well by saying 'I am in pain' as by saying 'I know I am in pain'?

12. Let us call the two positions, 'I alone am real' and 'I cannot know that anyone else exists', 'ontological' and 'noetic' solipsism, resp. The one position seems quite distinct from the other, inasmuch as 'I cannot know that anyone else exists' appears to imply nothing whatever about what exists. Certainly noetic solipsism appears to leave quite open the truth or falsity of 'I alone am real', i.e., of 'No one but me exists'. To cite a parallel, 'I cannot know that there are gold deposits on the moon' implies nothing about whether there are or are not such deposits. Is it the same

with 'I cannot know anyone else exists'? Do the following considerations show that there is a difference in the relationship of noetic and ontological solipsism, that unlike the nonphilosophical propositions, an implication relationship holds? Supposing the following argument (patterned after the one used in 8) is correct, how is the difference to be explained? Taking 'I cannot know that anyone else exists' to mean that this is *logically* impossible, it will follow according to the argument in 8 that I cannot conceivably believe anyone else exists. But the only circumstance under which it is logically impossible to believe *p* is where *p* is logically impossible, in our present case, that it is logically impossible for anyone else but me to exist.

There is an objection to this argument which needs to be assessed. It could be objected that the argument is beside the point since its conclusion is the *logical* impossibility of there being anyone else but me, whereas 'There are others besides myself' if factually false is not impossible. Can this be maintained? If it is correct to do so, then the matter of fact truth of 'I am the only one who exists' will be exactly analogous to other matter of fact truths. Consider the words 'I alone exist', uttered by a solipsist, and the same words uttered by the last survivor of a world catastrophe. Are these the same? That there is a last survivor implies it is true that there *were* other people, and false that there now are other people, from which the logical impossibility of there being a last survivor *and* other people as well follows. How is it with the philosophical proposition? Would the solipsist accept any evidence as falsifying his claim that he alone exists? Does he give a demonstrative argument for his position, or would he be content with empirical evidence such as the last survivor could make use of? The last survivor's evidence would not show that there had never been people other than himself. Would it put the solipsist's position fairly to say there could never have been, nor could ever be, people other than himself? Note the difference between its being logically impossible for others beside oneself to exist, and its being logically impossible that a last survivor and others besides himself exist.

Construing 'I alone am real' as implying that the existence of others than oneself is logically impossible, let us examine the function of the word 'I' in this statement. Does the statement say *who* it is that is real? Can it be argued that if it denies the possibility of anyone else being real, then the first person pronoun loses its use to single out a person? Is 'I' opposed to 'you'. or' he'? Wittgenstein remarked that what the solipsist wants is not a notation in which the ego has a monopoly, but one in

15

which the ego vanishes (Notes taken at roughly the time of dictation of material on solipsism, *The blue book*). If it is true that 'I' has lost its antitheses in the language – that these have been deprived of application – can it be argued that ontological solipsism is inexpressible? Is Wittgenstein's dictum á propos here: 'Whereof one cannot speak, thereof one must be silent'?

Note, however, that *being silent* implies the possibility of not being silent – of making one's thoughts public. Is the ontological solipsist not only condemned to silence but also prevented from thinking what he cannot express?

13. Suppose language were changed in such a way that 'know' and 'believe', 'certain' and 'probable', no longer applied, as they now do, to the same proposition, the first member of each pair being deprived of its present use so that it would no longer be correct to say, 'I know there are squirrels in the attic', 'It is certain virus x is the cause of her illness'. Would anything be gained? Would we have to introduce a new pair of terms to express the distinction which each pair at present expresses (for example, 'believe with a high degree of probability' and 'merely believe', 'highly probable' and 'probable')? Would the sceptical difficulty reappear in connection with the applicability of the new pair?

14. When we say that 'All prime numbers except 2 are odd' is certain, and that 'Water freezes at 32 °F' is certain, are we ascribing the same property to each proposition? Consider the pairs, 'certain', 'probable' and 'mathematically certain', 'probable'. How are they connected with the logical character of propositions? What similarities and differences exist among the following pairs: 'certain', 'probable'; 'swift', 'slow'; 'mathematically certain', 'empirically certain'; 'odd', 'even'?

15. Suppose one wished to reckon the probability of death within a random group of people between ages 45 and 70. On Reichenbach's view the mortality statistics on the basis of which the frequency of death is computed are themselves only probable. Does this consideration in any way affect the computation of the desired probability? How would one reckon the probability that Brown, Smith, and Jones, whose headstones we seem to see, have actually died? Is the actuary proceeding carelessly in not basing his probabilities on antecedent probabilities of his statistical evidence?

16. If the inductive principle is *a priori*, can adjoining it to the observational premises of an induction validate, or justify, a conclusion drawn from them? Compare an induction augmented by this principle with the

inference, which lacks a general premise: 'This is a square; therefore, this is four-sided'. Will the addition of the *a priori* general premise 'All squares are four-sided' make it possible to infer a conclusion that was not possible before? Compare the truth-table of a function $p \cdot q$, representing premises, with the conjunctive function $p \vee \sim p \cdot p \cdot q$.

17. Kant says that concepts of objects transcending sense-experience 'retain no meaning whatever', yet says he does not exclude the possibility of there being objects of this sort. Kant must mean here by 'concept having no meaning', a meaningless term. For a concept is the meaning of a term and it makes no sense to speak of its having meaning or being meaningless. Rephrasing Kant's claim as 'objects transcending sense-experience' is a meaningless term, can he say his philosophy does not exclude transcendent objects? *What sort* of object is denoted by a meaningless expression? If a term refers to an object it is not meaningless, and if it is meaningless it cannot refer to an object. Compare the following expressions: 'Transcendent objects exist', 'Oval triangles exist', 'Runcibles exist'.

18. When a philosopher ignores the consequences his position has with regard to language, how is this to be explained? Bradley argues that it is logically impossible for material things and relations between them to be real, Hume that it is logically impossible to know that they are real. The linguistic facts, if there were such facts, which would provide the backing for such claims, would be that words and phrases like 'chair', 'north of', 'knowledge of wild life' have no application. But there are no such facts, and the philosopher can scarcely make the mistake of supposing there are. His own discourse belies any such explanation as that he is mistaken about the use of these terms.

As a hint at a possible explanation consider Wittgenstein's remark on the solipsistic claim, 'I can only *believe* someone else is in pain, but I *know* it if I am': 'Yes: one can make the decision to say "I believe he is in pain" instead of "He is in pain". But that is all – What looks like [...] a statement about a mental process is in truth an exchange of one expression for another which, while we are doing philosophy, seems the more appropriate one' (1953, p. 102).

15*

REFERENCES

Recommended reading:
  Hans Reichenbach (1948), 'Rationalism and empiricism: an enquiry
  into the roots of philosophical error', *The philosophical review*, Vol. 57,
  pp. 330–346.
Further readings:
  A. J. Ayer, *British empirical philosophers*, Introduction.
  Brand Blanshard (1967), 'Internal relations and their importance to
  philosophy', *The review of metaphysics*, Vol. 21, pp. 227–236.
  Immanuel Kant (1929b), *Prolegomena to any future metaphysics*, Intro-
  duction.
  —(1929a), *Critique of pure reason*, Introduction.
  Morris Lazerowitz, *The Structure of Metaphysics*, Ch. 1.
  —*Philosophy and Illusion*, Ch. 6,
  Frederick L. Will, 'Will the future be like the past?', *Mind*, Vol. 56,
  pp. 332–347.

8. Freedom of the Will and Theories of Ethics

I. Differences between metaphysical systems often have their focus in divergent positions on the nature of the proposition that every event has a cause. When it is said that every causal statement is a special case of the general law that future events arise from past events, and furthermore, that they *must* arise from them, what is being asserted has to be clarified, whether, for example, the necessity imposed by a causal law is contingent or *a priori*. And there is even some question as to whether there is any necessity at all. Hume held that the necessity we seem to find in causation is nothing more than a feeling of expectation that has been built up in our minds. Constant conjunctions exist in nature, but no necessary connection. Other philosophers hold that such conjunctions can only be accounted for by supposing them to be logically necessary, and amongst such philosophers it is in dispute whether the relation is analytic or synthetic. In either case every causal statement would be *a priori* true or *a priori* false. But then an explanation is required for what Hume pointed out, that causal statements can have no *a priori* proof inasmuch as their opposites are conceivable. Some philosophers are ready to allow that the immutable laws of nature of which Galileo spoke do not have the unalterable truth of $2+2+4$, that is, that causal inevitability is not logical necessity; but they hold that a tie such as Hume denied is to be found nevertheless in fact exists. If the tie between occurrences is contingent merely, it is of course theoretically possible that it not exist, that an event might occur without having a cause. That is, the position that 'All events have causes' – unlike 'All effects have causes' – is empirical implies the possibility that some events are not brought about by events which precede them, but are 'free'.

Whether there are uncaused events as well as caused events, and what is the nature of the relation we take to be causal, are questions which belong to the field of metaphysics. But they also belong to the field of ethics. They have a direct bearing on a longstanding controversy in this field over whether man has freedom of will. Taking into account all of the events leading up to an act a man does or the choice he makes, the question is whether he could do otherwise than he does do or make a different choice than the one he in fact makes. This question is of special importance in connection with actions classified as moral – those which are duties, or are right, or are wrong. Is man a 'moral free agent'? When he does an act which is judged to be right, or to be wrong, could he have done otherwise or chosen otherwise? And is he morally responsible for performing such actions or choosing to perform them?

Ethics has as a central concern the nature of moral actions. Another concern is the nature of intrinsic goodness. Whether there are intrinsically good states of affairs, that is, states of affairs which are desirable in themselves without regard to anything else, is independent of whether man does or does not 'have free will'. But the existence of right actions and wrong actions seems to be in a different case. Some if not all accounts of moral actions make their existence depend on the existence of alternative courses of action which the agent could have launched on instead, this latter being a necessary condition for having free will. For example, one ethical theory about rightness, utilitarianism, explicitly incorporates into its account a reference to alternative possibilities which the agent has open to him: An act is right if its consequences are no less good, or no worse, than any alternative act the agent could have done instead; and analogously for a wrong act. According to most ethical views, and perhaps quite independently of anything explicit in the mind of the ordinary person, if whatever the agent does he must do, that is, if he could not do otherwise, then what he does will be ethically neutral – neither morally right nor morally wrong. Thus the existence of moral actions, with their concomitant moral responsibilities, presupposes that courses of action are possible to the agent which are different from the ones taken. And whether different courses of action are possible to an agent depends upon whether a choice of a different course was possible for him. Ultimately, whether he can act differently rests on whether he can choose to act differently. Freedom of the will – freedom to will any of a number of alternative acts – is thus taken to be a precondition of both right and wrong action. We shall therefore turn first to the question whether it is possible for freedom of choice to exist.

This appears to be the question whether choices are free from the determining influence of causes, and thus to be a form of the more general question about the nature of the universe. If *all* events, including mental events, are causally determined, then the consequence appears to be that there is no freedom of choice, and that whatever takes place is inevitable. That is, if all events without exception are brought about by causes, both their existence and nature being what they must be in virtue of their antecedents, then alternative possibilities are precluded. Whether this is the inference to be drawn from the premise that all events are subject to causal laws is uncertain. Some philosophers have held that it is, others have held that the existence of possible alternatives to the act the agent engages in is compatible with the universal presence of causation, and still other philosophers have accepted the inference but have denied the premise, namely, that all events, in particular, acts of choice, are necessitated by their antecedents. What William James (1897) called 'hard determinism' is the position that all events have determining causes and that it follows from this that no man can do other than he does do. Indeterminists claim that one can do otherwise and can choose otherwise, and that this implies that some occurrences are spontaneous. The compromise position, which James called 'soft determinism', maintains that man has freedom of will and at the same time that causation is universal. One form of it is to the effect that there is a sense of 'could' such that it is true to say one could do otherwise than one does do, even though everything that happens is predetermined.

The position taken on whether a person can do otherwise than he does do not only bears on the existence of right and wrong actions. It is at once evident that it has implications with regard to moral responsibility. Barring special conditions, which in some cases have been specified in legal codes, a person is said to be responsible for his actions; and society in fact holds him responsible, by giving him credit for doing right or for doing his duty, and censuring or punishing him for doing wrong. The two extreme positions on free will both put in question whether anyone can justifiably be held responsible for his actions. The following interchange between two characters in Somerset Maugham's *Of human bondage* puts the position of the hard determinist:

Philip: 'Have you never done anything you regret?' 'How can I regret when what I did was inevitable?' asked Cronshaw in return ... 'The illusion which man has that his will is free is so deeply rooted that I am ready to accept it. I act as though I were a free agent. But when an action is performed it is clear that all the forces of the universe from all eternity conspired to cause it, and nothing I could do could have prevented it. It was inevitable.

If it was good I can claim no merit; if it was bad I can accept no censure.'

Thus 'what must be, must be', because of whatever forces are operative, and since what one does or chooses is the necessary resultant of those forces, praise and blame are no more intelligible when directed to human agents than they are when directed to inanimate objects. It makes no sense to blame a stone which shatters a window, and on the determinist view it makes no sense to blame the person who throws the stone. Given one's heredity, one's natural and social environment, including education, and one's past actions, the decisions one makes are predetermined, and it is an illusion to suppose they are not. 'Man's life', says Baron d'Holbach, 'is a line that nature commands him to describe upon the surface of the earth, without his ever being able to swerve from it, even for an instant. He is born without his own consent; his organization does in nowise depend upon himself; his ideas come to him involuntarily; his habits are in the power of those who cause him to contract them; he is unceasingly modified by causes, whether visible or concealed, over which he has no control, which necessarily regulate his mode of existence, give the hue to his manner of thinking, and determine his manner of acting' (1770, Ch. 11).

The determinist points out that there is no reason to exempt human volition from the operation of causes. The indeterminist replies that there is the best of reasons, namely, that we are held accountable for our actions, and in fact consider ourselves responsible for them whenever we pride ourselves or blame ourselves for what we have done. If we could not have done differently then Cronshaw's observation would be the appropriate one. But we assent to responsibility for our actions, and however irrational it may be, we take pride in some and regret others. If this is irrational because it implies that we could have done otherwise, then how much more irrational is a system of things in which taking pride in our actions or feeling remorse for them should be *necessitated*. Only in a universe in which possibilities are precisely coextensive with what is actual must it be granted that what one does is the only thing one could do. Apparently, the alternative to denying that anyone can do other than he does do is to deny that choice of an action, or the doing of an action which is voluntary but not chosen, is causally determined. Either choice is free from the determining influence of causes or else no one can make a different choice from the one he in fact makes; and when no conscious selection among alternatives is made, as in the case of many voluntary acts, if there is no possibility of preventing them by choosing to prevent them then it is an empty claim to say one would have done differently had one chosen to.

'Men think themselves free', said Spinoza, 'inasmuch as they are conscious of their volitions and desires, and never even dream, in their ignorance, of the causes which have disposed them to wish and desire' (1901a, Pt., Appendix). Why does the indeterminist not accept this account and concede that it is an illusion that man possesses freedom of will? Can he support his claim to freedom by anything more substantial than an argument to the effect that without freedom no one is morally responsible for his acts? Perhaps no one *is* morally responsible for his acts. It is entirely possible that we should all have the illusion of freedom and that there be no freedom. The indeterminist replies that he does not need to argue for the existence of freedom. Nor does he need to rely on any indirect evidence. He lays claim to the positive evidence of his own immediate experience. He claims to be as conscious of his freedom to choose among alternatives as he is of the presence of any other immediate datum. On this point Henry Sidgwick writes:

'It is impossible for me to think ... when confronted with several alternatives that my volition is completely determined by my formed character and the motives acting upon it. The opposite conviction is so strong as to be absolutely unshaken by the evidence brought against it. I cannot believe it to be illusory. So far it is unlike the erroneous intuitions which occur in the exercise of the senses: as (e.g.) the imperfections of sight and hearing. For experience soon teaches me to regard these as appearances whose suggestions are misleading: but no amount of experience of the sway of motives even tends to make me distrust my intuitive consciousness that in resolving after deliberation I exercise free choice as to which of the motives acting on me shall prevail' (1874, p. 51).

But if one's selection of one of these motives is free, does this mean that it has no necessary connection with the past? Indeterminists answer this question affirmatively: Insofar as it is free it is independent of what has gone before. Some indeterminists have held that failure of causal laws to operate where volitions are concerned is a direct consequence of the intuitive perception that we can either will to do an act or will not to do it. Determinists are quick to point out that man is then indeed not morally responsible for his acts. In fact it is a misnomer to call them *his* acts. If moral acts and moral choices occur spontaneously, that is, quite independently of any antecedents, then they are like accidents: They happen, but they are beyond the control of one's character, one's environment, one's past actions. They spring from nowhere. One becomes a mere bystander, a spectator of the acts his body or mind engages in, not an agent who is accountable for what is happening.

We thus find ourselves in a dilemma with respect to the forms of determinism and indeterminism expounded here: If every chosen or voluntary action is causally determined no one is morally responsible; and likewise if they are free from causation no one is morally responsible. It is a commonplace that we are held accountable and that we hold ourselves accountable, both for deliberately chosen actions and for actions which could have been prevented or could have been done had we chosen. The thought suggests itself that the consequence common to both views, that no one is morally responsible, stems from a common tenet. And indeed there is an assumption on which they both rest, namely, that there is a logical incompatibility between the statement that events are determined by their antecedents and the statement that one can equally choose to act and choose not to act. Proponents of the two views merely insist on the truth of different statements within the pair, and discard different statements as untrue. Possibly it would not occur to anyone to doubt the existence of two possibilities, choosing to act and choosing not to act, but for the doubt that this is compatible with the determinist thesis that every event has its sufficient conditions. The strict determinist takes it to be impossible that an event should not occur, given its sufficient conditions. From this it follows that it is impossible for more than one volition to occur. In consequence he challenges the 'intuitive consciousness' of free choice which Sidgwick laid claim to. The controversy thus has the form of a debate over which of two incompatible theses is true, that all events are causally determined, or that it is equally possible to make two different choices.

The ordinary man behaves as though both of these theses are true. This fact can be explained in one of two ways: either by saying that the ordinary man is capable of living comfortably with mutually contradictory beliefs or by holding that there is in fact no incompatibility between the two tenets in dispute, that is, by holding that 'all events are the results of their causal antecedents' does not entail that one can never do other than he does do or choose other than he does choose. The latter is the position of so-called 'soft' determinism: that volitions as well as events in nature are subject to causal laws and yet that man is, in any important sense, free. The obvious task is to show how the two claims can be reconciled with each other, in particular, to specify a sense of 'free' which will make a reconciliation possible. The idea very naturally suggests itself that some obscurity in the meanings of key terms lies at the bottom of this longstanding and recalcitrant dispute over freedom of the will. This was Hume's approach to the problem. 'From this circumstance alone', he says, 'that a controversy has been long kept on foot, and remain still undecided, we may presume there is some ambiguity in the expression, and that the disputants affix different ideas to the terms employed in the controversy. For as the faculties of the mind are supposed to be naturally alike in every individual ... it were impossible, if men affix the same ideas to their terms, that they could so long form different opinions of the same subject' (1902, Sec. VIII, Pt. I, Par. 62) . Accordingly, his program is 'to make it appear that all men have ever agreed in the doctrine both of necessity and of liberty, according to any reasonable sense, which can be put on these terms; and that the whole controversy has hitherto turned merely upon words' (*Ibid.*, Par. 63).

What needs to be made clear is the connection between possession of free will and the power of acting differently from the way in which we actually do act, and the connection between the latter and the tenet that everything has a cause in what precedes it. Moore says that it is 'a mere abuse of language' to hold that our wills are free 'if we *never* can, in any sense at all, do anything except what, in the end, we actually do do ... We certainly have *not* got Free Will, in the ordinary sense of the words (1912, p. 203), if this is the case. That is, that we *can* do something which we do not do is a necessary condition for having free will. But he questions whether it is a sufficient condition. 'Whether we have it or not will depend upon the precise sense in which it is true that we can (*Ibid.*).; and merely showing that we sometimes can do differently will not show that we have free will unless this is shown to be true in the relevant sense of 'can'. As for 'Everything has a cause', he says it does follow in one sense of 'can' that nothing ever can happen except what does happen. But if 'can', or 'could', is ambiguous, then the fact that some things could have happened which did not happen need not contradict the principle that everything has a cause.

He then proceeds to argue that in at least one sense of 'could' it is true to say we could have done otherwise than we did do. His reasoning is that there is a distinction, understood by everyone, between two events, neither of which happened, one of which is possible and the other not. We say of the cat that she could have climbed the tree, though she did not, and of the dog that did not climb the tree, that he could not have. In the one case it is true to say it could have been done, in the other case not. That is, the fact that neither climbed the tree does not do away with the distinction between what could and what could not be done. Nor does it imply that what the cat does and what the dog does not do is undetermined: The cat's desire and the dog's incapability are sufficient for each.

What the courts accept as excusing one from liability for one's actions is a clue to the sense in which moderate determinists take an action to be freely done. It also indicates acceptance of the same causal uniformities where voluntary or chosen acts are concerned as operate in the world of nature. A verdict of guilty is precluded in those cases where a plea can be supported that the offense was either done in ignorance of certain facts or done under compulsion. One contemporary writer, H. L. A. Hart, sets out the list of defenses or exceptions as 'Mistake of fact, coercion, duress, provocation, insanity, infancy' (1948, p. 179). A man who receives stolen goods in ignorance of their origin is counted not culpable, unless his ignorance is inexcusable. A drug addict is conceded not to be responsible for a theft, although he may be considered responsible for having become an addict. Certainly one would not be held responsible if an accident occurred as a result of a patellar reflex action or as a result of paralysis. But in general, as another contemporary writer points out, we should not accept as reasons for absolving a person from responsibility for an act that he did it (a) because he wanted to, (b) because he did not have a good character, or (c) because his past acts have formed his character (Nowell–Smith, 1959, Ch. 20).

What is to be concluded from these considerations? Given that a man's moral character, however formed, is the resultant of various forces, are we to allow that he could not have done differently but is nevertheless answerable for what he did? Or are we to say that he could have done differently because the action flowed from his character, and that the kind of character he possessed was in his power? The latter seems to be the answer of Hume, Mill, and a number of other philosophers up to the present day. Hume comments that 'the conjunction between motives and voluntary actions is as regular and uniform as that between the cause and effect in any part of nature (1902, Sec. VIII, Pt. I, Par. 69), and Mill that given the motives, character, and disposition of a man, he will in fact act in only one way unless some other antecedent interveness. 'When we' think of ourselves hypothetically as having acted otherwise than we did', says Mill, 'we always suppose a difference in the antecedents' (1872, p. 567). Mill is convinced that one often could have chosen another course, had it been preferred. But this is by no means the same as supposing that one could have chosen it if another was preferred. One cannot act in opposition to the strongest desire or aversion.

In what sense then has one freedom? Hume specifies it as 'a power of acting or not acting, according to the determinations of the will' (1902, Sec. VIII, Pt. I, Par. 73). This is the power which the prisoner does not have: however much he wills to escape, nothing changes. Without this power, Hume says, no actions can be 'objects either of approbation or dislike ... Actions are objects of our moral sentiment, so far only as they are indications of the internal character, passions, and affections.' Accordingly, moral responsibility is assessed in proportion as actions stem from these sources. We all proceed on the assumption that how we act is determined by the kind of characters we have, and our efforts to alter people's characters by moral exhortation and by rewards and punishments is sufficient indication that we take for granted that behavior is uniformly connected with type of character. W. K. Clifford, a writer with views similar to Mill's, expresses forcefully the point usually insisted on by the strict determinist, viz., that one cannot conceive of responsibility without uniformity (1879, p. 325). An act which does not have its source in a man's character is a mere accident for which *he* is not accountable. Freedom cannot mean exemption from causal laws, but only from the control of circumstances outside one.

To say that a man is responsible for conduct determined by his character, and that he is free in proportion as it is his character and not external circumstances which guides him, leaves a question unanswered which the strict determinist is sure to ask: Is one responsible for one's character? Is the formation of character in one's control? Mill answers this in the affirmative: Character is not only made *for* us, but *by* us. In Clifford's words, 'within certain limits I am ... responsible for what I am now, because within certain limits I have made myself ... The habit of choosing among motives is one which may be acquired and strengthened by practice, and the strength of particular motives, by continually directing attention to them, may be almost indefinitely increased or diminished ... I am responsible for a very large portion of the circumstances which are now external to me; that is to say, I am responsible for certain of the restrictions on my own freedom' (1879, pp. 324–325). We can alter our character, says Mill, *if we wish,* just as others can form and alter our character by willing the requisite means, if they wish. That is, we, like others, can place ourselves under the influence of certain circumstances, can modify the motives activating us by feeding or starving them, can engage in actions which build or destroy character by choosing to strengthen the motives eventuating in those actions. According to Mill, people object to the idea that our conduct is determined because they confuse it with the idea that no matter how we strive, either to do an action or prevent an action, what happens is predestined. Whatever is to happen will happen, regardless of our efforts. Our character and motives being what they are, Mill grants we shall act in only one way unless some other antecedent intervenes. But one such intervening antecedent is the wish to resist a motive, or to encourage it. And this antecedent makes a difference to what follows. It is not that some force guides history to a foregone conclusion by negating our efforts and wishes. One need not subscribe to this fatalistic tenet in order to hold that whatever exists at any given time has its causal determinants.

But does one escape, in the end, into anything less compelling than fatalism? Do *we* cooperate in the formation of our characters, and if so, were there not sufficient reasons for our cooperation in the form of determining causes? Let us allow that we can alter our characters *if we wish.* Does the wish have its source in our character, and if so, was it not determined? Could that particular wish have failed to occur? If a hardened criminal has no such wish we can only assume that there are no causes within him (or outside him) to bring it about. Now the statement, 'If he wished to improve his character, he would do so', is quite empty if he cannot wish it. And if his character is determined by all the influences operating on him from birth onward, and his wishes in turn are determined by his character, and his actions in turn by his wishes, then the sense in which he is nevertheless a free agent seems to be a sense which is irrelevant to the free-will controversy. A moderate determinist says 'I am a free agent when my actions are independent of the control of circumstances outside me' (Clifford, pp. 326–327), or that by liberty is meant 'a power of acting or not acting, according to the determinations of the will' (Hume, 1902, Sec. VIII, Pt. I, Par. 73), or 'Freedom means the opposite of compulsion; a man is free if he does not act under compulsion' (Schlick, 1939, p. 150). Perhaps no one would deny that 'freedom' in nonphilosophical contexts is the antithesis of 'constraint': I have freedom when I am unhindered in the realization of my desires. But whether its antithesis in the freewill controversy is something quite other than constraint, namely, causal determination, is the core of the dispute. Indeterminists and strict determinists, as we have seen, are agreed that they are antithetical. Moderate determinists seem to say they are not.

Moore tried to support this latter view by specifying a sense of 'could', as it is used in 'I could have done differently', which permits one to accept causal determination of actions and also the truth of 'one can do otherwise than one does do'. 'I could have' is analyzed as 'I would have if I had chosen', and this is compatible with the principle that everything has a cause. He thinks that those who deny that we ever could have done differently than we do in fact do deny it because they think no one would act differently *even if* he chose to. This is the fatalist position. But he admits the possession of free will is often denied for another reason: that we never could have chosen differently. His reply is that to say that we could have chosen otherwise implies that we would have chosen otherwise had we chosen so to choose, that in this sense it is true that we could have chosen otherwise, and that this again is compatible with the causal principle.

It is clear that the difficulty here is similar to the difficulty of holding that one's acts are free insofar as they result from one's character – insofar as they are not determined by causes external to the person. The question is whether the person, as a complex of tendencies, desires, motives, principles, is or is not an original undetermined cause. Moore's claim that one can do otherwise in the sense that one would if one chose to, prompts an unending chain of questions: Could one have chosen otherwise? Could one have made a different choice to choose?, etc. The strict determinist maintains that to put off answering the crucial question is not to answer it. He reiterates the position expressed by Schopenhauer: 'A man can surely do what he wills to do, but he cannot determine what he wills'. Our volitions, and our characters, are the result of our inherited equipment and environmental influences; the belief that we can do otherwise or choose otherwise is due to ignorance of determining forces. The springs of human conduct are largely unconscious. Leibniz's observation that 'we do not always perceive the often imperceptible causes upon which our resolution depends' (1900, p. 293), is borne out by modern-day work of psychoanalysis in disclosing unconscious motivations.

J. L. Austin has raised crucial objections to Moore's analysis of 'could have done' as 'would have, if', though it remains possible that some similar analysis may be correct. But any such analysis is subject to the kind of determinist objection cited in the preceding paragraph. Accordingly, C. D. Broad raises the question whether there is a *categorical* sense of 'could', one which does not analyze as 'would have, if' (1952, pp. 206–207). Kant said that 'ought' and 'ought not' imply 'could': If what was done ought not to have been done, then the act done *need not* have been done, i.e., *could* have been avoided, and if what was not done ought to have been done, then the act not done *could* have been done. The question is whether a meaning can be attached to 'could' which is expressible without the conditional 'if certain antecedents had been present which were not present'. And if such a meaning can be singled out, the further question is whether in that sense 'I could have done otherwise' ever asserts what is true. In Broad's view it does not, because he thinks it entails unacceptable consequences. One consequence he admits to be logically possible: that events which are factors in the total cause of a given action may themselves have no 'causal ancestors'. That is, the series of causes stops with them 'just as the series of ancestors stops with Adam' (*Ibid.*, p. 211); they are 'causal progenitors'. Determinists hold that every event has causal ancestors. The indeterminist view is that there are in the world causal progenitors, for example, deliberate efforts made by us to reinforce some desire or stifle some other. But now such efforts are nothing more than accidents; they happen to occur and they happen to reinforce one desire rather than another. The indeterminist, who holds that complete causal determination precludes moral responsibility, is driven to maintain that it is these accidents and their consequences for which we are responsible. The efforts we happened to put forth categorically could have been otherwise.

Broad thinks that this is not the position of those who hold that one could have done something other than one did. He takes them to be implying that although there are no *events* which are causal ancestors of efforts we make, these efforts are nevertheless determined by something which is not an event, namely, the agent or self. This rather than events in in the agent is the total cause. Broad's objection to this tenet, which he thinks is entailed by the categorical possibility of alternative actions, is not that what the agent is is itself determined. It is, rather, that an event, which has a date, could not conceivably have as its total cause something which 'contained no factor to which the notion of date has any application' (*Ibid.*, p. 215). It will be recognized that the position against which these objections are raised is the position which attempts to reconcile 'every event has a cause' and 'man can do other than he does do'.

Whether such reconciliation is possible rests on whether analysis does show that the falsity of 'every event has a cause' is entailed by 'man can do otherwise than he does do', where the analysis of 'can' does not involve the notion 'would, if'. Moore admits that the *truth* of the determinist tenet that everything has a cause entails, in some sense of 'could', the falsity of the indeterminist claim that man could do what he does not do; but he does not specify this sense. One contemporary writer, Keith Lehrer, makes no attempt to come to a decision, by analysis, concerning the relation between these two tenets, and devotes himself to supporting the claim made by Sidgwick, Thomas Reid, and others that introspection discloses that we have free will – regardless of what this implies concerning the principle that every event is causally determined. The question thus shifts to what looks like an empirical examination and away from logical analysis. It is worthwhile trying this approach, for if the possibility both of choosing to do an an act and of choosing not to do it is an introspective datum, then the consequences must take care of themselves.

It will be recalled that Sidgwick claimed an 'intuitive consciousness' of exercising free choice in reaching a decision after deliberation. Mill denies that consciousness certifies any such thing. This is one type of challenge to the claim that freedom to choose exists and can be known by introspection. It is curious that there should be any disagreement over what one is conscious of. One is reminded of the similar disagreement over whether we are aware of universals. Mill's denial does not indicate any misapprehension of what his contemporaries affirmed or that he thought he and they were talking at cross purposes. 'To be conscious of free will must mean', he says, 'to be conscious, before I have decided, that I am able to decide either way' (1872, p. 564). But he denies that 'what I am *able* to do, is ... a subject of consciousness. Consciousness is not prophetic; we are conscious of what is, not of what will or can be. We never know that we are able to do a thing, except from having done it, or something equal or similar to it' *(Ibid.)*. A rather different objection is raised by the determinist: that introspection does not show we could have chosen differently under exactly the same conditions, external and internal; we merely feel we could have chosen differently if a different motive had been present. Mill grants that we do often believe or feel convinced of the latter, but that 'if our so-called consciousness of what we are able to do is not borne out by experience it is a delusion' *(Ibid.)*.

16

Another type of challenge to the claim that we are immediately aware of freedom to decide 'either way' is that such introspective evidence is inadequate inasmuch as it can in any instance be deceptive. We can feel that we are free, and be deluded. To use an illustration of this point from a contemporary writer, 'the timid man in a hypnotist's audience . . . who gets up to make a speech, may truthfully protest a feeling of complete freedom in choosing to do so: this is quite compatible with the possibility that his choice was determined . . . by the instructions he received earlier under hypnosis' (Hempel, 1958, p. 161). His evidence is as inconclusive as it would be if his senses testified under hypnosis that there was a butterfly before him when there was not.

This argument will be recognized as a variation on the sceptical argument against the possibility of sense knowledge. Because one may in any given case be deceived it is concluded that one cannot in any circumstances whatever know that one is not deceived. As we have seen in Chapter 3, the claim is that it is *logically* impossible to know this, not that it is merely in fact impossible. It should be noted also that the force of Mill's claim is that freedom of choice *could not* be a datum of consciousness – that introspection can only tell one what one feels, not what one is able to do. Thus by *argument* various writers dismiss as an illusion the perception Sidgwick and Reid claimed to have. Sidgwick said this perception was 'absolutely unshaken by the evidence brought against it'. But note that the 'evidence' is not counter-evidence of the same sort, but argumentation which musters neither direct nor indirect evidence against what is asserted to be an empirical fact. It is demonstrative. Like Parmenides' argument against the reality of separate things, which purported to show plurality to be self-contradictory, the arguments against direct awareness of freedom purport to show its impossibility. Yet in the case of the argument against plurality and of all arguments against free will an admission is made which throws suspicion on the argumentation: that there is the appearance of plurality and the illusion of freedom. The appearance of plurality implies its possibility, and on the face of it constitutes some evidence for its reality. And analogously, the illusion of having freedom of choice implies that this is logically possible.

Now it is of course allowed that like the timid man under hypnosis we could all have a feeling of freedom in choosing and not have freedom. The existence of this feeling is compatible with there not being freedom of choice. Since there is no additional and decisive reason for taking sides in the dispute over whether there is direct consciousness of freedom of choice, in particular for siding with those who assert the existence of freedom on the ground of direct evidence, it is worthwhile investigating whether there is *indirect* evidence for it, that is, evidence which at least makes its existence probable. Were an outsider to drop into the world, would he find factual evidence from which he could infer the likelihood that earthlings have freedom of choice? Certain facts of human behavior would at once be apparent to him: that people seriously deliberate over whether they should do one act in preference to another, as though it were both possible to choose it and possible not to choose it; that people praise and blame each other and themselves for actions done, and have feelings of satisfaction or remorse for them, as though they could have done differently. When, for example, the prophet Nathan presented David with the parable of the rich man who seized the one ewe-lamb of the poor man, the most natural construction to place on David's judgment on himself for having seized Bathsheba, the wife of Uriah the Hittite, is that he believed it possible to have resisted temptation. Admission of being rightly taken to account for one's deeds, the prevalence of feelings of regret for having done what should not have been done or for having left undone what should have been done, the existence of praise and blame could not fail to impress an observer as utterly inappropriate were different choices and different courses of action not possible. It is theoretically possible that deliberation over courses of action, praise and blame, and feelings of guilt should exist without there being any fact to which they are relevant. But the probability of everybody being fooled all of the time is not impressive, although this improbable thesis is what the determinist insists on. If we could fall back on theological grounds, we could arrive at something better than probability. For example, on the Cartesian view that God is our creator, it could be argued that it would be incompatible with his nature to deny his creatures free will and at the same time to make them such as to suffer feelings of guilt. If He did, we should have to suppose Him more wicked than the Cartesian demon. So from the hypothesis that He is our creator it could be argued that it is impossible that our choices are all determined. If, however, God is removed from the cosmic picture, it merely becomes a tremendous improbability that deliberation, praise and blame, remorse and satisfaction exist in the absence of freedom. The more instances there are of these phenomena of human behavior, the more likely it becomes that we are not all deluded about all of our actions and choices. If empirical evidence is at all relevant to establishing the

16*

existence of freedom, then the evidence there is makes it at least probable.

II. Whether any action can occur other than the one which does occur
is a question which not only arises about acts which are morally indifferent, so-called amoral acts which count as neither right nor wrong; it
gives rise to the further question whether there are any moral acts.
Given that every act of an agent is such that it must occur and there
is no possibility of its not occurring, the critics of determinism claim it
follows that no act is either right or wrong. An action that is either right
or wrong is one that the agent could have avoided. If there is no such
possibility then there are no freely willed actions, with the consequence
that no right or wrong actions exist. What constitutes the rightness or
wrongness of an act can of course be investigated independently of the
question whether such acts exist, just as one can ascertain what is implicit
in being a unicorn whether or not unicorns exist. Criteria for judging
the moral character of an act, and thus for assessing moral responsibility
for it, have been of tremendous practical concern, although usually the
crucial question in practical affairs is whether an action in question in fact
meets criteria generally agreed on. It is sometimes the case, however,
that a moral issue arises because different criteria are operative in the
minds of the disputants. It then becomes a theoretical question of fixing
the features which are essential to an act's being right or wrong, rather
than a practical question whether the act has certain agreed on features.
It is this theoretical question which falls within moral philosophy, or
ethics, and to this we shall now address ourselves.

In fixing responsibility for an action we often consider the agent's
motives or intention, but there is some reason for supposing that these
are independent of the act's rightness or wrongness. There is a group of
views in ethics according to which the moral character of an act is a
property of the act, on a par with such features of material objects as
length and weight, and that what goes on within the breast of the agent
in no way bears on the character of resultant actions. That is, ethical
terms such as 'right', 'wrong', 'morally obligatory' name features of actions, and sentences such as 'Act x is your duty', 'Act y is wrong', 'Act z is
right' express something true or false according as the acts referred to
have these features. These views, called cognitive or objectivist, stand in
sharp contrast to so-called relativist or subjectivist views according to
which the moral character attributed to an act is only a property of the

act in a secondary sense, as it depends upon the attitude of someone or some group towards the act and would not exist independently of that attitude. That is, rightness and wrongness are 'relative'. On cognitive views rightness and wrongness are properties of actions, 'objective' in them, whereas on relativist views they have no objective status.

Possibly the earliest form of relativist views in the moral development of mankind was theological. The final authority in moral matters is a supernatural being, whose commands and proscriptions provided law and set the standard for duties and wrongs. Protagoras' account of how man came to acquire justice reflected in the form of myth a current ethical view, which in fact is still current. According to Protagoras, through a blunder of Epimetheus in providing all creatures with the means of preserving their species, man in his most primitive state was left helpless in the face of his natural enemies. His life was, as Hobbes described it, 'solitary, nasty, brutish, and short'. Plato writes that 'after a while the desire of self-preservation gathered [men] into cities; but when they were gathered together, having no art of government, they evil intreated one another, and were again in process of dispersion and destruction. Zeus feared that the entire race would be exterminated, and so he sent Hermes to them, bearing reverence and justice', which were distributed, not to a few, but to all. And Zeus instructed Hermes to 'make a law by my order, that he that has no part in reverence and justice shall be put to death' (1907e, sec. 322). An explicit account of the conveyance of a specific moral code is given in the Bible. Moses receives from the hands of God the Ten Commandments, which in consequence have their moral status guaranteed by divine sanction. No other guarantee for a moral rule beyond the fact that it is God-given is required.

This tenet has been made explicit in a theory about the nature of rightness propounded throughout the centuries up through the present. In the eighteenth century Archdeacon Paley wrote: '. . . to inquire, what is our duty or what we are obliged to do, in any instance, is, in effect, to inquire what is the will of God in that instance' (1859, p. 70). '*Right* signifies being consistent with the will of God', and correspondingly, *wrong* signifies being contrary to the will of God, or forbidden by him: '. . . God's will is the measure of right and wrong' (*Ibid.*, p. 87). Various contemporary writers have expressed the same view: '. . . a thing is not right simply because we think it is, still less because it seems to be expedient. It is right because God commands it . . . There is a real distinction between right and wrong [which] is rooted in the nature and will

of God' (Mortimer, 1950, p. 8)., . . . God gives content to the good . . .
The good is what God rewards and the bad is what he punishes . . .
God's laws, then, define the duty of man' (Carnell, 1948, pp. 154, 329).
These laws, like human laws, are products of a will, and neither right
nor wrong actions would exist but for God's permitting of forbidding
them. The justification of a moral judgment passed on a given act would
thus consist in showing the act to be permitted, commanded, or forbidden by God.

It is clear that this view precludes proceeding from God's goodness
and wisdom to the inference that an act is permitted *because* it is right,
or forbidden *because* it is wrong. For this would imply that what God
wills is governed by prior knowledge of what is right or wrong, that is,
that He operates in accordance with a standard outside himself to which
his will conforms. Emil Brunner, a contemporary theologian, sees this
consequence clearly and denies the assertion which implies it: 'The Good
has its basis and its existence solely in the will of God . . . the idea of a
law which is even higher than God Himself, is unthinkable in the Old
Testament. God is not merely the guardian of the Moral Law and of the
moral ordinances, but their Creator...' (1937, p. 53). Moreover, on the
view Brunner objects to, rightness and wrongness, instead of being constituted by God's fiat, are properties He recognizes as being already
present in the actions about which He wills. If God wills what is right
because it is right, then no action can be said to be right because it is in
accordance with his will but rather because of the nature of the act.
An act would be made right or wrong by what it is and not by anything
external to itself. Moreover, God's volitions, like our own, would be the
subject of moral judgment, as being either choices he ought to have
made or ought not to have made. Morally speaking, God, apart from
his superiority, would be in like case with ourselves, subject to the rules
we ourselves are subject to. It is clear that a view according to which an
act is right merely because it is in accordance with God's will, theoretically, will permit acts to be right which bring harm and destruction to
mankind. And this implication cannot be avoided by countering that a
perfect being wills what is right. For various arguments for God's perfection rest on the purported fact that he wills what is best for man.
Paley, as we have seen in Chapter 5, argued from the adaptations of nature
to man's needs to the beneficence of God. It is a *conclusion* that '. . .God
Almighty wills and wishes the happiness of his creatures' (1814,
p. 59).

The difficulties of any analysis of rightness by reference to theological considerations are obvious. Consider the moral atheist. He believes certain actions are right without believing that God, however conceived, exists. He sees no contradiction in the conjunction of propositions, right and wrong actions exist but God does not. But on the present view this conjunction would be self-contradictory. Without gods of any kind no actions are either right or wrong. To escape the contradiction the atheist must choose between denying that an act's being right entails the existence of God and denying that any acts have moral value. A moralist who grounded ethics in theology would have to hold that an atheist's or agnostic's uncertainty about the existence of God requires a corresponding uncertainty about the existence of moral actions. And given that "rightness" means conformity to the will of God, people who have no theological conceptions would either be said to have no conception of right and wrong or be held not to know what they meant when they judged an action right or wrong. It is little comfort to possess the proper conception of rightness. The spectre of God's death is at the same time the spectre of an amoral world. The crucial weakness in any theological view is summed up in Protagoras' comment: 'With regard to the gods, I cannot feel sure either that they are or that they are not, nor what they are like in figure; for there are many things that hinder sure knowledge, the obscurity of the subject and the shortness of human life' (*On the gods*).

This comment, coupled with a principle he announced concerning the nature of things, makes it natural to carry over the principle to morals. This principle was that man is the measure of all things. What one might call the anthropological view of morals is a natural alternative to the theological view that God's will confers rightness and wrongness on actions. Not the authority of God but the authority of society, expressed in its accepted moral views and legal codes, creates the standard by which actions are to be judged. Man, and not God, is the measure. Society's approvals and disapprovals become crystallized in laws, and in institutions which support and enforce the laws. The mores of a social group are coextensive with its customs in moral matters. As W. G. Sumner puts it, 'For the people of a time and place, their own mores are always good, or rather for them there can be no question of the goodness and badness of their mores...' (1934, p. 58). For purposes of critical appraisal and for the contrast with other relativist views it is worthwhile considering this extreme form of relativism, expressed as follows: 'Right acts are those approved of by the majority of a society, wrong acts those which are disapproved'. That this is an unequivocal example of a relativist view is clear; the moral character of actions is bestowed on them by the attitude of society and would not exist but for that attitude.

It is natural to wish to amend this view by going behind the approvals and disapprovals of a particular society during a given period for some justification, either by appeal to a wider society over a longer period of time or to a reason for the attitudes in the nature of the acts approved or disapproved of. The wish to amend is prompted by certain unpalatable consequences. Apart from the objection that the notion of a society, its bounds in place and time, is vague, if a majority of a society does not either approve or disapprove of a type of action, e.g., inflicting suffering on animals, then the action becomes amoral. And if there were no majority attitude because attitudes exactly counterbalanced each other, then again actions on which they bear would be amoral. This consequence could be avoided in the first circumstance by looking for the essential feature of rightness in the act itself rather than in attitudes towards it. This would not constitute an amendment of the view but would jettison it. In the circumstance where there is a split in society – in the circumstance where there clearly is 'a moral issue' – the view as it stands cannot take care of the fact that each segment of a divided society is ready to say the other segment *ought* to take the same attitude it does. This suggests a concealed acceptance of some sort of objectivism with respect to rightness and wrongness. But on the present view each segment would be saying that the majority of society would approve of the dissenting segment taking a different attitude. The only amendment of this 'approval' view which would provide for such an evaluation of group approvals would be one in which a wider group was referred to in the analysis of rightness, say, all of mankind during a given time interval.

But which time interval? The length of the period of time is arbitrary and the choice of time period likewise. If a society is taken to be the inhabitants of a certain geographical area, then since the moral code current in one period of history may differ greatly from that in another period, the moral status of a particular act or type of act will correspondingly vary. On objectivist theories of rightness and wrongness a particular act, say of incest, once wrong is always wrong. *That* act has the attribute of wrongness as surely as a particular sphere has a certain diameter, even though other acts of that class may not have that attribute. No act loses its moral attribute or acquires a new one any more than it loses or acquires any other feature, such as date, circumstances, consequences. On the society approval view under consideration one and the same act, as well as the same kind of act, can change its moral character from one era of time to another. A homicide at one time can be approved of and later disapproved of, and with this shift in attitude the act which was right becomes wrong. The same change can occur during a single specified period with a shift of public feeling. A moral judgment to the effect that a certain type of act is right will be true or false according as it is true or false that a majority approval exists, but the truth-status of the judgment can alter with time. And with the change in feeling the former judgment does not become false; the only circumstance under which a moral judgment is false is when the majority attitude fails to support it. Two members of a given society who disagree with each other over the moral character of a given act will be disagreeing merely over what a poll would show about society's attitude. And moral deliberation would consist in conjecturing the general reaction. People who make their moral decisions in this way are often condemned as opportunistic. Curiously, in a situation where one's own reaction made the difference between an act's being right or wrong, that is, was decisive, one's judgment as to whether the majority approved, if one knew forces were equally balanced, would only require knowing what one's own reaction would be. Coming to a decision on the moral status of an act in this circumstance might be less difficult than it in fact is, though were one in a state of ambivalence the status of the act would remain in suspense and the difficulty of coming to a decision would be insurmountable since there would be no appeal possible to what one's reaction ought to be. In most cases, knowing whether an action was right or wrong would be theoretically possible, as a poll is always possible, though counting heads makes attaining knowledge more difficult than it in fact usually is, and is not a procedure usually engaged in.

It is a known fact that different cultures have different attitudes towards actions of certain kinds and also that members of one culture may consider the attitude current in another culture morally insensitive. Thus, for example, one country will send missionaries into another country, not only to bring religion but to bring morals. Verbally the members of different cultures appear to be in disagreement when those of the one say, for example, that binding the feet of infant girls, or the immolation of a widow on the funeral pyre of her husband, or the exposure of infants and the aged is wrong, and those of the other defend its rightness. It is unhesitatingly accepted that what appears to be in dispute is in fact in dispute. But on the relativist view under consideration, members of two cultures A and B who know the moral attitudes of their cultures and on this basis say, the one that an act is right, the other that it is wrong, cannot be in disagreement. For each is saying what is true, namely, that society A approves and that society B disapproves. One moral judgment will not constitute a denial of the other since two true statements cannot be inconsistent with each other.

Similarly, in the case of a kind of action that is approved of by both socieites, it would be normal to speak of the two societies being in moral agreement. Members of the two societies who pronounced on a particular act of that kind would be said to be in agreement if their words were the same. Nevertheless, when a member of society *A* says that act is right, he is not saying anything about the attitude of society *B*. He is only saying something about his own society, and the fact that another society approves does not on this view enter into his judgment. Similarly for a member of society *B*. Both will be saying what is true, but they will not be saying the *same* thing. They will each be attaching a different meaning to the word 'right,' the one, 'approved of by society *A*', the other 'approved of by society *B*'.

In spelling out these implications of the society approval view, con-sequences have been brought out which some philosophers consider to be reasons against it. Relativists, however, recognize these consequences and accept them without relinquishing their view, however odd it may seem that people of different societies who use the words 'right' and 'wrong' appropriately are talking at cross purposes when they suppose themselves to be agreeing or disagreeing. There are, however, some consequences which can less easily be taken in stride. Consider a moral judgment by a member of society which denies the feature conferred on it by the majority of that society. This judgment must always be false. That is, an opposing minority, or a prophet, or a social reformer can never be in the right. Of course by sustained effort a single person or a minority can change the status of an act by winning a majority to their side, in which case what was morally reprehensible becomes morally correct. An act's acquiring a new status is something like its being made right or wrong by majority vote. And there will be a point in the process where it will be morally neutral.

Another unwelcome consequence rests on the commonplace that the attitudes of a society are subject to moral evaluation. One can concede the fact, as did many Germans under the Nazi regime, that one's society reacts with approval and yet hold it to be morally in the wrong. A mob can feel approval of a lynching, but even a member of that mob can later sit in judgment on the mob's feeling. Now just as the view that rightness is constituted by God's will precludes passing moral judgment on his will, so this view precludes passing judgment on majority attitudes. To make such a judgment is in either case to turn away from the proposed standard of rightness.

There is reason to suppose that acceptance of a different standard is also implied by seeming disagreement. It is clear of course that two people within a society can on this relativist view disagree if one of them has a false idea of what the majority attitude is. But suppose each knows how the majority reacts, so that there is no disagreeing over this, and yet that disputation continues. In this case some other feature of the act under discussion must be in dispute. The same sort of conclusion can be drawn from the occurrence of continued dispute between two people of different societies, each of whom knows the attitudes of his own and the other's society. If disagreement implies that both statements cannot be true, then some other feature of the action must be in dispute.

Perhaps the most crucial objection to this approval view is what it implies for moral discourse. Sentences which no one takes to be self-contradictory must be interpreted as such on this view, for example, 'He killed a man in a duel and his society approved of his action, but nevertheless it was wrong'. And a statement such as 'I believe this is wrong though I know my fellow men approve of it' reduces to: 'I believe this is wrong, even though I know it is right'. Yet both of these sentences, as English is used, describe possible situations. On the present relativist view they lese their descriptive use and become self-contradictory nonsense.

It might be held that the inadequacies of society approval views stem from ignoring the reason for which people band together into social groups, namely, their own self-interest, and that one must recognize the central position of this fact in arriving at a correct analysis of rightness and wrongness. A society is a group of individuals with a community of interests, and what attracts individuals to a group, whether it is a group pitted against society or society itself, is self-interest. Society approval is compounded of reactions of the greatest number of individuals, each individual governed by his own interests. The fact that a number of people approve of a type of action because it is in some way advantageous to them is no justification for resting rightness on the number of approvals rather than on the ground for each of them. Just as a 'normal' perceiver is one whose perceptions fall within those of the majority, so the conventionally moral person is one whose actions come under majority approvals; but in neither case do numbers make a perception veridical or an action right. To behave as if it did is, to use Wittgenstein's comparison, 'as if someone were to buy several copies of the morning paper to assure himself that what it said was true' (1953, p. 94). Protagoras' dictum that man is the measure has two possible interpretations, one that the mjority of mankind is the measure, the other that each individual man is his own measure. This latter interpretation is the one accepted by some ethical relativists who look for something more basic in the concept of rightness than the group attitudes which societies codify and enforce. Underlying the group attitude towards types of acts is the attitude of the individual member. What is right is relative to him. As Bishop Butler said, 'When I reflect in a cool moment I see that nothing can be good which is not in my own interest'.

It is clear that what an individual approves of and what is to his interest are not coincident concepts and that distinct ethical views about rightness could be formulated in terms of each concept. And each formulation has variants. For example, to say an act is right might be held to mean that I (exclusively) approve of it, or that some specified person approves of it, or that whoever passes judgment on it approves of it. Similarly, it might be held to mean that it is to my interests exclusively, that it is to the interests of some specified person, or that it is to the interests of the agent. When the moral judgment is made by a dictator or absolute monarch, the first two views in each series coalesce. Presumably when Louis XIV said 'L'État, c'est moi' or Boss Hague 'I am the Law', the implication was that in making a moral judgment they were saying both that they themselves approved and that the criterion of rightness for everyone was the approval of the king, or of Hague. Similarly, when Thrasymachus said justice was what was to the interests of the ruler (*Republic*, Bk. I), a moral judgment, whether made by the ruler or by anyone else, would be a judgment solely about the ruler. Such views would allow the possibility of agreement and disagreement in moral matters, as concurrence or dissent would merely concern the question whether a certain act was approved of, or was to the interest of, the ruler. But the ruler himself, on the view that he need consult only his own attitude, would be in a privileged position, and could resolve moral issues with an ease which does not exist in fact. As with society approval views, no one could say one ruler's decrees were morally better than another's, any more than members of two religious sects could, on the theological view, place moral evaluations on their respective gods' commandments.

If one took the view that one man's feelings were as good a criterion of rightness as another's, and one man's interest as important as another's, then two views involving each concept, approval and interest, are possible: either the extreme egoistic view that what is right is what I approve of, where 'I' can be anyone passing judgment, or the view that what is right is what the agent approves of, where the agent can be anyone; and similarly for views connecting rightness and interest. Some of the consequences of these views are similar, and also the objections to be raised against them. For example, if the word "I" occurring in judgments at different times stands for one and the same person, then the view that what is right is identifiable with what I at any time approve of allows the moral status of a particular act (or class of acts) to vary from day to day with shifts in my attitude. Similarly, if a class of acts, say of theft, are to my interests at one time but not at another, then at one time theft is right and at another time wrong. On the other hand, if 'I' functions like a variable, to stand for any one of a number of people who use it making judgments, then when both of two persons assert that a given act is right they are not agreeing with each other, despite appearances, since their two statements are about different persons. Nor, for the same reason, can they disagree, for they will be making true statements about distinct persons. There can of course be dispute, on the 'agent approval' view, over whether the agent approves, or whether it is to his interest, and hence over whether a given act is right.

What the connection is between the fact, if it is a fact, that every individual acts so as to promote his own interests, and the ethical view that the standard of rightness is the agent's self-interest need not be gone into here, for there is an objection to the view which seems unanswerable. This is that taken as an analysis of rightness, that is, as an account of the meaning of the term 'rightness', it implies the self-contradictoriness of saying that it is sometimes right for an agent to act against his own interest, whether short run or long run. But there is no contravention of usage in saying the virtuous sacrifice of the burghers of Calais was not in their own interests even though it was what they chose. Moreover, there is a parallel to the objection Moore raised against ethical egoism, namely, the view that *the* good is identical with *my* good, which applies to the assertion by each of a number of ethical egoists that right is what is conducive *solely* to his own interests. This is that one and the same thing is identified with many distinct things.

A similar objection can be raised against identifying rightness with what each person passing judgment approves of. In fact the objections to holding that what is meant by 'act x is right' is that whoever makes the judgment on x approves of it, parallel in a number of respects those which can be made against the view that what is meant by this is that x is to the interest of the agent. But some are unique to it, for example, the surprising ease of knowing whether an act is right, an act's lack of moral character when one's feelings are ambivalent, the unplausibility of the implied account of moral deliberation. But there is one objection deserving of special mention and this is one directed by Moore against the claim that what one is doing in asserting an act is right is stating one's approval of it. His objection rests on a distinction between what is implied by the fact that one makes such an assertion and what is logically entailed by it. Making the assertion does indicate that one has a feeling of approval, and it is proper to say the fact of assertion implies this; but the assertion itself does not entail it. By analogy: The fact that one says someone has drawn a triangle on the blackboard implies that one believes this, but does not entail it; what is entailed is, for example, that someone has drawn a three-sided figure.

The same objection holds against saying that what one means in asserting that an act is right is merely that one thinks it is right. Thinking an act is right presumably is a different attitude from approving of it, but in addition to being subject to the same sort of criticism it is subject to another, namely, that as an account of the meaning of 'right' it is circular. If 'right' in the analysans is replaceable by 'S thinks x is right' then the explanation of 'x is right' launches one on an infinite regress of explanations, which is to say that no explanation is given. Instead of the theory being an account of the meaning of 'right', the meaning is made permanently elusive. A curious feature of this view that in asserting an act is right one is merely saying one thinks it is right is that it is sometimes 'justified' by the claim that no one ever *knows* an action to be right or wrong. On this claim Moore remarks that 'so far from implying the untenable view that to assert an action to be right or wrong is *the same thing* as to assert that we think it to be so, we imply the direct opposite of this. For nobody would maintain that I cannot know *that I think* an action to be right or wrong...' (1912, p. 127).

One of the sharpest divisions among writers on ethics concerns the question whether the criterion of rightness permits apparently opposed judgments both to be true. Most of the relativist, or subjectivist views imply the possibility of judgments on a given type of action varying from culture to culture, and era to era, and at the same time being true. By some ethicists this consequence constitutes an objection to all such views. The view that what is right or wrong is relative to God's will only escapes the objection when coupled with the common assumption that God's wisdom and goodness preclude his commanding the same kind of action which at some other time or place He forbids. He could not escape the charge of being heedless of man and forgetful of his announced decrees if the operation of his will were wayward and inconstant. God, or at least the Christian God, being what He is, the standards by which an act is judged right or wrong will not vary from one culture, or one period of time, to another. The criterion of conforming (or failing to conform) to God's will assures invariant rightness and wrongness to actions. For this reason the ethical view which makes the moral character of a class of acts relative to a mind has an objectivist, or 'absolutist' feature: that their moral status cannot change.

We have already detailed the objections against this particular view. But there is a view, which has appeared in the history of ethics and is still current, that at least allows an atheist or agnostic to pass moral judgments without committing himself by implication to the existence of a supernatural being, and that at first sight preserves an objective standard. This is the so-called 'ideal observer' view. Some idea of this view can be got from the words of Frances Hutcheson who in the early 1700s laid down as one of the things we mean by being 'obliged to an Action': 'that every Spectator, or he himself upon Reflection, must approve his Action, and disapprove his omitting it, if he considers fully all its circumstances' (1897, p. 408). The requisite qualities of such a spectator have been spelled out by contemporary writers (for example, Firth, 1952, and Brandt, 1955) as impartiality, being fully informed and vividly imaginative, having mental calm and being otherwise normal. In explication of these qualities R. B. Brandt writes: '(1) A person is "fully informed and vividly imaginative" if he has all true nonethical beliefs and lacks all false nonethical beliefs that would affect his reaction of feeling or desire; and if he has these beliefs in mind as vividly as if he were perceiving the facts believed; (2) A person is "impartial" if ... his reaction ... would have been the same no matter what ... individuals or groups are involved ...; (3) To be "calm" means that one's reaction is not influenced by prior states of anger, depression, fear, grief, and so on. To be "otherwise normal" implies ... that one is not

insane, debilitated by fatigue, seriously ill, and so forth' (1959, p. 174).
The view differs from the theological view in not committing one to the
existence of God, however similar an ideal observer may be to Him, nor
in fact to the existence of an ideal observer.

It might be supposed that any ideal observer, if there were one, would
make the same moral judgments as any other. But there is no contradiction involved in saying that two beings who were fully informed, imaginative, impartial, etc., differ in attitude. The attitude of such beings with
regard to a class of actions cannot without begging the question be incor-
porated into the description an ideal observer must answer to. This means
that from the fact that S is an ideal observer it cannot be deduced that
he would approve of x as against y, any more than it could be inferred
that he would prefer red to blue. To put it in Protagorean terms, each of
a number of ideal observers becomes the measure of right and wrong,
and no contradiction would be implied by their differing in attitude.
Unless there is a way of demonstrating that when any ideal observer
approves or disapproves of an action, every other one must do likewise,
there is only an assumed advantage of this theory over other approval
theories. It will not, in principle, prevent two divergent moral statements
from being true, and it will not guarantee the same meaning to 'x is right',
nor, consequently, a single standard by which every act can be judged.

There is one thing which all the views so far discussed, including the
theological and ideal observer views, have in common. This is that moral
judgments are taken to express something true or false. A view may
allow the possibility of the truth-value of a moral judgment changing,
but it nevertheless is the case that the judgment always has a truth-value.
Such views stand in sharp contrast to theories according to which moral
judgments do not *describe* acts at all but instead have an entirely different
function. One such view is the so-called emotivist theory according to
which moral jugments *give vent* to feelings but do not assert that any
feeling exists. To say an act is right is not to say it has a natural or superna-
natural property, such as having general approval or having divine sanction, but to give expression to an emotion. Moral words are said not to
function like normal predicates. Whereas 'being approved of by the majority of people' is a descriptive phrase for which empirical tests are available for ascertaining whether it applies or not, 'right' and 'wrong' are
held to have no descriptive use. How differently they function Ayer eluci-
dates as follows: '. . . in saying . . . [that the man acted rightly] we are not
elaborating or modifying our description of the situation in the way

that we should be elaborating it if we gave further police-court details, or in the way that we should be modifying it if we showed that the agent's motives were different from what they had been thought to be. To say that his motives were good, or that they were bad, is not to say what they were. To say that the man acted rightly, or that he acted wrongly, is not to say what he did'. (1954, p. 235). If I say to someone, "You acted wrongly in stealing that money", I am not stating anything more than if I had simply said, "You stole that money". In adding that his action is wrong I am not making any further statement about it. I am simply evincing my moral disapproval of it. It is as if I had said, "You stole that money", in a special tone of horror, or written it with the addition of some special exclamation marks. The tone, or the exclamation marks, adds nothing to the literal meaning of the sentence' (1951, p. 107). 'It is for this reason that these ethical predicates are not factual; they do not describe any features of the situation to which they are applied' (1954, pp. 235–236).

If they are non-descriptive, then judgments in which they occur are neither true nor false. In this respect the theory differs radically from what Ayer calls 'the orthodox subjectivist theory'. 'The orthodox subjectivist does not deny, as we do, that the sentences of a moralizer express genuine propositions ... His ... view is that they express propositions about the speaker's feelings ... They would be true if the speaker had the relevant feelings, and false if he had not. And this is a matter which is, in principle, empirically verifiable. Furthermore, they could be significantly contradicted. For if I say, "Tolerance is a virtue", and someone answers, "You don't approve of it", he would on the ordinary subjectivist theory, be contradicting me. On our theory, he would not be contradicting me, because, in saying that tolerance is a vriue, I should not be making any statement about my own feelings or about anything else. I should simply be evincing my feelings, which is not at all the same thing as saying that I have them' (1951, p. 109).

How then is moral disagreement possible? Moore's argument against the usual relativist views detailed above, is that they preclude the possibility of disagreement in circumstances in which we all should say disputation does take place. To square with the fact of disputation emotivists must give a different account of it than disagreement over the truth-values of incompatible moral judgments. Ayer's means of doing this is indicated in the following: '...we find, if we consider the matter closely, that the dispute is not really about a question of value, but about a question of

17

fact. When someone disagrees with us about the moral value of a certain action or type of action, we do admittedly resort to argument in order to win him over to our way of thinking. But we do not attempt to show by our arguments that he has the "wrong" ethical feeling towards a situation whose nature he has correctly apprehended. What we attempt to show is that he is mistaken about the facts of the case. We argue that he has misconceived the agent's motive; or that he has misjudged the effects of the action, or its probable effects in view of the agent's knowledge; or that he has failed to take into account the special circumstances in which the agent was placed. Or else we employ more general arguments about the effects which actions of a certain type tend to produce, or the qualities which are usually manifest in their performance. We do this in the hope that we have only to get our opponent to agree with us about the nature of the empirical facts for him to adopt the same moral attitude towards them as we do' (1951, pp. 110–111).

C. L. Stevenson, who also holds an emotivist theory, describes argument over moral issues in much the same way. Moral disagreement is described as a disagreement in attitude, and 'A and B will be said to disagree in attitude when they have opposed attitudes to something, and when at least one of them is trying to alter the attitude of the other' (1942, pp. 82–83). 'The *seeming* incompatibility of "x is right" and "x is wrong" springs from the fact that the judgments exert a different sort of emotive *influence* – that the judgment at t_2 undermines the work of the judgment at t_1' (*Ibid.*, p. 85). The use of the words 'right' and 'wrong' to influence others likewise operates in the same way with self-exhortation, to influence moral decisions. And when we ask the question 'Is x right?' we are of course not asking what our present attitude is but asking for assistance in reaching an attitude. Moral deliberation is described by the emotivist as an attempt to bring conflicting attitudes into harmony so that one can come to a decision on whether to approve or disapprove something. For this purpose we review facts which are relevant to the issue, just as we do in moral debate, where the aim is the different one of influencing people to take the same moral attitude as ourselves. It is clear that the same facts may influence different persons to make different moral decisions, that whether they influence one to have an attitude of approval or of disapproval is relative to the participants in a moral disagreement. Supposing that the outlook of one disputant is hatred of an ideology, then to point out that a certain type of action will cause suffering, e.g., use of nuclear weapons, may bolster his position that a bomb ought to be dropped. Ayer says we point out facts 'in the hope' that our opponent will adopt the same moral attitude towards them as we do; but this is a hope, not an assurance.

Some emotivists have augmented their view that moral statements are expressions of attitudes with a further claim, that they are prescriptive, that they operate something like imperatives. 'You ought to' has the force of 'Do!' Stevenson has called them quasi-imperatives, to indicate their similarity to and their difference from ordinary imperatives. 'You ought to quit smoking' has something of the force of 'Do not smoke any more', though not quite. (One can without redundancy say 'You ought not' and follow it by 'Anyway, don't'.) Although moral judgments are in the indicative mood, too much weight should not be placed on this fact, as directives are often so expressed: 'The audience will remain seated during the procession'. And even a clearly factual statement may have the same function: 'For each hour of smoking your life span is by that much diminished', which is indirectly prescriptive. Sometimes 'ought' has this indirect guiding function. Sometimes it functions more directly, to coerce or coax, as does an outright imperative. 'Ought', to use W. D. Falk's comparatives (1953), can guide or goad. Whether or not guiding and goading succeed in influencing conduct or attitudes, this is the aim of asserting a moral opinion.

R. M. Hare has elaborated a theory around this feature of moral language which has in addition some affinity with a theory shortly to be expounded, set out by Kant. According to Hare, sentences of the form 'x ought to be done' are prescriptive, and their utterance expresses one's own resolve or decision to carry the prescription out, which is something quite different from being merely expressive of an attitude. Moreover, moral prescriptions are universal, or involve universal prescriptions. For example, 'Lies ought never to be told' comes to 'Tell no lies to no one at any time', and 'You ought not to lie to your child' to 'Do not lie to your child else you will be infringing a universal moral maxim I subscribe to'. To say to someone that *he* ought or ought not do x has backing it the more general 'ought': any person in circumstances of this kind ought (or ought not) do this sort of thing when other people involved are of such-and-such a sort (Hare, 1954, p. 306). The injunction clearly applies to the speaker as well, so that a moral statement not only issues a directive to others but is an expression of one's acceptance of it for himself.

In light of what is to be said for the thesis that moral predicates

17*

have a special emotive function, the question naturally arises why many writers on ethics are not content to accept emotivist accounts of the nature of moral judgments. Let us grant that 'right' and 'wrong' often have a use to commend or condemn, and that the fact that one utters sentences containing them indicates an attitude of the speaker, perhaps even that the speaker subscribes to a moral rule. What then are the objections to emotivist theories? Al of them eventually rest on the charge that what is *meant* by such sentences as 'Infliction of pain needlessly is wrong and ought to be prevented', 'His revenge on his enemies' relatives was morally inexcusable', is not what Ayer, Stevenson, and Hare imply it is. If it were, then it is difficult to explain the persistence of the delusion that moral judgments are factually descriptive, say something true or false. On the face of it, sentences of the form 'x is right' and 'x is wrong' do not appear to mean 'How splendid...', 'How terrible...', 'Would that ...', or 'Do ...', even granting that evaluative terms like 'right', 'wrong', and 'ought' do not describe an act the way 'swift', 'planned', 'reluctant' do. They appear to convey information about the character of x. It is unplausible to charge writers who analyze their meaning as they would that of any other sentence in the indicative with having been misled by the factual idiom into a failure to see they are like exclamations, or like imperatives. For there is no similar confusion about other sentences in this idiom, e.g., 'The audience will remain seated'. The emotivist is open to the countercharge of confusing a feeling that accompanies a moral judgment with the moral judgment itself, of taking as the content of the judgment something which in fact is external to it although perhaps always accompanying it.

Taking value terms to have only emotive and evocative meaning, as does Ayer, involves difficulties of a number of different kinds. For example, do the same words, 'That is wrong', referring to the same action, undergo a change of meaning if uttered with a less vehement feeling at a later time? And suppose the infliction of needless suffering, say, on an animal, were accompanied by no moral judgment at all. Is it senseless to raise the question whether this action was wrong even though no one gave vent to any feeling? Suppose someone who learned of this action said, 'That was most reprehensible'. This statement entails that the act referred to occurred, and so would have a truth-value. On Ayer's theory it would imply nothing further, and thus would be made true by the act's occurrence and by nothing else. Where moral judgments are more complex in form than 'x is wrong' it is difficult to see how any of the emotivist theories serve for their analysis, e.g., for the analysis of 'If U.S. policy in Vietnam was morally wrong, history will make this evident.'

A number of considerations suggest that 'right' and 'wrong' are more than emotive in function and furthermore, that they are attributive terms. Consider what we usually describe as a change of opinion, when we use the word 'right' where we once used the word 'wrong', or vice versa. The fact that we use different words indicates that we have different attitudes, but on Ayer's and Stevenson's theories there would be no implication that one attitude or the other was mistaken. And when we censure ourselves, as we sometime do, for the attitudes we have had, using such words as 'It was wrong of me to feel as I did', we should only be expressing a feeling about a feeling. We frequently censure feelings as well as actions, and we attempt to induce others to change their feelings. In such cases our language, according to emotivists, evinces our disapproval of feelings towards a given action, but we cannot justify our disapproval by reference to the moral character of the act to which the feelings we censure are directed. We could not say, 'Your attitude is immoral because the act is wrong,' unless the value term 'wrong' in this statement is taken to make an attribution.

The emotivists whose views are considered here have supported them by looking at the *language* of morals. Language is a complex instrument (Wittgenstein has compared it to a box of tools), which has a variety of jobs to perform. It would be well to see whether linguistic examination shows anything further that bears on the controversy between emotivists and cognitivists. There can be no doubt that value terms have an emotional environment, sometimes emphasized by exclamation marks or tone of voice, and that they are able to express and evoke feelings. Balanced against this is the fact that moral judgments are expressed in the indicative. This form of speech, in which 'good', 'bad', 'right', and 'wrong' appear as grammatical predicates, represents the recognition that ethical terms have cognitive content. They are quite unlike ejaculations such as 'Oh!' and 'Ah!', which have no adjectival use whatever. The fact that the grammar of these two sets of words is so different may be taken as *prima facie* evidence that their semantic jobs also differ in important ways. Even though to the exclamation, 'Wrong!', there corresponds the sentence 'That is wrong', and both serve to evince an attitude, the ejaculatory 'Wrong!' differs in the following important way from the pure ejaculation 'Oh!'. 'Oh!' does not expand into 'This is Oh!' It is literal nonsense to say 'This act is Oh!', but perfectly intelligible to say 'This act is morally wrong'. This difference can legitimately be taken to signalize a basic likeness between 'This action is wrong' and 'This action is final', and a dissimilarity between property-denoting, or attributive terms and exclamations.

We shall now consider two theories which claim that value predicates denote properties of actions and that moral judgments either truly or falsely attribute these properties to them. The first, put forward by Kant, has the feature operative in Hare's view: the 'universalizability' of the determining principle of an action. Without going into special features of Kant's view we can take cognizance of its central feature, his criterion for the moral worth or reprehensibility of our actions which operates in so much of moral discourse, particularly when we ask or are asked, 'What if everyone acted on that principle?' Such a question is intended to stir any rational mind into consideration of the principle determining his action. Is it a moral principle, and how is this to be tested? 'The essence of morality', Kant says, 'is that our actions are motivated by a general rule. If we make it the foundation of our conduct that our actions shall be consistent with a universal rule, valid at all times and for everyone, then our actions exemplify the principle of morality' (1969). And the overriding universal rule, what Kant calls the imperative of duty, is that one act on a principle which one could will should become a universal law. To be moral the maxim the agent adopts when he decides to act must conform to this rule. Now whether one can will that a maxim become a universal law, i.e., wish that all men adopt it, or alternatively, whether it can 'by thy will become a universal law of nature' *(Ibid.)*, i.e., have the force of a law that binds all men to adopt it, is not to be decided by consideration of the results it will secure, or by its conformity to God's commands or to feelings towards or opinions about the action. The test to be applied is as follows: 'If the principle of the action can, without self-contradiction, be universalized, it is moral; if it cannot be so universalized without contradicting itself, it is immoral. That action is immoral whose principle cancels and destroys itself when it is made a universal rule' *(Ibid.)*.

Leaving aside appraisal of the stricture 'universalizable without self-contradiction', let us confine attention to a weaker form implied by it: capable of being universalized without defeating or destroying itself. We shall take it that a maxim which cancels or destroys itself when made universal is one whose continued operation is impossible. Kant's illustrations concerning promises, telling the truth, payment of debts, indicate what he has in mind. About promises he writes: 'May I, when in distress, make a promise with the intention not to keep it? Considerations of prudence aside, would such an act be moral? The shortest way to answer this question is to ask, "Would I be content that the principle (getting out of difficulties by making false promises) should hold good as a universal law, for myself and all others?" If I ask, "Can the principle of making deceitful promises to get out of difficulties be universalized?" I realize that it cannot. For with such a law there would be no promises at all. With such a principle made universal, it would be in vain to allege my intentions. As soon as it were made a universal law, the principle would necessarily destroy itself, necessarily defeat its own end ... No one would consider such promises as binding, and all would ridicule them as vain pretenses' *(Ibid.)*.

'Promises ought to be kept' is enjoined then on everyone, oneself included. And this injunction is categorical. It is not obligatory merely as a means to some end. That is, the precept is not short for: 'You ought to keep your promises *if* you wish to stand well in the community, or be able to borrow money in future, etc., ...' As Kant puts it, what one morally ought to do is not a hypothetical 'ought', dependent on some condition. Nor is it subject to exception. What one ought to do everyone else in the same circumstances also ought to do. This is how the test of universalizability is to be understood. To say that S ought to do *x* is to say that the maxim S adopts in doing *x* can, without defeating itself, be adopted by everyone similarly placed. What Kant lays down as the necessary and sufficient condition for an act to be morally obligatory he maintains is in conformity with how ordinary people think about moral questions. 'If we attend to ourselves, on the occasion of any transgression of duty', he writes, 'we shall find that we do not will that the principle of our action should become a universal law. On the contrary, we will that the opposite should remain a universal law, only we assume the liberty of making an exception in our own favor – just for this time only, it may be. This cannot be justified to our own impartial judgment...' *(Ibid.)*.

Critics have been quick to point out difficulties in Kant's theory. For one thing, principles considered entirely moral would by Kant's test be no one's duty to abide by, for example, the principle of sharing with those less fortunate than oneself. As a maxim for all to live by it would not remain permanently in operation. Since eventually there would be no one less fortunate than anyone else, it would destroy the possibility of its own continuance. For another thing, principles which cannot be universalized, and hence are immoral, could conceivably be acted on rightly in some cases. The principle 'not to beget a new generation', as a maxim for all to adopt could not long remain in operation. For it would destroy the possibility of its continuing as a principle of conduct by bringing human society to an end. Yet for people with serious hereditary disease it is a duty not to procreate.

Even if it were conceded that actions in accordance with principles which cannot be universalized are wrong, it would appear that actions which are *not* wrong, i.e., whose principle can be universalized, are not thereby necessarily right; there is no entailment between the universalizability of a principle and the moral rightness of an action falling under it. The principle 'to indulge one's sexual appetites' can evidently be universalized. Missionaries who persuaded natives to wear clothing were under no illusion that the principle 'to wear an amount of clothing suitable to the climate' could be universalized, yet had no doubts that the natives' practice in accordance with this principle was wrong. The principle 'to cut one's hair in such a way as to distinguish one from gorillas' can govern the grooming of everyone; yet cutting one's hair would under most circumstances count as a morally indifferent action. In general, one can always ask concerning any universalizable principle, 'Are the actions falling under it right?' And to ask this is not to ask again, 'Is their principle universalizable?'

Inasmuch as the test of universalizability can be met by actions which could count as amoral, the question arises whether Kant's criterion is an *ethical* one. It has been characterized as a 'purely formal' criterion for determining the rightness of a class of actions, which suggests the criticism that the principle of universalizability has no ethical content and thus cannot be used as a standard by reference to which moral attributions are to be evaluated. Moore claims to have discovered a fallacy, frequent in ethical theory, to which he gave the name 'the naturalistic fallacy'. Put very briefly, the fallacy consists of the attempt to define ethical terms by means of terms which have no ethical content, or to express it differently, the attempt to analyze ethical properties in terms of natural, non-ethical properties. Kant's attempt to define duty in terms of universalizability would seem to fall under Moore's fallacy.

Let us, however, suppose that universalizability is a criterion for determining duties. Further serious objections against Kant's theory remain: (a) that it gives rise to a conflict among duties, (b) that it leaves us with no guide concerning the principle to which the test of universalization is to be applied. To illustrate (a), suppose we take it that Kant intended to hold that the principle motivating a lie can never be universalized (see his essay of 1797, 'On the supposed right to tell lies from benevolent motives'). And suppose, as in the example discussed in Book I of the *Republic*, a man intending murder asked for the return of his weapons for destructive purposes. Ought one to lie to him by denying that one has the weapons in his possession? If the principle on which one acts is 'to prevent murder whenever possible', a principle which can be put into operation permanently by everyone, then this is in conflict with one's duty always to tell the truth, inasmuch as the principle 'to lie so as to avoid difficulty' cannot according to Kant be universalized without defeating itself. One is in the dilemma of acting wrongly if one lies, and wrongly if one does not, since not to lie makes one an accessory to a murder. Most people would not hesitate to say that one has no duty to tell the truth to a person who has no right to the truth.

If one tries to defend Kant's theory by formulating the principle of action differently, namely, 'to lie so as to prevent murder', one meets with difficulty (b), that there is no guide as to which principle the test of universalization is to be applied to. One's lying would fall within two classes, the general class, lying to avoid difficulty, and the more specific class, lying to avoid aiding and abetting a crime. The principle characterizing the latter class seems capable of operating without destroying the possibility of its continuance. To which maxim is the test of universalizability to be applied, the more general or the more specific one? Nothing in Kant gives a means for deciding which, and hence for deciding whether an act falling under two such maxims is right or wrong. Pairs of maxims involving this difficulty can be multiplied indefinitely; for example, 'to provide for one's family', 'to provide for one's family by opening a pet shop', 'to advance knowledge', 'to advance knowledge by archaeological exploration'.

It might be thought that Kant's test would serve to decide between different moral codes, as a type of act approved of in one society and frowned on in another, e.g., polygamy, would be determined by a maxim which either could or could not become a universal law. But it is not clear what maxim is to be tested, and hence whether it could or could not be universalized. Nor is it clear that two different but compatible maxims, each embodying a reference to a specific setting, might not be framed.

Kant's wish to provide a shield against the impact of one's desires – against one's proneness to justify acting for one's own convenience – led him to castigate theories which made the rightness of an action depend upon its results. Nevertheless, when Kant comes to consider certain admitted duties we find him abandoning his test of maxims and appealing to results. When he raises the question whether he can wish that the maxim on which he acts should be adopted by everyone, his answer in some cases appeals to the goodness of the results brought about by such adoption. W. D. Ross makes this point in connection with two types of duties Kant discusses, as follows: First, the duty to oneself of fostering certain of one's potentialities. Suppose 'a man is tempted to lead a life of pleasure without developing his talents. He sees that such a system could subsist without self-contradiction (as in the case of the South Sea Islanders), but finds that he cannot *will* that it should come into existence. "For ... he necessarily wills that his faculties be developed, since they serve him ... for all sorts of possible purposes" (Kant, 1969, pp. 46–47). Here there is a frank appeal to purposes, i.e., to desires of his own. The reference to universalization is neither here nor there; he directly sees the utility of his own talents, and sees that he should behave in a certain way simply in order to get certain results' (Ross, 1954, pp. 46–47). Again, consider one's duty to alleviate the suffering of others. 'A man in prosperity is tempted to say that the misery of others is no concern of his, and to act accordingly. This system, again, might subsist, but he cannot will that it should; for by such a law he would deprive himself of the love and sympathy of others when he needs it. Here again the appeal is to results, and in this case to definitely hedonistic results; benevolence is justified by an appeal to far-sighted selfishness' (*Ibid.*, p. 47). Mill said of the categorical imperative, '...when [Kant] begins to deduce from this precept any of the actual duties of morality, he fails, almost grotesquely, to show that there would be any contradiction, any logical (not to say physical) impossibility, in the adoption by all rational beings of the most outrageously immoral rules of conduct. All he shows is that the *consequences* of their universal adoption would be such as no one would choose to incur' (1863, Ch. 1).

When one takes stock of the kind of considerations entering into moral deliberation on an action one is inevitably driven to recognize the central place which the results of the action occupy: Will they be as good as those consequent on the alternatives open to one? Would the results of other acts be better? One can be mistaken about what consequences will ensue, but in practice no one doubts the relevance of the consequences in measuring right and wrong. The English utilitarians took these consequences not only as being *in fact* a sign of rightness or wrongness but as being of their essence. (For discussion of this, see Urmson, 1953.) There are a number of variations on utilitarianism – egoistic, hedonistic, ideal utilitarianism, 'act'-utilitarianism and 'rule'-utilitarianism – but a common thread runs through them all, that consequences are the *criterion*. This is to say that actions are right *because* they produce a certain kind of effects, as compared with those which would be produced by alternative actions, and that they would be right *under any conceivable circumstances*. G. E. Moore, whose 'ideal' utilitarianism we shall concentrate on, makes this claim in a number of places. In *Principia ethica* (1922) he writes: 'It is always the duty of every agent to do that one, among all the actions which he *can* do on any given occasion, whose *total* consequences will have the greatest intrinsic value' (p. 232; see also *Ethics*, 1912, Ch. 2). In saying this he is aware of the radical divergence of such a view from one like Kant's, which holds that 'certain rules ought *absolutely always* to be obeyed, *whatever* the consequences may be...', i.e., '*even if* the world as a whole were the worse because of our action' (1912, p. 181). On this Moore commented: 'It seems to me self-evident that knowingly to do an action which would make the world, on the whole, really and truly *worse* than if we had acted differently, must always be wrong' *(Ibid.)*. The maxim basic to this pronouncement is that a state of affairs containing a lesser balance of good over evil, or a greater balance of evil over good, than some other state of affairs is the less preferable of the two.

Before proceeding to the detail of Moore's position, certain features should be noted: First, that it is the character of the *total* consequences of an action, not of its consequences for the agent or for some privileged person or group, which determines an act's rightness or wrongness. Egoistic utilitarianism gives as a criterion for the moral character of an action its effects on the agent. John Stuart Mill was emphatic that the utilitarian view he was putting forward 'does not dream of defining morality to be the self-interest of the agent' (1871, Ch. 2), that is, of making an act's character depend on effects on the agent alone. Henry Sidgwick also makes this point clear in saying 'I ought not to prefer my own lesser good to the greater good of another...' (1874, p. 183).

A second feature to be noted, which is a consequence of the first, is that since there can be only *one* totality of effects, no act can change its moral status. Utilitarianism, in fact all forms of it, is an *objectivist* view: The consequences of an act are a genuine part of its nature, so that members of any number of societies will all judge correctly or incorrectly that such is its nature. Further, whether it has that feature does not depend on those who judge it. That an action is right, or wrong, i.e., is productive of certain effects, is a fact about it in no way dependent on any attitude towards the action, any more than the fact that an effect of impact between bodies is dependent on any attitude towards it. Moral disagreement over consequences bears directly on the moral character of an act, not, as Ayer asserts, as a means of crystallizing an attitude. Moral deliberation is coextensive with deliberation on consequences. We can now give a more careful statement of ideal utilitarianism. To say a specific act is right is to say its total consequences are at least as good as those of any alternative the agent could do; to say it is one's duty is to say its consequences are better than those of any alternative; to say it is wrong is to say its consequences are less good than those of something else the agent could do. These analyses reflect the recognized distinction between the concept of duty and the concept of rightness. If an act is mor allyobligatory it is right, but the converse does not hold: a number of acts may be right without a specific one being one's moral duty (their consequences and those of their alternatives might be the same). But if an act is one's duty then any other act would be wrong; that is, the alternatives would bring about a less good state of affairs. That there is this distinction is reflected in the fact that we often blame people for an action which has good consequences, but less good ones than of an alternative that could have been chosen. The importance of explicating the moral character of an act in terms of alternatives possible to the agent is thus clear. The mere fact that an act brings about a good state of affairs is no guarantee of its rightness. An act can be right, even one's duty, which brings about a preponderance of bad over good. We have a recognition of this fact in the maxim 'Choose the lesser of two evils.' It will be right to choose an act whose consequences are preponderantly bad if those of the alternatives are worse.

The utilitarian view that Moore sets out, unlike Kant's view, gives a criterion for testing the moral character of a *specific* act without doing this for the class of acts to which it belongs. It is clear that Kant's criterion for a specific act's being morally obligatory, or for being wrong, is at the same time a criterion holding for all acts of its class. But acts of the same class may have quite different consequences, and therefore on Moore's view quite different moral attributes. Circumstances alter cases. The consequences of lying, for example, may differ greatly, in their total of good and bad, from one case to the next. It is conceivable but unlikely that all acts of lying bring about a less good state of affairs than not lying.

One can only say that all acts of a given class are wrong if in every case some other act would produce better results. Two acts will be right, and one not morally preferable to the other, only if their consequences are the same and the consequences of their alternatives the same.

The motives which govern one's choice have on this view no bearing on whether the act resulting from them is right or wrong. Only the actual consequences are relevant. It is thus possible that an act motivated by the desire to bring about the worst possible state of affairs should produce, through some mischance or miscalculation, the best possible state of affairs. And such an act would be right. Also, if one acted in such a way that one could wish the maxim of one's action to become universal law, where the maxim usually operated to insure consequences far better than anything else, such motivation could not save the action from being wrong if in fact its consequences were less good than they might be. Some critics have objected to the ethical view that permits this. Moore's reply (1912, pp. 182–190) is that the requisite distinctions between, on the one hand, judgments on motives, judgments on the goodness of states of affairs, and judgments on the praiseworthiness or blameworthiness of the agent, and on the other hand, the moral character of an action leave his criterion of rightness intact. A man might be praiseworthy for a wrong action because his motive was good, or blameworthy for a right one because his motive was bad. A state of affairs might be better for the presence in it of a benign motive as against a malicious one. And a motive might be condemned because it is of the kind which usually leads to wrong action, even though in a given case it did not. But all of these judgments are distinct from judgments on the moral character of an act.

Certain criticisms directed against the kind of doctrine held by Bentham, Mill, and Moore concerning individual acts – given the name 'act-utilitarianism' by contemporary writers – have suggested the need of revising it or even of abandoning it altogether. These criticisms center on the answers act-utilitarians give to two questions, 'What justifies punishment?' and 'Why should promises be kept?' It has usually been considered that the justification of punishment and the obligation to keep promises present special difficulties for utilitarianism, particularly for the form set out by Moore. Two views of punishment lie comfortably together in the ordinary man's mind until the circumstances of a particular case bring them into conflict. One view is that wrongdoing merits punishment, and punishment to fit the crime. This is the retributive view, according to which it is morally fitting that a person should suffer in proportion to his wrongdoing. The other is the utilitarian view, which justifies the evil of suffering punishment, not on the ground that what one has done merits it but on the ground that inflicting it promotes the good of all, either by deterring or reforming the miscreant or through the peace and security it creates in society. This principle can be applied directly to each individual case of wrongdoing, and if punishment does not produce a better state of affairs than non-punishment, then it cannot be justified.

A common objection is that such a view would justify subjecting the innocent to punishment. E. F. Carritt writes: '. . . the utilitarian must hold that we are justified in inflicting pain always and only to prevent worse pain or to bring about greater happiness. This, then, is all we need to consider in so-called punishment, which must be purely preventive. But if some kind of cruel crime becomes common, and none of the criminals can be caught, it might be highly expedient, as an ex- ample, to hang an innocent man, if a charge against him could be so framed that he were universally thought guilty' (1947, p. 65). In order to meet this objection John Rawls revises act-utilitarianism on the basis of the distinction between the practice of punishment 'specified by a system of rules which defines offices, . . . penalties, defences . . . which gives the activity its structure' (1955, p. 3), and particular applications of these rules to particular cases. His thesis is that utilitarian considerations apply to the practice rather than to particular actions falling under it. That is, the practice specified by the rules is justified by conformity of the rules with the utilitarian criterion, the applications by their conformity with the rules. (See also Smart [1961, p. 4]: 'Rule utilitarianism holds that the rightness or wrongness of an action is to be judged by the goodness and badness of the consequences of a rule that everyone should perform the action in like circumstances.') John Austin, a nineteenth century writer, put the distinction as follows: 'Utility would be the test of our conduct, ultimately, but not immediately: the immediate test of the rules to which our conduct would conform, but not the immediate test of specific or individual acts. Our rules would be fashioned on utility; our conduct, on our rules' (1954, Lecture 2). This distinction, together with a distinc- tive conception of the nature of rules, characterizes so-called 'rule-utili- tarianism'.

Rawls' defence of utilitarianism against Carritt's objection consists in exposing what the objection presupposes: that each official is without restriction entitled to bring utilitarian considerations to bear on whether *he* should condemn an innocent man. The practice of punishment does not allow him such discretion. Punishment as a practice has to be defined by reference to a system of accepted authorities, statutes, law-courts, etc. Apart from stipulations governing it the practice does not exist. Carritt's example suggests that the institution of punishment stipulates that the officials set up by it have authority to condemn the innocent if they believe it will promote the good of society. With this latitude each particular act of an official would be justified, not by conformity to rules for meting out punishment, but by the utilitarian criterion. Considering the danger of increased suffering from the discretionary powers of officials, both to innocent victims and to those who feared becoming innocent victims, such an institutional practice would be unlikely to satisfy the utilitarian criterion; and it is to practices that this criterion applies.

Were such a practice in operation no particular case of inflicting suffering for the good of society would be an exception to it. An official who deliberated over whether punishment should be meted out to an innocent man would be operating within a practice which had no limits on his discretionary authority, either understood or written into it. Such can hardly be called a practice, for there are no rules defining exceptions and acceptable defences. Rules are qualified by referring to exceptions, and in the case of the practice of punishment, by specifications of the people to wield authority, the actions appropriate to their office, and the limits of their discretion. These qualifications and specifications are governed by utilitarian considerations. The practice defined by the rules involves giving up the liberty to act on an ethical principle – such as the good of society – independently of the rules. Nevertheless, an individual case of inflicting suffering can raise questions about the need for change in the practice, as well as questions whether the rules, hedged about as they are by understood or specified limits, apply.

A similar defence of the utilitarian principle, by confining its application to a practice where a practice exists, is offered in connection with the practice of promise-keeping. Critics of utilitarianism have made punishment and promises the test cases of the theory. They have held that the utilitarian criterion justifies much more than punishment of the guilty and that it cannot justify at all the strictness with which we feel obliged to keep promises. This charge is made against act-utilitarianism, according to which the only justification for keeping a promise in a particular case is that a less good state of affairs would result from breaking it. The general rule, 'Keep promises', becomes 'a mere rule of thumb which we use only to avoid the necessity of estimating the probable consequences of our actions at every step' (Smart, 1956, p. 334); and we are justified in following the rule only if doing so has as good consequences as not following it. Among consequences of promise-breaking, of course, must be reckoned people's weakened faith in the custom of promise-keeping. Critics like W. D. Ross point out that we still consider a promise binding even though the consequences of breaking it, including the damage done to the practice of promising, are better than those of keeping it. Cases can be imagined where this damage is minimal or nonexistent, for example, a promise made to a dying man which is known only by the promiser. Though we might accept as a defence for breaking a promise the severity of unforeseen consequences, we should not accept the general defence, offered without further explanation, that it was better on the whole to break it.

Rule-utilitarians admit that this is true, and defend utilitarianism by maintaining the utilitarian criterion is applicable only to the practice of promise-keeping, rather than to particular promises. Although this practice is not defined explicitly, as is the practice of punishment, still there is a general understanding about the conditions of promising: that a promise is given only if one intends to keep it, that only certain defences of promise-breaking are acceptable, etc. The institution of promising denies to the promiser the liberty to decide in each case whether the promise is to be kept. It allows this liberty only within a small area. A person who engages in the practice of promising can defend his act of keeping or breaking the promise by reference to the rule 'Keep promises' together with its understood or specified exceptions. Whether the rule applies to his case is what he must decide when he deliberates over whether to keep his promise. But it is not open to him to use the reasons which justify the rule to justify his particular action. The 'practice conception' of a rule is that it is legislative rather than a rule of thumb guide enabling one to short-circuit calculations of consequences. Some rules are of this latter kind, for example, always to tell the truth to someone who asks about the gravity of his illness. This rule, which is not part of a practice, is merely a generalization which sums up past decisions arrived at by applying the utilitarian principle directly. One is always entitled to reconsider a generalization and by-pass it to apply the principle directly to the case in hand. The distinction between the two sorts of rules may not always be clear-cut. But where there is a practice, the practice conception of the rules governing it applies. The traditional test cases of utilitarianism, punishment and promise-keeping, are cases of practices, and are held not to present difficulties for the theory if they are properly construed.

It has of course been questioned whether the distinction between rules defining a practice and rules which merely summarize the result of applying the utilitarian principle to similar cases can save the principle from permitting the infliction of suffering on the innocent or can leave it any justification for promise-keeping. Suppose it is granted that an institution of punishment which gives officials the authority to condemn the innocent for the good of society is *unlikely* to have a utilitarian justification. Is this enough to save utilitarianism from the criticism that it justifies more than it should? If it is always wrong that officials in the exercise of their discretionary powers make the innocent suffer, then the *possibility* of its being on utilitarian grounds right is enough to constitute an objection to utilitarianism. Again, suppose a promise is exacted knowing the consequences of keeping it are extremely severe for the promiser, and that although the practice does allow of certain defences for not keeping a promise, among them that the consequences are severe, the foreseeable consequences to the promiser are not severe enough to permit a defence of not keeping it. (The purpose of exacting the promise is to disallow this sort of defence.) But suppose it turns out that keeping this promise would in fact produce much less good *on the whole* than breaking it. Is this consideration irrelevant to deliberation over whether it should be kept? Is it clear that the utilitarian test is relevant only to the practice and that in a particular case one can only deliberate over whether the promise falls under the exceptions built into the practice?

Whether or not the practices of punishment and promise-keeping present difficulties for utilitarianism, there is a difficulty, implied by considerations noted by Russell, which Moore took as constituting the most serious objection of all. This is that if the rightness of an act depends on its *actual* consequences then the utilitarian may have to hold that it is sometimes right to act on evidence that the consequences will be the worst possible and sometimes wrong to act on evidence that they will be the best possible. If an act produces as great a balance of good over bad or as small a balance of bad over good, on the utilitarian view it is right. Russell simply calls such an act fortunate, 'but we cannot maintain that the most fortunate act is always the one which ... a

18

wise man will hold that he ought to do' (1910, p. 22). Antecedently the evidence at one's disposal might make it probable that a certain action would have the best possible results (although it in fact brings about the worst possible). How ought one to act? Plainly choice is not rational unless governed by the available evidence. To choose a course of action without regard for evidence is tantamount to making a decision depend on the toss of a coin. It seems clear that we ought not go against evidence, from which it follows that it will be right not to go against it, and therefore right to do the indicated act. But were the utilitarian to assent to this, one and the same act would be both right and wrong. Similarly, if the evidence makes it probable that an act's consequences will be the worst possible, it would be one's duty not to do it even though doing it produces the best possible results. So long as one holds that it is one's duty to act on evidence, it will be right so to act, regardless of the *actual* consequences. Accordingly the utilitarian criterion is modified to read: An act is right if and only if the evidence available to the agent makes it probable that its consequences are as good as those of any alternative act. An act which on the basis of the evidence one ought to do will then be right even though its actual consequences are less good than those of some other act.

Moore admits that it may seem 'outrageous' to say that a man who had evidence that his act would not produce the best consequences could be said to act rightly in virtue of an accident defeating his purpose (1912, pp. 191–192). He nevertheless thinks it proper, after an act has been done and many of its results known, to judge the act right and to judge the agent blameworthy. Similarly, after an act has been done for which the probabilities were all in favor of its producing the best results, it is proper to judge the agent praiseworthy, but to let the judgment on the act's moral character rest on its actual consequences. But he admits that the judgment we apparently ought to pass on it *beforehand* involves the utilitarian in a paradox. We should undoubtedly say, beforehand, that the agent ought to choose the course whose consequences would most probably be the best, and that it would be wrong not to. Moore grants that we would be *justified* in saying this, but that 'we may be justified in saying many things, which we do not know to be true' (*Ibid,*. pp. 194–195), and which in fact are not true. And he is willing to accept the paradox that a man may deserve the greatest praise for choosing to do an action which *actually* is wrong. What undermines this reply is the defence a person often makes *after* the act: that if he had it to do over again, he would make the same choice as he did make – in other words, that what he did was right even though its consequences were less good than those of another choice. Moreover, it seems paradoxical to hold that it is *ever* true to assert that one ought to act against evidence for believing a certain course will produce the best possible results. One can miscalculate the probabilities and so do a wrong because the evidence available did really make it probable that the course chosen would have less good consequences than some other course; but it would seem that if one calculates correctly the probabilities that there will be as good results as any one could possibly bring about, then action in accordance with it is always right.

Nevertheless, Russell's view also commits one to a paradox. Suppose the evidence available to S makes it probable that the consequences of his chosen course of action x will be the best possible, but that S' has evidence that they will be the worst. Suppose also that it is impossible for S' to communicate this information but that nevertheless he is in a position to prevent S from doing x. On Russell's view S's act x will be right, since the evidence available *to S* makes it likely that the consequences will be better than those of any alternative. But it will also be right for S' to do the act y which prevents S from doing what is right.

One of the merits of the various utilitarian theories is that the criterion formulated by reference to consequences is in conformity with the test we apply when we deliberate over alternative courses of action. By way of objection it has been claimed that there is a difficulty, which the various forms of utilitarianism have in common with other ethical theories, and this is that if they are correct then it is impossible ever to know an act is right, or at least more difficult than we in fact find it to be. Consider how difficult it would be to know what the attitude of society, or of the world, is, and how difficult, if not impossible, to know God's will. Similarly, supposing the human race does not die out, so that the consequences of an action, or of conforming to a rule, are unending, it would be impossible either to reckon the total consequences or their probability. If one takes the view that every event is part of a causal chain, so that every event has an infinite number of effects, then the rightness or wrongness of the simplest act could not, in principle, be known.

This sceptical conclusion is on a par with the sceptical conclusion concerning our knowledge of the external world. It would seem to have the astonishing consequence that moral discourse is without sense. In brief outline, justification of this claim is as follows: A person who says

18*

no one really knows an act is right or wrong is unable to describe a situation in which he would know that a judgment of the form 'x is right' is true, which means he would never know the terms 'right' and 'wrong' had correct applications. He would not, in Wittgenstein's words, 'know what it is like' for these terms to apply correctly. Not knowing what it is like to establish the truth of 'x is right' implies not knowing what it is like for x to be right. The underlying implication would seem to be that these terms have no correct use, which of course destroys moral discourse.

Up to the present no ethical theory that has been formulated has turned out to be free from difficulties, and this fact has been highlighted in the present chapter. We might well ask the question Wittgenstein raised in another connection: 'Where does our investigation get its importance from, since it seems only to destroy everything interesting, that is, all that is great and important? (As it were all the buildings, leaving behind only bits of stone and rubble.)' (1953, p. 48). It is plain that if we are to have an objective appraisal of a theory we must not only articulate it clearly but make explicit the considerations which in fact or in appearance go against it. To arrive at any secure results in ethics we must first break the hold that a favored theory has on us by facing the objections to it. It may be that none of the theories so far formulated by philosophers will survive this scrutiny, in which case, as Wittgenstein said in answer to his question, 'what we are destroying is nothing but houses of cards' *(Ibid.)*. But it may be that rival theories, for example, act-utilitarianism and rule-utilitarianism, contain within themselves elements which seen together will lead to a firm theory. One thing the investigation with its negative outcome can give is a better understanding of the related uses of the words 'right', 'wrong', and 'morally obligatory'. J. L. Austin, for example, was of the opinion that before a correct theory could be established in philosophy it was necessary to make an extended investigation of the terminology, and closely related terminology, used in the expression of the theory. The two processes, linguistic discrimination and concept refinement, are bound up with each other, and together they are a precondition for constructive work in the field. Attention to the language of morals has been an invariant feature of our investigations, whether explicit or not, so that if houses of cards have been destroyed, 'we are clearing up the ground of language on which they stand' *(Ibid.)*.

III. One notion operative in theories about right conduct, and very explicitly in utilitarian theories, is a notion which has so far been left unexplored, the notion of goodness. With utilitarianism, as Russell says, 'what is called good conduct is conduct which is a means to other things which are good on their own account...' (1910, pp. 3–4). Hence 'the study of what is good on its own account must be included in ethics, which then ceases to be concerned only with human conduct. The first step in ethics, therefore, is to be quite clear as to what we mean by good and bad' *(Ibid.)*. When Plato said virtue was knowledge of the good he gave only a metaphorical account of the good, as being like the sun which illuminates the objects of sense. Just as these are seen by the light of the sun, so truth, and thus ethical truth, is known when illuminated by the idea of the good. Some interpretations of this obscure statement identify the good with God, so that virtue would be knowledge of God's will. Socrates begs off giving a sober account, however: 'Sweet sirs, let us not at present ask what is the actual nature of the good, for to reach what is now in my thought would be an effort too great for me'. (*Republic*, Bk. VI. Sec. 506). In that dialogue he would only assert emphatically what it is not – that it is not pleasure. In the *Philebus*, pleasure is conceded to be a good, and a number of goods are ranked in a scale. The question here is what, if anything, they have in common.

As with positions on rightness, we find the same cleavage of positions as to whether 'goodness' denotes a quality at all, or whether it is a merely emotive term. Until recently this did not come into serious question; value terms were taken to stand for apprehendable characteristics. Moore said: 'My business is solely with that object or idea which I hold, rightly or wrongly, that the word "good" is generally used to stand for' (1922b p. 6). However puzzling it may be that people who know the meanings of 'right' and 'good' can disagree over whether they denote a quality, we leave aside this question to examine some of the theories which agree that goodness is a quality. The word 'good' is used in several quite different contexts. We speak of good motives, good people, good instrumentalities, good states of affairs. Our concern now is with goodness as an attribute of states of affairs, in distinction to rightness, which is a property of actions. On utilitarian views, rightness is a property of actions which eventuate in states of affairs having the attribute of goodness or badness. As Moore put it, 'right' denotes a property of actions which are 'good as means' (*Ibid.*, p. 18), which, without going into qualifications, are good-producing.

It is important to demarcate clearly the concept *good as a means*, or *instrumentally good*, from the concept *good as an end*, or *good in itself*

– what Russell called 'good on its own account'. In the literature of ethics the term 'intrinsic good' is used to denote the latter concept, so that when *the* good, the highest good, and what they have in common, namely, goodness are referred to, the characterization 'intrinsic' is tacitly understood. Moore explicates this predicate as follows: '... that a thing is *intrinsically good* ... means ... that the existence of the thing in question *would* be good, even if it existed quite alone, without any accompaniments or effects whatever ... Very often ... when we say that a thing is "good", we mean that it is good *because of its effects*. We are, for instance, familiar with the idea that it is sometimes a good thing for people to suffer pain; and yet we should be very loth to maintain that in all such cases their suffering *would* be a good thing, even if nothing were gained by it – if it had no further effects' (1912, p. 69).

Classical utilitarianism as propounded by Jeremy Bentham and John Stuart Mill, specified pleasure as the sole intrinsic good, and held a thing to be good only to the extent that it is pleasurable. Pain alone is intrinsically bad. As Bentham wrote: 'Nature has placed mankind under the governance of two sovereign masters *pain* and *pleasure*. It is for them alone to point out what we ought to do, as well as to determine what we shall do' (1907, p. 1). And Mill: '...actions are right in proportion as they tend to promote happiness, wrong as they tend to produce the reverse of happiness. By happiness is intended pleasure, and the absence of pain; by unhappiness, pain, and the privation of pleasure ... Pleasure, and freedom from pain, are the only things desirable as ends; ... all desirable things ... are desirable either for the pleasure inherent in themselves, or as means to the promotion of pleasure and the prevention of pain' (1871, Ch. 2). As has already been pointed out, this form of utilitarianism is hedonistic but not egoistic: 'The standard is not the agent's own greatest happiness, but the greatest amount of happiness altogether ... of mankind and of all sentient creatures' *(Ibid.)*. To take the position that *the* good to which right action is a means is in the case of each person identical with *his own* good is as Moore points out, a contradiction. For it declares that 'several different things are *each* of them the *only* thing desirable' (1922b, pp. 104–105).

It is of some importance to distinguish *the* good, which the property *goodness* characterizes, from the property itself. Hedonists have held that what is good is pleasant and what is pleasant is good, and have come to two conclusions, one that *the* good and pleasure are identical, and the other that what is *meant* by "being good" is being *pleasant*. Moore in

Principia ethica denied both claims, but for different reasons. As for identifying *the* good with pleasure, he accepted the distinction made centuries earlier by Plato in the *Philebus* between pleasure and the consciousness of pleasure, and then argued that to hold pleasure alone to be intrinsically good (good if it existed by itself) is to maintain it is good whether we are conscious of it or not (*Ibid.*, pp. 88–91). If, as Moore held, consciousness of pleasure is more valuable than pleasure, then pleasure cannot be the only good. Going further perhaps than either Plato or Moore, we might say that pleasure without the consciousness of pleasure has no value whatever. For pleasure without the consciousness of pleasure would imply pleasure without the enjoyment of pleasure; and this, like an unfelt pain (if that is possible), would seem to be in itself value-neutral, neither intrinsically good nor intrinsically bad. Only the enjoyment of pleasure has intrinsic value, but the enjoyment of pleasure implies consciousness. Pleasure is worth having only insofar as it is a content of consciousness.

As for the property *goodness*, Moore says that any attempt to identify it with what he terms a 'natural' property involves the fallacy, already mentioned in a criticism of Kant's theory, of defining an ethical term by reference to non-ethical properties. What he calls the naturalistic fallacy is committed by all theories which claim that to be good means to possess some natural property such as *being pleasant, being desired, being liked, being approved of*. His reason is that the goodness of a state of affairs is different in kind from natural properties, which we apprehend perceptually. 'It is not *goodness*, but only the things or qualities which are good, which ... can be objects of *perception*' (*Ibid.*, pp. 110–111). Our senses do not disclose it as they do redness, swiftness, pleasantness, or being desired, and there is a corresponding difference between a quality of which we are non-perceptually aware and those other qualities. It may well be that what is good is pleasant, or desired, or approved of, but these features are not defining properties of it. 'The naturalistic fallacy', Moore says, 'consists in the contention that good *means* nothing but some simple or complex notion that can be defined in terms of natural qualities' (*Ibid.*, p. 73).

In further specification, value attributes are distinguished from 'intrinsic' properties, on which they are nevertheless held to be dependent. Of the two types of property Moore says: 'I can only vaguely express the kind of difference I feel there to be by saying that intrinsic properties seem to *describe* the intrinsic nature of what possesses them in a sense in which predicates of value never do. If you could enumerate *all* intrinsic properties a given thing possessed, you would have given a *complete* description of it, and would not need to mention any predicates of value it possessed; whereas no descritpion of a given thing could be *complete* which omitted any intrinsic property' (1922a, p. 274). 'Good' thus denotes an attribute having a special place amongst attributes. It is not a natural property but is possessed by a thing in virtue of its natural properties. To use Broad's terminology, some natural properties are 'good-making' (1942, p. 63), but the good they produce is itself non-natural.

This terminology suggests that natural properties are the causes of a thing's having value, which implies the possibility of a thing's having the good-producing qualities without the good they normally produce. And it would then be possible, with regard to two exactly similar things, for one to have value and the other not. Moore denies the suggestion that this is possible; on his view natural properties of what is good might better be called good-entailing. The connection between the natural properties in virtue of which a thing is said to have value and the value attributed to it is not contingent. Two things which are exactly similar could not conceivably have different value properties. As Moore put it, a value property is such that 'if one thing possesses it and another does not, the intrinsic nature of the two things *must* be different' (1922a, p. 275). A value judgment to the effect that a thing having certain natural properties is good thus is *a priori*, and furthermore, synthetic *a priori*. In Broad's words: 'The necessary connexion between those natural characteristics of a thing which are good-making and the goodness which they confer on it could not possibly be analytic. For this would involve the absurdity that the *non-natural* characteristic of goodness is contained as a factor in the analysis of the purely *natural* good-making characteristics' (1942, p. 66). To bring out the difference between natural properties and goodness in another way, to say pleasure or friendship or aesthetic enjoyment is intrinsically good, unlike saying it is desired or approved of, is not an empirically verifiable assertion. The value property has a necessary dependence on the nture of the thing rather than a connection with it which is contingent on circumstance, people's psychological make-up, or the laws of nature.

Value properties are thus unique among properties. It is Moore's contention that goodness and badness are unique in the further respect that they are simple and hence indefinable. The notions of rightness and and wrongness are defined by ideal utilitarians in terms of intrinsic goodness and badness, but the latter have no definition. This implies that any true statement about goodness (as contrasted with one about *the* good, to which the adjective 'good' applies and which he thinks to be definable), will not be analytic. It will be *a priori* synthetic. Goodness, like the sense-quality yellow, is not analyzable into component parts. If it were, then in any sentence employing the adjective 'good' we could substitute the complex expression with which it is synonymous without change of meaning. Moore holds that since we can always sensibly ask concerning the complex denoted by such an expression whether it is good there cannot be an identity between the two; we are not asking something as contentless as 'Is what is good good?' To illustrate he considers the definition of 'good' as 'what we desire to desire'. To ask whether A is good is thus the same as to ask whether A is one of the things we desire to desire. But we note that it is also sensible to ask whether it is good to desire to desire *A*. Of this Moore says that it is 'apparent that the meaning of this second question cannot be correctly analyzed into "Is the desire to desire *A* one of the things we desire to desire?"' 'That we should desire to desire *A* is good' does not translate into the redundancy 'that *A* is good is good' (1922b, p. 16). It is always an open question whether what we desire to desire is good, but not whether what is good is good. The same type of argument holds against all attempts to equate *good* with natural properties, for example, with what is desired. 'This is desired, but is it good?' is not the same as 'This is desired, but is it desired?', and 'This is desired but not good' is not a contradiction. Similarly for equating goodness with what is **pleasant** or with what is approved of.

Moore's non-**naturalism** clearly rules out subjectivist accounts of goodness, that is, accounts according to which the assertion that something is good implies that certain feelings are being had towards it. Subjectivist views, such as '"goodness" means being desired', or 'being found pleasant', not only involve the naturalistic fallacy. They also make the goodness of a thing depend for its existence on the accident that these feelings towards the thing exist, whereas on Moore's view whatever has it has it in virtue of its natural properties and it is equally objective with them. As Ross puts it, goodness 'is a quality resident in the object itself, independent of **any** subject's reaction to it' (1930, p. 89). This thesis is graphically illustrated by Moore's treatment of another value attribute, beauty. Imagine, he says, two worlds, the one exceedingly beautiful and the other repulsively ugly. 'Is it irrational to hold that it is better that the beautiful world should exist, than the one which is ugly?' (1922b, p. 84), assuming that no human being ever has lived, or can live on either. It is his view 'that the beautiful world is *in itself* better than the ugly' (p. 85), even though it would be better still if there were human beings to whom it gave enjoyment. At a later time he wrote, 'I think now, as I did not when I wrote *Principia*, that the existence of some *experience* ... does follow from the hypothesis that there exists a state of affairs which is good' (1942, p. 168). But the fact that it is only states of affairs involving consciousness that are intrinsically good does not mean that goodness is subjective, i.e., depends on any attitude towards the experience, any more than that the rightness of an action depends on an attitude towards it.

Assuming that good is a quality of a state of affairs 'containing *both* some feeling and also some other form of consciousness' (1912, p. 249), and that this quality is not perceived by any of the physical senses, the question arises how one is aware of it. Supposedly one is aware of it as immediately as one is aware of the yellowness of an image. How this is effected needs to be specified. Some have supposed us to have a special sense by which we intuit the value inherent in an experience or state of affairs. Philosophers such as M. Schlick, who notes that 'its organs cannot be pointed out as can the human eye' (1939, p. 6), evidently suppose they are objecting to an empirical view, one, moreover, which is 'out of harmony with modern psychology' (Urban, 1930, p. 56). This is one form of so-called intuitionism in value theory. But another and different form of it escapes this criticism. On this view, when one perceives that something is good one has rational insight into an *a priori* connection between the thing's natural properties and goodness. Goodness and its connection with natural properties are, as Ross put it, 'discerned by the intelligence' (1930, p. 87). One is reminded of Plato's account of our apprehension of universals and their logical connections.

Critics, especially naturalists, have objected that neither a special sense nor a non-perceptual faculty of the mind is required to intuit goodness, which in any case they do not take to be a non-sensuous property. The dispute between naturalists and non-naturalists on this point is curious, particularly since both know the use of the word 'goodness'. Especially curious is the idea one must have of the disputants: the one must take the line that the other is value-blind, after the analogy of being color-blind, the other must suppose his opponent to be suffering from sort of delusion. But leaving this aside, Moore's claim that between natural properties and value properties there is a synthetic *a priori* connection clamors for examination. Do we know the truth of an evaluative judgment in the way in which we know the truth of '$2^{2^2}+1$ is prime'? It is clear that Moore's view makes value disagreements understandable: one person merely fails to see a logical connection which the other sees, and only one of the opposed judgments can be true. But the difficulty is that one of the two judgments is an inconceivability of thought, comparable to '27 is prime'. And when one changes one's mind about the value of a state of affairs, one must consider oneself either to have relinquished an inconceivability or to have embraced one. The way one would convince oneself or another person that one's value-judgment was true would be by using demonstration from concepts. If one considers any of the disputed value-judgments, for example, that certain traits of character, or knowledge, are intrinsically good, it has to be admitted that unlike *a priori* propositions in mathematics their truth or falsity remains unresolved.

Considerations of these kinds have prompted some philosophers to maintain that the nature both of value and of value-judgments has been misconstrued by non-naturalists and naturalists alike. Philosophers of both sorts have taken 'good' and 'bad' to denote properties, descriptive or non-descriptive, and value-judgments to be either true or false. Their critics hold that these terms are used emotively, to commend or condemn, and judgments in which they occur have quite different functions than to assert or report a fact. Stevenson and Ayer take the function of these terms to be emotive – to give vent to feelings. Any disputes about what is good are disputes about facts which determine the attitudes which one's value-statements indicate (but do not assert). Value-words are in no sense attributive, and the great difference between descriptive statements and value-judgments is concealed by their common grammatical form. There is no such thing as knowing the truth-value of a value judgment, as it has none – hence the characterization of this position as 'noncognitivist' – and reasoning where values are concerned cannot be a demonstration, either empirical or *a priori*, that a value-predicate belongs to something. It merely provides inducements for approving it.

R. M. Hare presents a somewhat different account of value-judgments, but which is nevertheless like the noncognitivist view just described in insisting that value-words have a nondescriptive function. 'Good' not only expresses a pro-attitude on the part of the person who uses it. The value-judgment in which it occurs both commends something and is used to guide choices. This latter function it can perform because we are appealing to certain standards applying to all things of the class to which the object commended belongs. Commending and censuring are done in connection with a particular thing, but their function is to apply to all things like it. Value-judgments are 'covertly universal' (1952, p. 129). Now one can always ask of someone who says '*A* is good' *why* it is good. This is to ask which empirical good-making characteristics *A* has. So in saying *A* is good, one is appealing to the general principle that all things like *A* will be good, and one is *making an assertion* that *A* has certain properties (not always specifiable) in virtue of which it meets the standards applicable to its class. Hare distinguishes between the meaning of the word 'good' and the criteria for its application: Its meaning is its commendatory function; the criteria for its application are the good-making characteristics of the things of its class. These characteristics will vary with the class. A good hunter and a good draft horse, for example, will have different good-making properties which satisfy different standards of evaluation. When one supports a value-judgment one cites these properties. But the connection between an ascription of such properties and a value-assertion is *not* a logical one. Hare denies that a nondescriptive statement follows from a descriptive one. He thus explains quite differently than does Moore our being unable to say of two exactly similar states of affairs, *A* and *B*, that one is good and the other not. 'It is the purpose of the word "good" and other value-words to be used for teaching standards.' Hence to use it of *A* but not of *B* would be to 'defeat the purpose for which the word is designed. I should be commending one object, and so purporting to teach my hearers one standard, while in the same breath refusing to commend a similar object, and so undoing the lesson just imparted ... The effect of such an utterance is similar to that of a contradiction' (p. 134).

Hare maintains that a person could know the meaning of the word 'good' if he recognized its commendatory function, even though he did not know the criteria for its application to a thing of a certain class. i. e. the good-making characteristics of things of its class. He allows it is natural to say one learns its meaning by learning its application to things having certain characteristics (pp. 116–117), but claims for the word 'good' 'the primary function' (p. 127) of commending a thing so as to guide choice. It may, however, also function descriptively if one is acquinted with the standard for the thing's class (e. g., for the class of horses, the class of acts affecting one's happiness, the class of acts indicative of one's moral character). If one understands the word 'good' and knows the criteria for its application, then '*A* is good' gives information about A. Hare characterizes it as having 'this peculiar combination of evaluative and descriptive meaning' (p. 127). So it would appear that a value-judgment is either true or false, since it conveys the information that a thing satisfies certain criteria even though these cannot be specified. But if the standards which the good-making properties of a thing must satisfy vary, then the truth-status of the evaluative judgment will likewise vary. Standards are laid down by custom and convention; as Hare says, 'The standard of "goodness" ... is normally something which is public and commonly accepted' (p. 114). But we know that standards can change. In fact one reason Hare takes the evaluative meaning to be the primary meaning of 'good' is that its evaluative force can be used to change its descriptive meaning, i.e., the criteria for its application (p. 114; see also p. 119). Once one's standard is challenged one needs to do something more than cite good-making characteristics of a thing in order to support a value-judgment.

With this compromise between cognitivism and noncognitivism we close our account of ethical theories. As in the case of the investigation of the concept *rightness*, we have not arrived at a position free from difficulty and therefore have not come to a position that would be acceptable to all philosophers. Nevertheless the gain from the critical examination of a parade of theories cannot be doubted. Apart from reaching secure results, which ethics cannot boast of as yet, the progress of philosophy consists of continuous clarification, and analytical criticisms of theories is an important component in that process. Many years ago Moore wrote: 'It appears to me that in Ethics, as in all other philosophical studies, the difficulties and disagreements, of which its history is full, are mainly due to a very simple cause: namely to the attempt to answer questions, without first discovering precisely *what* question it is which you desire to answer' (1922b, p. VII). The fact that such a number and variety of conflicting theories about intrinsic goodness exist suggests that philosophers have not as yet reached a sufficiently clear view of the central question, or questions, they are asking.

DOUBTS AND QUERIES

I, 1. Suppose that we have a hand in the formation of our characters, as Mill and Clifford assert, and that even though every event including decisions, are caused, does such an ability to form our characters give us control over our decisions? Character is supposedly formed by our placing ourselves in circumstances where some desires are encouraged and others stifled. When we place ourselves in such circumstances are we determined to do so? That is, if the decisions we make follow from our characters, do our characters determine those decisions which are prior to the formation of our characters?

According to psychoanalysis character formation takes place in large part by unconscious identification with parents and other educators. Since this process is unconscious we have no control over it. Is there any room for control of character formation, given this early determination of it?

Once character is formed, actions and choices are causally determined by it. They flow from it as automatically as does any effect in nature. Can we be said to have freedom if we have no control over an automatic operation of character?

2. Suppose that when we accept responsibility for an action, praise or blame ourselves for it, and feel regret or self-satisfaction, it is a mere delusion on our part that another act or choice was possible, and that we could equally have chosen to do it or not to do it. If we free ourselves of this delusion, then the purpose of praise and blame bears only on *future* behavior, to encourage or deter. In this case what is the explanation of our lauding, holding blameworthy, and even exonerating those who are dead?

3. If God knows the future and therefore knows what we are going to do, then what we are going to do is already predetermined: we cannot fail to do what he knows we are going to do. How does this square with the possibility of deliberating on how we should act? If deliberating on a future course of action implies it is not yet determined, is God's fore-knowledge inconsistent with the possibility of such deliberation?

4. Kant held that 'ought' implies 'can'. Let us consider the consequences of conjoining this claim with the view of Hobbes and Locke that the notion of an uncaused action is self-contradictory, and with the strict determinist view that the concept of a freely willed action implies an uncaused action. Does it follow that the notion of duty implies a self-contradiction? Does it follow that feeling regret and remorse, in implying, as it would seem, the possibility of having acted differently, is logically impossible? In connection with regret, is the wish that one had acted differently on a footing with the 'wish' to see a five-sided triangle?

5. Suppose we reject the analysis of 'could' as 'would, if', on the ground

that it generates an infinite regress, and turn to a categorical sense of 'could' such as Broad expressed in the statement: 'Given *all* the antecedents of an act of choice, I nevertheless could have chosen differently'. Broad concludes that this statement implies a causal progenitor, i.e., an uncaused event. Is this the only possible conclusion?

Compare the notion of an original undetermined cause with Plato's notion of the soul as a self-mover.

6. In maintaining that the problem of free will is a pseudo-problem Schlick claimed that in any ordinary sense of 'freedom', freedom is opposed to constraint. Is it thereby implied that an action could be free even though its occurrence is causally determined? Does his position differ from that of moderate determinism that freedom and causal determination are not incompatible?

Strict determinists hold that no action is free which is causally determined. What is the mode of verification relevant to adjudicating between the rival claims of strict and moderate determinism, and how decide between these two views and the view that the problem of free will is no problem at all? Rival philosophers are aware of each other's conflicting positions as well as of the lines of reasoning given in their support. A question which seems bogus to one philosopher seems quite genuine to equally competent philosophers. If this problem is bogus what kind of procedure will convince the strict determinist that it is, and if it is not bogus, what procedure could be resorted to if a philosopher like Schlick is to be convinced that it is not?

The dispute over whether there is freedom to act or to choose has all the appearance of being empirical. At least three connected questions bear on whether in fact it is what it seems: (a) Is the connection between cause and effect, believed by some philosophers to be necessary, a contingent one? (b) Does the appeal to introspection show that the question whether freedom exists is an empirical one? (c) Does the probabilistic argument, from indirect evidence, show the same thing?

7. If, as it seems, the connection between events in a causal transaction could conceivably be otherwise but nevertheless has to hold, given the state of the world, then there is an identity between what must be and the actual, and between the impossible and what does not occur. Will this identity be a factual one, like that between the evening star and the morning star? What becomes of the category of the possible? Will what is possible be *in fact* the same as what is necessary? When the indeterminist insists that several alternatives are possible and the determinist denies

conflict of duties by arranging duties in an order of precedence such that some duties would override other duties? How would the principle of universalizability be affected by this addition to Kantian theory? Does the ranking of duties imply a higher-order duty which is not ranked in the scale of duties? How would this higher-order duty be related to the principle of universalizability?

14. It was plainly not self-evident to Kant, as it was to Moore, that 'knowingly to do an action which would make the world, on the whole, really and truly worse than if we had acted differently, must be wrong'. How would one justify this moral maxim if the appeal to self-evidence is ruled out? Kant held that justice should be done even though the heavens fall. There are major injustices and minor injustices. Would prevention of a slight injustice warrant making the heavens fall?

15. Could one justify Sidgwick's claim that 'I ought not to prefer my own lesser good to the greater good of another'? Compare with Butler's assertion: 'When I reflect in a cool moment I see that nothing can be good which is not in my own interest'.

16. Suppose the criterion of rightness in two different worlds were utilitarian, but that in one world, unlike ours, half of its people were sadists, who enjoyed inflicting pain, half were masochists, who enjoyed suffering it, and that an action was only wrong if it inflicted just enough pain on a sadist that its total consquences contained a greater balance of evil than some alternative, or so little pain on a masochist that the total contained a lesser balance of good than some alternative. Suppose a sadist inflicted pain on a masochist. Would people in the two worlds judge the act in the same way? Can a case be made out for holding that the utilitarian view is relativist?

17. Suppose we grant that we *feel* ourselves morally bound by a promise even though we can see that the consequences of keeping it are less good than those of breaking it. Does feeling bound imply that we *are* bound to keep it? Does the test of act-utilitarianism supposedly provided by promise-keeping rest on our *feeling* morally bound or on our being morally bound? Is this a possible distinction in Ayer's view?

18. Compare the following three general philosophical claims about assertions that an action is right: (1) they are made true or false by the property of the action; (2) they are made true or false by the attitude of a group of people; (3) they have no truth-value. What kind of investigation is relevant to the elimination of some or all of these claims – an examination of actions which are called right and wrong, an examination

of the meanings of 'right' and 'wrong', or an examination of the uses these words have in the language? Wittgenstein said (at a Moral Sciences Club meeting, as reported by John Wisdom, *Mind*, Vol. 41, 1952), 'Don't ask for the meaning of a word, ask for its use'; and he also said, 'For a *large* class of cases – though not for all – in which we employ the word "meaning" it can be defined thus: the meaning of a word is its use in the language' (1953, p. 20). Is there a difference between the literal meaning of a word and the use the word has in the language? If there is a difference, is the emotivist saying that purely ethical terms have no literal meaning but only a use?

19. One notion as to why philosphers continue to disagree is that they argue at cross purposes, each employing a somewhat different sense of the phrase, 'morally right'. Are the different theories about rightness simply explications of its different senses, comparable to explications of the different senses in the two expressions 'right angle' and 'right direction'? One objection to this explanation of the multiplicity of views is that if there were such differing uses, they would be recognized and the disagreements would be dispelled, inasmuch as the arguments for a view would provide the sense of the term on which the view is an elaboration. A further and connected point is the following: Philosophers who hold one view take the position that rival views are false. Does this imply that they think the sense of the term 'rightness' they have fixed on is the only ethical sense the word has in the language? In view of the fact that philosophers use ethical terms in their normal ways, how is their apparent obliviousness to some of the senses in which they themselves use the word to be explained?

III, 20. Moore said that '...the naturalistic fallacy is the fallacy which consists in identifying the simple notion which we mean by "good" with some other notion' (1922b, p. 58), and that 'Even if goodness were a natural object, that would not alter the nature of the fallacy nor diminish its importance one whit' (*Ibid.*, p. 14). On the basis of these statements W. K. Frankena (1939) concludes that what Moore calls the naturalistic fallacy is the fallacy of defining what is indefinable. If a definition is produced of what is indefinable then two properties are being treated as one and the same. Note that indefinability of a concept does not imply its being non-natural, since *yellow* is indefinable but natural. Being simple, in the sense of being indefinable, and being non-natural are logically independent. Now for a concept to be indefinable is for it not to be

19*

decomposable into components contained in it. That is, it is not resolvable into a conjunction of concepts. There will be no analytic statement of the form '"good" means φ and ψ' comparable to '"triangle" means three-sided plane figure'. But suppose there were an *a priori* synthetic connection between goodness and some other property, comparable to that between *being yellow* and *being colored*. Is it logically absurd to suppose that *being good* synthetically entails some natural property? Moore holds that a thing's natural properties can entail goodness. Does the consideration he put forward as showing that goodness is not a natural property also show that it cannot entail a natnral property?

21. Hume said that an *ought*-statement could not be deduced from a statement of what *is*, that is, no statement of the form 'x ought to be done' could be deduced from a non-ethical statement about what is the case. To use Hume's own words, it 'seems altogether inconceivable, how this new relation can be a deduction from others, which are entirely different from it'. Does Moore's claim that predicates of value are entailed by natural predicates go against Hume's claim? That it does might be argued as follows: That a statement about what is, one to the effect that such-and-such a thing exists and has certain natural properties, entails that the thing is good. An intrinsically good state of affairs is one which we ought to try to preserve, not to say create. Consequently it would seem to follow that a statement to the effect that a particular thing has certain natural properties entails a statement about how we ought to act. Evaluate this argument.

22. Moore held that a *complete* description could in principle be given of something which is good, without any mention of its value-property. Ross denies an analogous claim about beauty on the ground that 'its beauty might be for some purposes the most important fact about it' (1930, p. 121). Is this a verbal dispute over what is to be called a complete description?

Ross seems to rest his claim that beauty is a descriptive property of a thing on the fact that it might be the most valuable property of it. Now, beauty is a value-property. Is a value-property of a thing made descriptive by being more valuable than other of the thing's properties?

23. What does Moore mean by the phrase 'open question'? The question 'Is what is pleasant pleasant?' is not, according to him, an open question, whereas 'Is what is pleasant good?' is. Does he mean that a question is open when the statement corresponding to it is contingent? Or does he mean only that the corresponding statement does not state an identity

between concepts, but could state some sort of entailment between them? Does a hedonist who says that what is pleasant is alone good state an empirical proposition which he claims to be true on the basis of experience, or does he instead declare it is inconceivable for what is pleasant not to be good? If the latter, he would be making the entailment claim that being pleasant entails being good. Is this entailment made into an identity by the claim that pleasure alone is good?

24. Suppose goodness is a non-sensuous quality which is 'discerned by the intelligence'. Have we any comparable experience of an object describable in this way, other than grasping the meaning of a word? Presumably one grasps the meaning of 'good' when one understands the word, so something more must be involved in discerning it by the intelligence. Some philosophers claim it is grasped by a special sense. The way in which a quality is apprehended is connected with the type of quality it is. For example, that loudness of sounds is heard implies that it is an auditory quality, and conversely. But how goodness is apprehened and whether it is a natural quality are equally difficult questions to answer. What mode of verification is relevant to deciding between the theories that goodness is a non-natural quality and that it is a natural quality, that goodness is apprehended by a special sense and that it is apprehended by the intellect?

On Ross' view, is apprehending the presence of goodness in thing like apprehending that 32 is even (evenness being a non-sensuous quality)? Here we have two universals necessarily connected, both properties being descriptive. On the Moore-Broad view there is a necessary, synthetic connection between the descriptive property of a thing and the non-descriptive property *goodness*. Is there any more difficulty in supposing *goodness* entails some descriptive property, different from itself *in kind*, than in supposing a thing's descriptive properties entail *goodness?*

25. Is it possible for a person to perceive a thing's natural qualities and fail to apprehend its goodness which is entailed by them? Supposing it possible, when one apprehends its goodness does one make a deductive step from its natural properties to its goodness? And if so, does this imply that the value of a thing is always inferred and never itself directly apprehended?

When one changes one's mind about the value of a thing in the presence of the qualities which bestow value on it, and admits a mistake about it, is this comparable to giving up the mistaken idea that $2^{2^5}+1$ is prime?

26. Granting that value-words give expression to feelings and that one

recognizes their persuasive force, why do people still suppose that one is asserting an opinion, true or false, in uttering a value-judgment? Why do we suppose that when, as we say, we change our mind, one attitude must be mistaken, not just different? We are aware that preferences change with age. Why are we not content with supposing a new evaluation represents merely a changed preference? If, as Ayer says, the moral judgment 'That is wrong' is no more verifiable than a cry of pain or a command since it does not assert anything true or false, then one has a reason for holding it is not self-contradictory to say of a given act that it produces a greater balance of good over bad than any act possible to the agent, but yet is wrong. How would one argue with a utilitarian who insisted it *is* self-contradictory?

27. Normally we say that the criteria for the application of a word and the features by which the word is defined are one and the same. Hare says 'good' has two meanings, one evaluative, and one descriptive of the good-making characteristics of the class of things called 'good'. The first he says is its primary meaning because it is constant ('good' always commends) and the second variable, and also because evaluation can change the descriptive meaning of 'good' for the class to which it is applied. How are we to choose between these claims and the following claims: (a) that it is not part of the *literal* meaning of 'good' that it should express or arouse feeling or guide choice, but one of the constant accompaniments of its use, (b) that if one comes to apply 'good' to things having different descriptive properties from those it had in the past, it is being redefined?

REFERENCES

Recommended readings:
David Hume (1902, 2nd ed.) *An enquiry* . . ., Sec. 8.
G. E. Moore (1922a), *Philosophical studies*, 'The nature of moral philosophy'.
Further readings:
J. L. Austin (1962), *Philosophical papers*, 'Ifs and cans'.
R. M. Hare (1955), 'Universalizability', *Proc. of Arist. society*, Vol. 55.
M. Lazerowitz (1964), *Studies in Metaphilosophy*, Ch. 2.
G. E. Moore (1912), *Ethics*.
C. L. Stevenson (1942), 'Moore's argument against certain forms of ethical naturalism', in: *The philosophy of G. E. Moore*.

General Bibliography

Aetius, *Aetii de placitus reliquae*, in: Milton Nahm (1947, 3rd ed.), *Selections from early Greek philosophy*. New York, F. S. Crofts and Co.

Ambrose, Alice (1966), *Essays in analysis*. London, George Allen and Unwin.

Ambrose, A., and Lazerowitz, M. (1962, rev. ed.), *Fundamentals of symbolic logic*. New York, Holt, Rinehart and Winston.

Anaxagoras, *Fragments*, in: Milton Nahm (1947, 3rd ed.).

Anselm, St. (1939), *Proslogium*, trans. by Sidney Deane. Chicago, Open Court Publ. Co.

Aristotle, *Metaphysica*, in: *The works of Aristotle*, Vol. 8 (1928, 2nd ed.), ed. by W. D. Ross. Oxford, Clarendon Press.

– *Physica*, in: *The works of Aristotle*, Vol. 2 (1930), ed. by W. D. Ross. Oxford, Clarendon Press.

Austin, J. L. (1962), *Sense and sensibilia*. Oxford, Clarendon Press.

Austin, John (1954), *The province of jurisprudence determined*. London, Weidenfeld and Nicolson.

Ayer, A. J. (1937), 'Verification and experience', *Proc. of Aristotelian society*, Vol. 37, pp. 137–156.

– (1947), *Foundations of empirical knowledge*. London, Macmillan.

– (1951, rev. ed.), *Language, truth and logic*. London, Victor Gollancz.

– (1954), *Philosophical essays*. New York, St. Martin's Press.

Bentham, Jeremy (1907), *An introduction to the principles of morals and legislation*. Oxford, Clarendon Press, 1923 reprint edition.

Berkeley, George (1871), *A treatise concerning the principles of human knowledge*, in: *The works of George Berkeley, D. D.*, ed. by A. C. Fraser. Oxford, Clarendon Press.

Blanshard, Brand (1967), 'Internal relations and their importance to philosophy', *The review of metaphysics*, Vol. 21, pp. 227–236.

Bochenski, I. M. (1956), *The problem of universals*. A symposium with Alonzo Church and Nelson Goodman. Notre Dame, Indiana, University of Notre Dame Press, 54 pages.

Boswell, James (1893), *The life of Samuel Johnson*. New York, Crowell.

Bradley, F. H. (1922), *Principles of logic*, Vol. 1. London, Oxford University Press.

– (1925), *Appearance and reality*. London, George Allen and Unwin.

Braithwaite, R. B. (1938), 'Propositions about material objects', *Proc. of Aristotelian society*, Vol. 38, pp. 269–290.

Brandt, R. B. (1955), 'The defense of an "ideal observer" theory in ethics', *Philosophy and phenomenological research*, Vol. 15, pp. 407-413.

– (1959), *The problems of normative and critical ethics*. Englewood Cliffs, N. J., Prentice-Hall, Inc.

Broad, C. D. (1927), *Scientific thought*. London, Kegan Paul, Trench, Trubner and Co.

– (1942), 'Certain features in Moore's ethical doctrines', in: *The philosophy of G. E. Moore*. See under Moore (1942).

– (1952), *Ethics and the history of philosophy*. London, Routledge and Kegan Paul.

Brunner, Emil (1937), *The divine imperative*. New York, Macmillan.

Burnet, John (1920, 3rd ed.), *Early Greek philosophy*. London, A. and C. Black.

– (1928), *Greek philosophy*, Part 1: *Thales to Plato*. London, Macmillan.

Carnap, Rudolf (1935), *Philosophy and logical syntax*. London, Kegan Paul, Trench, Trubner and Co. ('Psyche miniatures').

Carnell, E. J. (1948), *An introduction to Christian apologetics*. Grand Rapids, Mich., Wm. B. Eerdman's Publ. Co.

Carritt, E. F. (1947), *Ethical and political thinking*. Oxford, Clarendon.

Church, Alonzo (1951), 'The need for abstract entities in semantic analysis', *Proc. of Amer. academy of arts and sciences*, Vol. 80, pp. 100–112.

Clifford, W. K. (1879), *Lectures and essays*. London, Macmillan.

Descartes, René (1901), *Meditations*, trans. by John Veitch. New York, M. Walter Dunne.

- (1927), 'De Mundo', in: *Descartes selections*, ed. by Ralph M. Eaton. New York, Charles Scribner's Sons.

Diogenes Laertius (1925), *Lives of eminent philosophers* [3rd century A. D.], trans. by R. D. Hicks. London, Wm. Heineman.

Empedocles, *Fragments*, in: Milton Nahm (1947, 3rd ed.).

Ewing, A. C. (1935), 'Mechanical and teleological causation', *Proc. of Aristotelian society*, Suppl. vol. 14, pp. 63–82.
Falk, W. D. (1953), 'Goading and guiding', *Mind*, Vol. 62, pp. 145–171.
Firth, Roderick (1952), 'Ethical absolutism and the ideal observer', *Philosophical and phenomenological research*, Vol. 12, pp. 317–355.
Frankena, W. K. (1939), 'The naturalistic fallacy', *Mind*, Vol. 48, pp. 464–477.
Freud, Sigmund (1943), *The future of an illusion*, trans. by W. D. Robson-Scott. London, Hogarth Press. First published in German as: *Die Zukunft einer Illusion*, 1927.
Galilei, Galileo (1914), *Dialogues concerning two new sciences*, trans. by G. Grew and A. de Salvio. New York, Macmillan.
Gardner, Martin (1964), 'Mathematical games', *Scientific American*, No. 211 (December), pp. 124–134.
Gaunilon (1939), *An appendix in behalf of the fool*, trans. by Sidney Deane. Chicago, Open Court Publ. Co.
Gellner, Ernest (1959), *Words and things*. London, Victor Gollancz.
Hardy, G. H. (1929), 'Mathematical proof', *Mind*, Vol. 38, pp. 1–25.
– (1940), *A mathematician's apology*. Cambridge, University Press.
Hare, R. M. (1952), *The language of morals*. Oxford, Clarendon Press.
– (1955), 'Universalizability', *Proc. of Aristotelian society*, Vol. 55, pp. 295–312.
Hart, H. L. A. (1948–49), 'The ascription of responsibility and rights', *Proc. of Aristotelian society*, Vol. 49, pp. 171–194.
– (1951), 'A logician's fairy tale', *The philosophical review*, Vol. 60, pp. 198–212.
Hartshorne, Charles (1962), *The logic of perfection*. La Salle, Ill., Open Court Publ. Co.
Hempel, C. G. (1958), 'Some reflections on "The case for determinism"', in: *Determinism and freedom in the age of modern science*, ed. by S. Hook. New York, University Press.
Hobbes, Thomas (1909), *Leviathan*. Reprinted from the edition of 1651. Oxford, Clarendon Press.
d'Holbach, Baron (1770), *A system of nature*, trans. by H. D. Robinson.
Hume, David (1888), *A treatise of human nature*, ed. by L. A. Selby-Bigge. Oxford, Clarendon Press.
– (1902, 2nd ed.), *An enquiry concerning human understanding*, ed, by L. A. Selby-Bigge. Oxford, Clarendon Press.
– (1938), *An abstract of a treatise of human nature* [1740]. Cambridge,

University Press.
- (1947, 2nd ed.), *Dialogues concerning natural religion*, ed. by Norman
    Kemp Smith. Edinburgh, Nelson.
Hutcheson, Francis (1897), *An essay on the nature and conduct of the
    passions*, and *illustrations upon the moral sense* [1700] in: *British
    moralists*, Vol. 1, ed. by L. A. Selby Bigge. Oxford, Clarendon Press.
James, William (1897), 'The dilemma of determinism', in: *The will to
    believe*. London, Longmans, Green and Co.
Joachim, H. H. (1906), *The nature of truth*. Oxford, Clarendon Press.
Jones, Ernest (1959), *Free associations*. New York, Basic Books.
Joseph, H. W. B. (1916), *An introduction to logic*. Oxford, Clarendon Press.
Kant, Immanuel (1929a), *Critique of pure reason*, trans. by Norman
    Kemp Smith. Toronto, Macmillan.
- (1929b), *Prolegomena to any future metaphysics*, ed. by Paul Carus.
    Chicago, Ill., Open Court Publ. Co.
- (1969), *Foundations of the metaphysics of morals*, trans, by Lewis
    White Beck. Indianapolis, Indiana, Bobbs-Merrill, Inc.
Laird, John (1942), 'Reality', *Mind*, Vol. 51, pp. 244–258.
Langford, C. H. (1942), 'The notion of analysis in Moore's philosophy',
    in: *The philosophy of G. E. Moore*. See under Moore (1942).
Lehrer, Keith (1960), 'Can we know that we have free will by introspec-
    tion', *J. of philosophy*, Vol. 57, pp. 145–157.
Leibniz, G. W. (1900), 'Extracts from Leibniz's *Philosophische Schriften*',
    trans. by B. Russell, as Appendix in: B. Russell's *A critical exposi-
    tion of the philosophy of Leibniz*. Cambridge, University Press.
- (1916), *New essays concerning human understanding*, trans. by
    Alfred G. Langley. Chicago, Ill., Open Court Publ. Co.
- (1951a), 'Letter to Bernouilli' [1698], in: *Leibniz selections*, ed. by
    P. Wiener. New York, Charles Scribner's Sons.
- (1951b), 'First principles: Foundations of the sciences, 4: New
    system of nature and of the communication of substances, as well
    as the union of soul and body [*Journal des savans*, June 27, 1695],
    in: *Leibniz selections*, see above.
- (1951c), 'On substance as active force vs. mere extension', Letter to
    De Volder [June 23, 1699], in: *Leibniz selections*, see above.
Lennes, N. J. (1928, 1st ed.), *College algebra*. New York, Harper and
    Brothers.
Lewis, C. I. (1946), *An analysis of knowledge and valuation*. La Salle, Ill.,
    Open Court Publ. Co.

Lewy, Casimir (1938–39), 'The justification of induction', *Analysis*, Vol. 6, pp. 87–90.

Locke, John (1812, 11th ed.), *Works*, Vol. 4. London, W. Otridge and Son.

– (1928), *An essay concerning human understanding*, ed. by A. S. Pringle-Pattison. Oxford, Clarendon Press.

Malcolm, Norman (1963), *Knowledge and certainty*. Englewood Cliffs, N. J., Prentice-Hall, Inc.

Melissos, *Fragments*, in: Milton Nahm (1947, 3rd ed.).

Mill, John Stuart (1956), *A system of logic*. New York, Harper and Brothers.

– (1871), *Utilitarianism*. London, Longmans, Green and Co.

– (1872), *An examination of Sir William Hamilton's philosophy*. London, Longmans, Green and Co.

Moore, G. E. (1912), *Ethics*, London, Oxford University Press.

– (1922a), *Philosophical studies*. London, Routledge and Kegan Paul.

– (1922b), *Principia ethica*. Cambridge, University Press.

– (1923), with G. F. Sout, and G. Dawes Hicks, 'Are the characteristics of particular things universal or particular?', *Proc. of Aristotelian society*, Suppl. vol. 3, pp. 95–128.

– (1942), 'A reply to my critics', in: *The philosophy of G. E. Moore*. Menasha, Wisconsin, George Banta Publ. Co. ('The library of living philosophers', Vol. 4).

– (1953), *Some main problems of philosophy*. London, George Allen and Unwin.

– (1959), *Philosophical papers*. London, George Allen and Unwin.

– (1962), *Commonplace book*. London, George Allen and Unwin.

Mortimer, R. C. (1950), *Christian ethics*. London, Hutchinson's. University Library.

Nahm, Milton (1947, 3rd ed.), *Selections from early Greek philosophy*. New York, F. S. Crofts and Co.

Selections from: Aetius, Anaxagoras, Empedocles, Parmenides, Sextus Empiricus, Xenophanes, Zeno, and others.

Nowell-Smith, P. H. (1959), 'Freedom and responsibility', in: *Ethics*. Harmondsworth, Middlesex, Pelican Books.

Paley, William (1813, 11th ed.), *Natural theology; or Evidences of the existence and attributes of the deity*. London, J. Faulder.

– (1859), 'Principles of moral and political philosophy', in: *Paley's moral philosophy, with annotations*, ed. by Richard Whateley. London, John W. Parker and Son.

Parmenides, 'Concerning truth', in: Milton Nahm (1947, 3rd ed.).

Paul, G. A. (1937–38), 'Lenin's theory of perception'. *Analysis*, Vol. 5, pp. 65–73.

Plato (1937a), *Parmenides*, trans. by B. Jowett. New York, Random House.

– (1937b), *Republic*, trans. by B. Jowett. New York, Random House.

– (1937c), *Theaetetus*, trans. by Jowett, New York, Random House

– (1937d), *Timaeus*, trans by B. Jowett, New York, Random House

– (1937e), *Protagoras*, trans. by B. Jowett. New York, Random House.

Price, H. H. (1953), *Thinking and experience*. London, Hutchinson's University Library.

Protagoras, 'On the Gods', in: Diogenes Laertius (1925).

Quine, W. V. (1951), 'Abstract entities in semantic analysis', *Proc. of American academy of arts and sciences*, Vol. 80, pp. 100–11.

– (1965, rev. ed.), *Mathematical logic*. Cambridge, Harvard University Press.

Ramsey, F. P. (1931), *The foundations of mathematics*. New York, Harcourt Brace and Co.

Rawls, John (1955), 'Two concepts of rules', *The philosophical review*, Vol. 64, pp. 3–32.

Reichenbach, Hans (1948), 'Rationalism and empiricism: An enquiry into the roots of philosophical error', *The philosophical review*, Vol. 57, pp. 330–346.

Ross, W. D. (1930a, rev. ed.), *Aristotle*. London, Methuen and Co.

– (1930b), *The right and the good*. Oxford Clarendon Press.

– (1954), *Kant's ethical theory*. Oxford, Clarendon Press.

Russell, Bertrand (1900), *The philosophy of Leibniz*, together with an Appendix consisting of Extracts from Leibniz, trans. by Russell. Cambridge, University Press.

– (1910), *Philosophical essays*. London, Longmans, Green and Co.

– (1917, 2nd ed.), *Mysticism and logic*. London, George Allen and Unwin.

– (1929, 2nd ed.), *Our knowledge of the external world*. New York, W. W. Norton and Co.

– (1936), 'The limits of empiricism', *Proc. of Aristotelian society*, Vol. 36, pp. 131–150.

– (1938, 2nd ed.), *The principles of mathematics*. New York, W. W. Norton and Co.

– (1943, 17th impr.), *The problems of philosophy*. London, Oxford University Press.

– (1945), *A history of Western philosophy*. New York, Simon and Schuster.

– (1948), *Human knowledge.* New York, Simon and Schuster.

Schlick, Moritz (1939), *Problems of ethics.* New York, Prentice-Hall, Inc.

Sextus Empiricus, 'Adversus mathematicos', *Fragments,* in: Milton Nahm (1947, 3rd ed.).

Sidgwick, Henry (1874), *Methods of ethics.* London, Macmillan.

Smart, J. J. C. (1956), 'Extreme and restricted utilitarianism', *Philosophical quarterly,* Vol. p. 344–34.5

– (1961), *An outline of a system of utilitarian ethics.* Victoria, Melbourne University Press.

Spinoza, Benedict de (1901a *Ethics,* trans. by R. H. M. Elwes. New York, M. Walter Dunne.,

  – (1901b), *On the improvement of the understanding,* trans. by R. H. M. Elwes. New York, M. Walter Dunne.

Stace, W. T. (1932), *The theory of knowledge and existence.* Oxford, Clarendon Press.

Stevenson, C. L. (1942), 'Moore's arguments against certain forms of ethical naturalism', in: *The philosophy of G. E. Moore.* See under Moore (1942).

Sumner, W. G. (1934), *Folkways.* Boston, Ginn and Co.

Taylor, A. E. (1912), *The elements of metaphysics.* London, Methuen and Co.

Turnbull, Herbert Westren (1961), *The great mathematicians.* New York, New York University Press.

Urban, W. H (1930), *Fundamentals of ethics.* New York, Henry Holt and Co.

Urmson, J. O. (1953), 'The interpretation of the moral philosophy of J. S. Mill', *Philosophical quarterly,* Vol. 3, pp. 33–39.

Whitehead, A. N. (1929), *Process and reality.* Cambridge, University Press.

Wittgenstein, Ludwig (1922), *Tractatus logico-philosophicus,* trans by C. K. Ogden. London, Kegan Paul, Trench, Trubner & Co.

– *Philosophical investigations,* trans. by G. E. M. Anscombe. Oxford, Basil Blackwell.

– (1958), *The blue book.* Oxford, Basil Blackwell.

– (1961), *Notebooks, 1914–1916,* trans. by G. E. M. Anscombe. Oxford, Basil Blackwell.

Xenophanes, *Fragments,* in: Milton Nahm (1947, 3rd ed.).

Zeno, *Fragments,* in: Milton Nahm (1947, 3rd ed.).

Index of Names